THERE'S NEVER BEEN NOTHING

THERE'S NEVER BEEN NOTHING

A PERSONAL JOURNEY TO SPIRITUAL misUNDERSTANDING

MATTHEW LEATHERWOOD

PERFECT STONE ENTERPRISES

OMAHA, NEBRASKA

THERE'S NEVER BEEN NOTHING:
A PERSONAL JOURNEY TO SPIRITUAL misUNDERSTANDING

Copyright © 2020 by Matthew Leatherwood

All rights reserved. No part of this publication may be reproduced, stored in a retrieval system or transmitted in any way by any means, electronic, mechanical, photocopy, recording or otherwise without the prior permission of the author except as provided by USA copyright law.

Perfect Stone Enterprises
www.perfectstoneenterprises.com

Paperback: 978-1-949067-05-7
Kindle: 978-1-949067-09-5
EPub: 978-1-949067-00-2
LCCN: 2019918215

Library of Congress data on file with the publisher.

Publishing and production by Concierge Marketing Inc.

Memoir/Personal

Printed in the United States of America

10 9 8 7 6 5 4 3 2 1

Contents

Introduction vii

Preface 1

PART ONE: CHILDHOOD CHREASTER 5

Lesson One:	Answers to the Big Questions Don't Come Easy 7
Lesson Two:	The Universe Provides Unexpected Gifts at Unexpected Times 11
Lesson Three:	The Definition of Unconditional Love Is…Mom 15
Lesson Four:	Killing Comes With a Price 21
Lesson Five:	You Don't Have to Have Higher Education to be Gifted 25
Lesson Six:	Everything and Everyone Are Completely Connected 33
Lesson Seven:	Church Isn't the Place for a Child to Find Answers 39
Lesson Eight:	Grieving the Dead Is Normal and Our Spirits Live On 45
Lesson Nine:	Your Best Friends aren't Necessarily the Most Obvious 51
Lesson Ten:	There are Forces at Work We Don't Understand 57
Lesson Eleven:	Children Need Mentors 63

PART TWO: COLLEGE YEARS/AGNOSTICISM 69

Lesson Twelve:	There Can Be Great News in the Biggest Disappointment 71
Lesson Thirteen:	Sometimes the Answer to a Problem Lies in Stepping Further Away 77
Lesson Fourteen:	Sometimes You Have to Get Dirty 81

Lesson Fifteen:	Dream Big. the Universe will Provide You the Opportunity to Fulfill It.	85
Lesson Sixteen:	Life Passes at an Exponential Rate and Will Control You If You Let It	93
Lesson Seventeen:	Baby Steps Aren't All that Risky and Running Won't Fill the Hole	97
Lesson Eighteen:	Choose Wisely and be Man Enough to Admit It When You Haven't	103
Lesson Nineteen:	If You Find Yourself Interested in Anyone Other than the One You're Dating, the One You're Dating Isn't the One for You	107
Lesson Twenty:	Marriage Is Something You Really Should Understand Before You Enter in to It. And It Better be with the One You Love	115
Lesson Twenty-One:	You Have to Make Time for Fun. It Fuels the Soul	121
Lesson Twenty-Two:	Some Things Just Shouldn't Come so Easy	129
Lesson Twenty-Three:	Giving Back Feels Good	137
Lesson Twenty-Four:	I Am Driven by My Restless Spirit	145
Lesson Twenty-Five:	Tough Times are an Effective Teacher	151
Lesson Twenty-Six:	Tough Times Don't Last; Tough People Do	159
Lesson Twenty-Seven:	Boundaries are Good; Sometimes You Just Gotta Let 'em Go	165

PART THREE: THE AL ANON YEARS 173

Lesson Twenty-Eight:	Great Things can Come From "Bad" Decisions	175
Lesson Twenty-Nine:	Desperate People Do Desperate Things	183
Lesson Thirty:	There Is Much You Can Learn From Those Who Have Been to the Abyss	187
Lesson Thirty-One:	"God" Is a God Of My Own Understanding and Things are in Numerical Order for a Reason	193

Lesson Thirty-Two:	It Isn't Enough to Say You're Sorry	199
Lesson Thirty-Three:	You Can Catch More than Germs in a Hot Tub	203

PART FOUR: BECOMING A "CHRISTIAN" 213

Lesson Thirty-Four:	Thirsty People Will Follow Anyone that Offers Them a Drink	215
Lesson Thirty-Five:	There May Not Always be Strength in Numbers, but Certainly Some Comfort	221
Lesson Thirty-Six:	Having a Religious Identity Doesn't Make You Immune to Change	227
Lesson Thirty-Seven:	After a Big Change, You Can Always Count on Something to Follow: More Change!	233
Lesson Thirty-Eight:	The Universe Has No Choice but to Come in to Alignment with Your Vision	239
Lesson Thirty-Nine:	Sometimes You Just Do What You Gotta Do	243
Lesson Forty:	Faith Has Deep Roots. You Can't Pull it and You Can't Argue with it	249
Lesson Forty-One:	The Grass May Actually be Greener on the Other Side, But It's Still Grass	253
Lesson Forty-Two:	Life Turns On A Dime	259

PART FIVE: INTRODUCING SCIENCE 269

Lesson Forty-Three:	No Matter How Much You Think You Know, There Is Much to Learn	271
Lesson Forty-Four:	You Have to Read Between the Lines	277
Lesson Forty-Five:	The Bible Was Not Written by God!	285
Lesson Forty-Six:	The Church Is a Corrupt Megacorp	293
Lesson Forty-Seven:	The Answers are in the Stars	299
Lesson Forty-Eight:	Be the Very Best "You" You Can Be	317
Epilogue		311

for everyone who is
searching for something

INTRODUCTION

It's been over ten years since I put together the original manuscript for *There's Never Been Nothing, A Personal Journey to Spiritual misUnderstanding.* To be perfectly honest, sitting down to write these words was more an exercise in patience than it was anything else. I wasn't sure I had the attention span to stay on task. It turns out, I did. And eighteen months after I began, I printed a raw manuscript and put it in a box. There is where I thought it would stay.

After finally getting the courage to let some friends read the manuscript, I set out to publish it. Who was to know if things I had gone through might make others feel less alone? And while it's certainly not on the *New York Times* Best Seller List (yet), it has certainly touched the lives of more than just a few.

Over that period of ten or more years, I have evolved. The title of this book is even taking on an "evolution," if you will. While my basic beliefs are the same, I continue to learn more about the Universe and those around me. I fall way short of my "Peace, Love, Joy, and Harmony" mantra on more days than I succeed, but I keep trying. Life is to be lived. That means making some mistakes. I've made my share.

When I discuss this book, or my blog, or my writing in general with people, I'm often asked where I stand on the "religion" scale. I'm not a Christian. When I disclose that to friends, and even perfect strangers, the question is nearly always the same, "So you're an Atheist?"

No, my dear friends, I am NOT an Atheist; far from it, in fact. In the past, I've tried labeling what I believe and it never seems to land on solid ground. I believe in a universal connectedness between all things, both animate and inanimate. Everything in our universe comes from one thing—energy. When you connect the little pieces, we're not so different.

So, I'm not an Atheist. Like our Founding Fathers who escaped religious tyranny from Britain, I'm more of a Deist. I believe in a higher power, higher consciousness, or supreme "being" of some sort. Every religious "God" I've ever learned about, wrapped up in dogma, has fallen far short of the enormity of the creator of my understanding.

There are two basic ideals that make it impossible for me to believe we're just a cosmic accident. The first is the concept of self-awareness. Biologically, we are basically identical. Yet, when I look in the mirror each morning, I'm aware of me. I see my face. I identify with my experiences and world view. I am not aware of yours. To me, that can only be explained by "soul."

The second ideal has more to do with physics as we understand it today. That said, I don't think we've even begun to scratch the surface when it comes to what we are or where we're going. But I do believe everything is on its way to somewhere.

Let me explain.

At our present level of understanding, we know you cannot create something from nothing. It's a basic premise of physics. Even anti-matter, dark matter, or any of that other stuff, is just that—stuff. It's something. Play with all the theories and dogma you'd like. Read all the texts and science you thirst for. At the end of the day, there's only one way we could have all we have today.

Because if humans can't create something from nothing, it's clear to me…

There's Never Been Nothing.

~Matthew Leatherwood

PREFACE

"There is great meaning in life for those who are willing to journey."

~Jim England

To this day I can see the young Native American boy, standing firmly in front of me, saying nothing with his mouth, yet speaking directly to my soul.

I was 10 years old at my favorite state park in Iowa, during my favorite time of year. Each autumn, my parents would load the camper and head for Waubonsie State Park, across the Missouri River from my home in Nebraska. The trees were vibrant and alive with an assortment of rich red, brilliant orange, and majestic purple leaves. It's difficult to describe the smell of fall in the Nebraska bluffs, but it is one I faintly catch even now as the wind finally comes around from the north in Texas, causing me to pause and long for home.

Waubonsie, nestled in the foothills along the borders of Nebraska and Iowa, is littered with hundreds of hiking trails. Some are man-made, yet many are trampled by the abundant wildlife native to the Great Plains. Every year, I spent hours discovering these wondrous trails, enjoying the freedom these simple times allowed a solitary boy.

As per my parent's instruction, I had previously always stuck to the marked trail, but on this day, I was somehow divinely led up a densely wooded ridge along a well-trodden deer path. From the crest of the ridge, I could look down over an open meadow unnoticed by me on previous excursions. In that meadow, at least one hundred yards from my vantage point, I spotted the young "Indian" brave. And then, he spotted me.

What happened next you may find unbelievable. You might even blame it on the vivid imagination of a child. Yet, I undoubtedly affirm it was real. In the instant the young boy spotted me, he began to run: right at me! In the blink of an eye, the young brave stood before me. He covered the distance between us in less than a second, running at supernatural speed. He wore only a loin cloth, moccasins and native jewelry, and spoke not a word. For ten seconds, he cocked his head as a dog would do while trying to listen. He looked directly at the heart of my young soul, then turned and disappeared.

Even at ten years old, I felt no fear, only peace and wonder. I calmly returned to the trail and back to camp, sharing my story with no one. Was it my imagination? Was it a visit from my spirit guide? I had been touched in a way I may never understand.

On another occasion, a decade later, I was on a weekend retreat with fellow students from the University of Nebraska. It was a weekend of bonding, learning and growing. I reflect on that retreat with great fondness, but another specific experience has claimed a major part of me and stayed with me through my years.

After a day of classroom work and team-building, I yearned for solitude. It's always been that way for me. I love people, yet for as long as I can remember, I've enjoyed those times when I could be alone with my thoughts. This was one of those times.

We took residence in cabins adjacent to a large wooded area, a perfect spot to soak up the gifts of nature and recharge while on foot. I walked through the trees and dense foliage, picking my way along the easiest path. As I emerged from beneath a particularly stubborn tree limb, I came face-to-face with a small wooden sign. It was in the middle of nowhere and completely random. The sign said simply, "Be still, and know that I am God."

So that is exactly what I did. I stood completely still and listened. The breeze was cool and clouds raced overhead the way they do in the fall, white horses kicking up their heels after a long summer. I was overcome with a feeling of peace and serenity. I took a deep breath of the brisk autumn air and returned to the lodge. I was different, but it took me a long time to discover how or why.

That's the way things were for me then. I had no spiritual direction or anyone to show me the way. My spiritual education came to me in surprising ways from the likes of "Indian" boys and random wooden signs. I had no idea what any of it meant. I only knew then, like I know now, those events were significant in my long journey toward finding spiritual peace and understanding.

And THAT is where I am today. I have reached the place in my life where I have a clear understanding of my spiritual purpose. I know where I fit in the universe. I know peace. I know love.

That isn't to say there isn't more to be done. Every day brings more clarity with new lessons from new teachers. I'm no longer trying to find my spiritual place. My focus now is to grow in the spirit I've come to understand.

I feel compelled to tell you that this isn't a "self-help" book. I offer no magic formula for you to discover your spirituality. What I DO offer you is an honest walk through a fifty year search for my truth. My sincere hope is you'll be reminded you are not alone in your endeavors. Others just like you are seeking spiritual truth every day. Perhaps reading about my search will help you in yours.

If you take just one thing from this book that helps you find your way, I will feel forever blessed. This work has been a labor of love for me and all who helped. Thank you for joining me in this little adventure. It has been truly that; and today, I have raised the curtain.

~Matthew Leatherwood

PART ONE: CHILDHOOD CHREASTER

"When I was a child, I spoke as a child, I understood as a child, I thought as a child; but when I became a man I put away childish things."

~Bible

Lesson One:

ANSWERS TO THE BIG QUESTIONS DON'T COME EASY

"I was born in a small town, taught the fear of Jesus in a small town..."

~John Mellencamp

Greenwood, Nebraska is home. It's where I was raised. Nestled between Lincoln and Omaha, Nebraska's two largest cities, Greenwood is what most would call a "bedroom community." With a population of just over 500 people, it serves as a resting place for those commuting to the larger cities for work.

While I was a child there forty-five years ago, this quaint little village boasted two bars, two grocery stores, an elementary school, a used farm implement dealer, two gas stations, a baseball diamond, park, train depot, gargantuan grain elevator and volunteer fire department. It was typical hometown America.

In addition to the local businesses, Greenwood also supported three churches. Catholics, Methodists and non-denominationals supported the local ministry. My family wore a Methodist label, which I accepted matter-of-factly, but it held no true meaning for me. But more on that later.

The town was evenly divided by a busy, two-lane highway. Parallel railroad tracks were constant thoroughfare for enormously long coal trains providing fossil fuels for heating in the Northeast. Black mountains of coal peered nonchalantly over the sides of stalwart train-cars as they rumbled by. The highway, used mostly for commuting to work throughout the week, became a colossal red river of cars filled with expectant Husker fans on home game Saturdays. Like the coal trains, there was an endless stream of speeding cars laced with banners and horns, brimming with the greatest fans in America donning bright red Husker jerseys waving the big Red N. Trying to cross the highway on "game days" was an effort in futility at best, a suicide mission if not quick on your feet.

Hunting and hiking were two things I loved most about living and growing up in a small Midwestern town. Conveniently located across the street from my parent's home awaited acres of silent, yet articulate farmland whose moods changed with the seasons. In the spring, freshly turned soil held the promise of bountiful crops. Summer cast a trance, corn standing hypnotized under the weight of suffocating heat waves. As the scorching heat gave way to fall, open fields of milo, crisp browning corn and mature soybeans sighed relief at the approaching harvest. Winter covered the somnolent fields with a restful blanket of shimmering snow.

I lived less than half a mile from the nearest creek where I would throw rocks or sticks into the whirling stream and hike for hours. Accompanied by my springer spaniel, Tammy, I would strap on a small backpack filled with homemade goodies and head out for a day of exploration. I don't remember wanting for companionship on those excursions, (excluding the dog, of course) and always embraced the solitude the plains provided. I guess that comes from being the youngest of three boys, separated from my next oldest sibling by seven years.

It was on these long hikes I remember having my first thoughts about God. Who WAS God? Where did he live? Is he really everywhere? Why can't I see him? Is heaven on a cloud? Are angels really crying when it rains? Is God really bowling when it thunders? I think you get the idea.

Questions like these, I realize now, came from two sources. First, I feel sure we all are born with an undeveloped knowledge of spiritual truths. A child trying to grasp the concept of "God" is probably a lot like a kid trying to figure out where babies come from! I still remember friends telling me girls got pregnant by taking a pill. Clearly, we can see a child may not be a reliable source of his or her own information regarding the spirit.

Secondly, leading to even more questions, well-meaning adults clouded my mind with stories of Christian lore that just didn't add up: questions I did not ask them, because I was either too embarrassed or could tell they just didn't know. But all that was fine with me to be honest. I was content at the time being at one with nature, pondering my own concepts of an almighty and all-powerful god. As it turns out, being at one with nature was closer to God than I realized.

In addition to the many questions I had about God, there was my unending fascination with death and sickness. I didn't share that obsession much for reasons that might be evident. How many kids truly spend that much time wondering about their mortality?

My dad was somewhat of a "germaphobe" and was an obsessive hand-washer. Mom kept the house so clean you could eat off the floor and I never once saw my parents drink out of the same glass or taste each other's food. How they ever had children is a mystery to me. I can't say I blame the cleanliness obsession on my concerns about illness, but I do know I spent a lot of time thinking about it. I wasn't a sickly kid nor was I prone to injury, but when I did get sick or cut a finger one of the first things I considered was, "Am I going to die?" To this day I find it odd that I harbored such thoughts and the idea of death no longer occupies my mind. In fact, I'd say I have more of a healthy curiosity about it today. But then, I've always felt a bit different.

As I reflect on my days as a child, I remember always feeling different. Not better or worse-than…just different. My mom frequently told me I was "special." I have NO idea what the hell that meant. Sometimes I think she actually meant "touched," but I choose to believe it meant she just liked me a lot. Whatever the meaning, the label of being special made me feel as though I had something to live up to. That isn't my mom's fault. I merely felt like someone special should grow up to accomplish great things. The problem was, I had no definition of "greatness."

Armed with my lack of spiritual direction and "special" label, I developed an internal sense that I was being groomed by "god" to play a major role in an astonishing event. Through the many phases of my spiritual wandering, that feeling has taken on numerous forms and at times has disappeared altogether. But some days, I still anticipate the wondrous event to come. Am I going to be asked to build an Ark? Will I cure cancer? Will I be the driving force in a rescue during some cataclysmic event? The answer to those questions could easily be "none of the above," but you just never know.

The comforting news is nearly every question I had as a child has been answered. My purpose has been made clear. It didn't happen without some seeking and listening, and except for the fact I don't know about the event for which I'm being groomed, my life has meaning. But again, you just never know!

Lesson Two:

THE UNIVERSE PROVIDES UNEXPECTED GIFTS AT UNEXPECTED TIMES

> *"I am the eagle, I live in high country, in rocky cathedrals that reach to the sky; I am the hawk and there's blood on my feathers, but time is still turning they soon will be dry; All those who see me, and all who believe in me, share in the freedom I feel when I fly."*
>
> ~John Denver

The snowflakes were the size of silver dollars and did not fall, but floated from the sky in slow motion like dry leaves from a tree. The air was breathless and the moisture-dense flakes lit carefully to earth, taking their place atop the soft, undisturbed, woolen blanket of fresh snow.

I was on one of my many winter "hunting" excursions and this time did not even bring the dog. Patience, or Pat for short, was the latest in the family brood of English Springer Spaniels and as yet lacked the calm I was hoping for in a companion that morning. Donned in my customary insulated green coveralls, fleece-lined hunting boots and carrying only my Remington 870 shotgun, I shuffled down the gravel road to the dry creek bed that ran west through the trees from my neighbor's house.

Although this would probably be a good place to talk about how the snow made crunching sounds beneath my boots, it wouldn't really be accurate. The blanket of snow we received the night before was soft and wet. When it made any sound at all, it was more like stepping on a thin layer of cork and sounded more like a slight "squeak." The snow continued to fall as I described and I entered the dry bed or "draw" in the early hours of a perfectly still, yet bitter-cold Nebraska morning.

Within moments of commencing my march down the middle of the winding, blanketed draw, I heard a twig snap to my right. I must admit I most commonly carried my shotgun across my chest in such a way as to make it quick to aim and shoot. Today, however, I was carrying it in my right hand, pointing forward at my side. The faint sound nearby gave me no cause to raise the weapon. I stopped dead in my tracks, my senses elevated to that of predator or perhaps even prey. I listened…watched.

And then she appeared. From the brush cleared by a harsh winter, stepped the most amazing doe I had ever seen. She stepped lightly into the clearing of the creek bed, turned her head toward me and froze. Neither of us twitched. The only sign of life between us was the steam from our breath. The quiet so overpowering it was as if you could hear the ice crystals forming from that steam and falling to the snow like tiny shards of broken glass.

Although I did a lot of bird hunting in those days (I don't hunt any more), I had never been interested in hunting deer. The thought of raising my shotgun to fire at this close range of only thirty yards never entered my mind. In fact, if I hadn't thought the movement would alarm her, I'd have lowered my weapon to the padded snow.

There we stood, two pawns in a chess match, watching and waiting to determine who would move. After what seemed like several minutes, I had a clear sign from my peaceful, brown-eyed friend that she felt no threat from me. From the same area where she had entered stepped a spotted fawn, faithfully following his mother who had obviously displayed a sign of "all clear." I almost stopped breathing altogether.

In a blanket of new snow, surrounded by the cotton balls of wet, falling snowflakes, entranced in the silence, the four of us stood. Yes, there were indeed four. In addition to myself, the doe and her brilliant spindly fawn, a new ally had entered the arena—Trust. We made a connection.

When I felt enough time had passed, I coughed and took one step forward. At my advance, the doe and her baby turned slowly and walked away. She didn't look back over her shoulder to see if I was following or if I might try to harm them. She knew. So did I.

I did no hunting that day. My gun stayed at my side and I walked the draw in wonder of the scene that had played before me. No postcard I've ever seen on a spinning display of any souvenir shop from the most breathtaking places in America has ever compared to the postcard I saw that morning. Not the Grand Canyon. Not Niagara. Not the Rocky Mountains.

That morning was my gift from the universe. It was a gift, and a message. It took me years to decode it, but today I get it loud and clear.

Lesson Three:

THE DEFINITION OF UNCONDITIONAL LOVE IS...MOM

*"Families are like fudge...
mostly sweet with a few nuts."*

~Author Unknown

My mother's homemade chocolate chip cookies were famous throughout town. Almost every friend I had was aware of these dark-speckled, mouth-watering treats. Our antique, clown-faced cookie jar, which sat right on the kitchen counter next to the toaster, always brimmed with the gooey delights. Every day after school I would grab six cookies and a glass of milk, head to the living room to watch some TV, then run outside to play. Is it any wonder I wore "Husky" pants?

Mom always was, and is to this day, the pillar of our family. She worked a grueling job at the local factory, then came home every night and started dinner. Laundry heaped high in the basket from just one day's worth of active boys was next on her list, followed closely by some cleaning. After a dinner that was usually devoured in minutes, which usually included some playful ribbing of siblings, it was on to dishes. There was almost always dessert.

On weekends, Mom baked, cleaned, did more laundry and even canned vegetables from our garden. There seemed to always be something wonderfully aromatic coming from the kitchen of our country, two-story home. If it wasn't cookies or candies for the holidays, it was bacon that had the power to send delightful redolence through the living room, up the stairs and into my room, tickling my nose to coax me from the abysmal sleep only a teen can realize. Mornings always made me smile.

I'm not sure what it was, perhaps just the joy of living, but something always made my mom smile, too. Mom just always seemed joyful, even jolly perhaps. Nothing seemed to get her down. I didn't ever hear her whistle, but it was common to hear her singing while she worked in the kitchen. Occasionally she even sat down at her piano and tickled the ivory with a little Ernest Tubbs. She taught me to play Chopsticks so we could play a duet together where the tune got faster and faster each time we played. That little game always ended in a belly sore from laughter. Mom was simply fun to be around.

Mom was a bit of a prankster. There was small window just above eye-level in our bathroom shower. (There was only one small bathroom for five people.) During the spring and often on cool summer evenings, mom would open the windows to the house so things could "air out." On more than one occasion, while in the midst of a nice hot shower after a long day of playing outside, I was blasted with the icy cold water that ran freely from our garden hose. If you recovered from the gasping breath and heart failure fast enough, you could catch a glimpse of my mom running around the corner of the house, giggling. Mom loved to play.

Halloween was big at my house. When I was a little older, mom let me have a big Halloween party. I invited all my friends and I'm pretty sure they all came. Just a year or so before, one of our local girls had been killed in a farming accident where a tractor had overturned on her. Since she lived way outside of town, none of us knew her well, but for weeks prior to the party we all decided we'd hold a séance to recall the spirit of Irene Graves.

The only light in the room came from candles dancing calmly in the middle of our dining room table. Ten eager subjects held hands as we began to chant. Irene Graves. Irene Graves. Irene Graves. Over and over we chanted, knowing we could recall the spirit of the local dead. I saw the flicker of light from the corner of my eye first. It was coming from our staircase which was across the living room, thirty feet from where we sat. As we continued to chant more gingerly, the ghost of Irene Graves appeared from our staircase holding a candle and a bowl. She was draped in sheer garment with a vale over her face. It worked. We did it!

More than one of the séance crew bolted under the table for shelter from the spirit. She made her way around the table, touching each and every one of us on the back of our neck with her icy, dead hands. Everyone was screaming and squirming and staring in utter disbelief. It was classic. The only catch was that it wasn't Irene Graves at all. It was my neighbor Jeanette and her icy cold hands came from the ice she was carrying in the bowl. She and my mother had planned this elaborate little play for weeks, hoping upon hope that it would indeed be Irene Graves we tried to raise from the dead. Jeanette had been hiding upstairs in our house for HOURS, waiting for just the right moment while we partied and played games. Only a loving mother and a devoted neighbor would go to that kind of trouble to make a memory for kids.

On every birthday I was made to feel special. Mom threw incredible birthday parties where all my friends were invited. Mom wasn't afraid of a mess. There was one particular party where mom bought water guns for everyone that came to the party. She set the stage with a tropical theme and my friends and I spent the warm, spring afternoon chasing each other with water pistols. I couldn't tell you what I got for presents that year. It doesn't matter. What I can tell you is that it was one of my most priceless memories, and mom created it.

Mom decorated for every holiday. You could tell the season by the color scheme in our home. Christmas, of course, was kind of a no-brainer. We had lights and a Christmas tree and fake snow covering the stereo and mantel. Winter wonderland scenes were set painstakingly upon the fluffy layer of polyester with ice skaters and little sleds and even animals. Mom even had ceramic trees with little lights. It was all like candy to a kid's eye at Christmas.

But Mom also decorated for St. Patrick's Day, Easter, May Day, July 4th, Halloween and Thanksgiving. We had four-leafed clovers all over the windows, or Easter bunnies, pumpkins, turkeys and Horns of Plenty. We had an American flag strapped to something in July and if there wasn't a flagpole available you could always find a sticker or pin-up of Uncle Sam somewhere on the Leatherwood property. Like I said, you could tell the time of year by the décor of our house. I'll never know how Mom did it, but there were smells that matched the colors. In the fall, our house smelled like fall; in March, like Irish Spring. There was a certain peace that fell over me when mom started the "spring cleaning."

Mom was the only woman at our house. As the mother of three boys she always had her hands full. I already mentioned the laundry and the cooking, but then there was the shopping and the mending and tending and hugging and doting and loving and discussing. Mom was the glue that held the whole thing together. When you wanted to spend the night at a friend's house, it was mom you asked for permission. Mom was the "go-to guy."

For all that mom was, there was one thing she wasn't. Mom was not a spiritual leader in the typical sense. Biblically speaking I realize that job falls to the "Man of the House," but that wasn't going to happen in our home. I'll get to that later. I understand today that mom's spiritual leadership came in the form of her love and devotion and joy for living. And that was pretty much as far as it went.

Mom did occasionally mention God and angels, but in general terms that I didn't understand. I had NO idea who or what God was. I had no concept of what it was to be a Christian (which is what I gathered we were by definition). To this day I have no recollection of my mother ever talking about attending church as a child. I knew we were "Methodists," but I'm not sure if that's because Mom was raised that way or if it's just the church we occasionally attended in town. You'll get the opportunity to read all about my trips to church, including vacation Bible school, but it all meant nothing to me and there was no one to explain it. And frankly, as a child, I wasn't wise enough to ask. I was already buying in to hollow explanations of a concept that would be foreign to me for years.

When grandpa died, he went to heaven. When my dog Tonka was killed, he went to heaven as well. Well, where the hell IS heaven? And better yet, WHAT is heaven? I have answers to those questions now, but if I told you I'd give the end of the story away. It'll just have to wait. Let's suffice it to say, for now, that heaven being an actual "place" where no one suffers and the streets are lined with gold and you're met at the Pearly Gates by Saint Peter, ad infinitum, was a comfort to me and other young kids like me then. It isn't now.

Lesson Four:

KILLING COMES WITH A PRICE

"Don't go into Mr. McGregor's garden:
your Father had an accident there;
he was put in a pie by Mrs. McGregor."

~Beatrix Potter, (1866-1943)
English author *The Tale of Peter Rabbit*

Before I graduated to the Remington 870 shotgun I got for Christmas at age fifteen, I did a lot of my "hunting" carrying a Daisy BB gun and a Montgomery Ward single-shot .410. The single-action Daisy was reserved, primarily, for short hunts around our two-acre home site where small birds like sparrows and pigeons were the primary prey. Occasionally my dad would let me carry it along on pheasant hunts with him and his friends as long as my antics didn't interfere with the "real" hunting at hand. It made me feel like one of the guys.

The .410, on the other hand, was my weapon of choice when I ventured farther from home in search of small game like rabbits and squirrels. It's on one of these small hunts where a rabbit entered the development of my spiritual nature. I realize, of course, that I keep rebounding to hunting stories, some of which may not be pleasing, but later on they play a important role in where I am today.

I was considerably younger than the last we discussed my excursions into the local wood. I still find it odd that this story takes place at nearly the exact same place where I encountered the doe and her fawn some years later, but in fact, it is in almost precisely the same area of the dry creek bed where I met the famed rabbit.

It was winter, but there was no snow to blanket the sea of dried leaves left abandoned by a typical Nebraska fall. In my teen years I always chose insulated coveralls as my hunting garb, but on this day, I was wearing my blue parka, complete with fur-lined hood, jeans and insulated rubber boots. It was bitter cold, but a sun brought closer by winter solstice warmed my face. It was another perfect day of hiking and hunting. The leaves crackled like a warm campfire beneath my feet. My trusty .410 poised ready across my chest. In my mind, I was a mountain man from 1850. This was my heaven.

From my left I caught a glimpse of something scurrying through the underbrush. Rabbit! I raised my gun and fired in the direction of the motion. It was an aimless shot which brought no death or destruction except to the dense undergrowth and decomposing soil. I opened the gun at mid-stock and reloaded. "Just let me get one more glimpse of you," I coaxed.

I stepped lightly toward the place I last saw my intended prey and looked deep into the heavy brush. My breathing slowed to near a stop as I let my eyes focus on the depth of the fallen tree branches laden with rotting wood from seasons past. Then, while squinting to filter the bright sun, I spotted the rabbit. He was no more than ten feet before me and was hunkered down low, nose twitching carefully, eyes full of worry. His only hope for survival was to rely on the forest surrounding him and beg to go unnoticed. Today was not that day. My eyes were too keen.

So as not to alarm the furry lapin, I slowly raised my weapon, carefully releasing the safety to avoid a 'click' that would send him into deeper cover. I looked through the site, down the cold steel barrel, and right into the eyes of the petrified bunny.

To the other animals of the woods, the explosion that followed must have sounded like a bomb that changed the face of time. I lowered the shotgun to my side to examine my kill. Where a terrified rabbit had stood only seconds earlier the carcass of my latest assassination now lied. A small, innocent life ended by the adventurous mind of a young boy. Guns don't kill. People do.

It tapped me softly on the shoulder at first; that question of "why?" I wasn't going to eat the rabbit. I wanted his fur to tan like they did in movies. I wanted to be a mountain man. I reached into the dense foliage and removed the limp bundle of softness and placed it in my game bag. At first I continued down the dry bed in search of more game, but what started as a gentle tap began a louder rhythm in my head and I turned to walk home. The look in the eyes of that hare was implanted in my conscience and I couldn't shake feeling the same fear he must have felt. And for what? Bragging rights? A pelt? It was my first introduction to remorse. Over forty years later, I can still see the face of the bunny with absolute clarity.

When I returned home, my mom, the ever-present pillar of the Leatherwood clan was working in the kitchen. I could see her through the window as I passed easterly across the front yard to the patio where I placed my spoil and double-checked to be sure my gun was unloaded. I entered the back porch, removed my boots and coat and slowly ascended the four stairs to our kitchen door, head down, shoulders sagging.

"Hi, Matthew. Did you get anything?" my mother inquired.

"I got a rabbit." I said.

The remorse suddenly found its way to my vocal chords and I related the entire story of the kill to my mother. She listened patiently as I ranted about how I had basically cornered this innocent furry being and then executed it. The tears streamed down my face as I struggled to catch my breath between the words and the pain. I don't remember what mom said to me then. I don't recall any words of comfort or if she even offered any. She just took me in her arms and let me sob.

I wish I could tell you this was the last of my hunting kills, but history speaks otherwise. I continued to hunt pheasant and quail with Dad and his friends. I still dreamed of being a mountain man and even trapped muskrat with my brother. But I never killed another rabbit. My young mind hadn't yet made the connection between THAT life and all life, but it was coming. In slow, painful, sometimes agonizing doses, it was coming.

Lesson Five:

YOU DON'T HAVE TO HAVE HIGHER EDUCATION TO BE GIFTED

"My father gave me the greatest gift anyone could give another person. He believed in me."

~Jim Valvano

As much as my mother was queen of the household, my father was king of all things garage. If there was a repair to be made, a lawn to be mowed (until the three of us boys were old enough), a contraption to be built or a room to be remodeled, my dad was the guy for the job.

Although dad was only officially schooled through the eighth grade (he later earned his GED from home while working and helping to raise three boys), he was a genius in his own right. There simply wasn't anything my dad couldn't build or fix. I've given it a lot of thought and I honestly can't remember a single time dad was ever completely stumped in his endeavors.

We moved to the place I called home in Greenwood when I was only two. The acreage sported a huge "back field" that measured nearly an acre. It was open grass where, as kids, we spent hours playing football, baseball and riding minibikes and go-carts that my dad built from scratch. Dad would take a piece of iron from here, a sprocket from there, a used motor from somewhere else, and using only drawings from the recesses of his mind, produce the kinds of toys many kids can only dream of.

From some of my earliest memories, I remember having a green mini-bike, a gold mini-bike, a white go-cart, a dune buggy made from Cushman golf cart parts, a three-wheeler made from an old Cushman Eagle and a Toro lawn tractor, all made with love in the middle of dad's garage. We also owned two riding lawn mowers that would rival anything you'd see today at Sears, complete with expanded metal grills and formed sheet metal fenders.

When I was younger, dad helped me build a soap box car for Cub Scouts complete with a complex steering mechanism. As teenagers, my brothers and I could always count on dad to keep our cars running, even when it meant major overhauls and body work. On one occasion, dad hauled home parts of an old Farmall tractor. It was basically a pile of junk with transmission and engine hulls full of grass and rat's nests. To us it was junk. To dad, it was a mowing and snow plowing machine complete with a five-foot mower deck and snow blade. After nearly forty years, the tractor continues to run and sits in my brother's garage on HIS acreage.

The garage was dad's domain. "Mom takes care of the inside stuff. I take care of the outside stuff. That works for us," I can still hear him avow. I loved walking into the garage where you could almost always find dad leaned over some piece of metal, the torch lit or the welder arcing.

"Don't look at the arc," he'd say. "The light will blind you." It was always all I could do to look away, but the smell of smelting iron still holds fast to my senses and the sound of a buzzing welder always brings me home. One of my few regrets in life has been that I didn't let my dad teach me to weld. He tried several times. But I was either too young or then too busy to take the time to learn something like that. There was just too much baseball, cars and dating. I couldn't be bothered. I have his welder and torch in my possession today. How I wish I knew how to use them.

On still another occasion, our house needed a new foundation. Dad probably could have hired it done, but instead rigged a way to lift our enormous house from its foundation, dig out the basement, remove the old blocks and completely rebuild the walls that held our home. He operated the backhoe that dug the trenches, dug and poured the footings and laid nearly every block. He had some help from my brothers, but basically tackled this gargantuan project alone.

When it was finished, the wall along the north side of the basement developed a crack caused by the vibration of passing grain trucks on the road in front of our house. Dad decided to have that issue examined by an expert who told dad, "It can't be fixed." I guess the expert forgot who he was talking to. Dad fashion screw jacks along the wall at about 45 degree angles and anchored them in the floor and along the wall. Each night and sometimes every few days, dad would go to the basement and turn all those jacks one turn. Just one. Ever so slowly, the wall was pushed back to its original position, the crack closed and dad secured the wall with I-beams that were fastened to the floor-joists. It was a genius display of engineering and patience. Couldn't be fixed? Indeed.

Although an aircraft welder by trade, Dad was an engineer and an artist at heart. He made copper barns to adorn walls and wire carriages pulled by little wooden horses. He designed and built the railing around our patio from square tubing and made patio furniture to match. He even designed the pillars that held the roof over the back porch which, of course, also matched the set.

For all dad's redeeming qualities, and there were several; he didn't smile much. In fact, many nights around the family dinner table, the side-aches caused by everyone else's obsessive laughter revolved around dad's stone face. The more serious he looked, the harder we laughed. It sounds like we were making fun of him, but in truth, I think dad enjoyed the laughter. He was just afraid to admit it.

There were only two things I remember making my dad laugh, or even smile. One was playing pranks on his friends. The other was a comedian named Justin Wilson.

I was with my parents on one winter afternoon as we were leaving Lincoln. I remember it well. We were coming down a hill from the Cornhusker Highway overpass when dad spotted one of his friends on the side of the road, seemingly dumping his Christmas tree. When we stopped to render aid, dad's friend explained that the tree had "blown off the top of his car and he was just picking it back up." We ventured only a few blocks down the road before dad turned around, suspicious of his friend's lame explanation. Sure enough, just as dad suspected, the tree remained where we had seen it last on the side of the road. The friend was nowhere in sight. Dad cheerfully picked up the tree, loaded it in the trunk of our car, and drove several miles out of our way to the friend's house. To my dad's delight, no one was home.

He opened the trunk of our '69 Chevy Impala, pulled out the tree, opened the door to his friend's red Dodge pickup truck and with a grin as wide as the Grinch, stuffed the tree in the cab and closed the door. The harvest green rotary phone mounted firmly to the wall in our kitchen was ringing when we got home. I can still hear dad's friend screaming through the earpiece as dad held it away from his face, the corners of his usually downturned mouth touching his ears.

The boy entered the lumber yard and told the man behind the counter, "My dad needs fifty 4x2s." To which the man inquired, "How long does your dad want 'em?" The boy said, "I'll be right back!" Upon returning the boy explained to the man tending the counter at the lumber yard, "My dad's building a house. He wants 'em a long, long time!"

Justin Wilson was a Cajun comedian who told that story and many others like it. Dad would place the circular LP on the record player, sit at the dark-stained dining room table by himself and roar with laughter at the antics of Justin Wilson. Tears would roll as he threw his head back in the chair and laugh until his belly shook. When friends came over, dad would sit them around the table and make them listen to Justin Wilson stories. Most would laugh with him. I think many were as puzzled as I that the usually stoic Bill Leatherwood had been moved to such humorous emotion. It's a puzzle I haven't solved to this day. I'm only happy my father found humor in something!

My father was a great dad. I already explained all the toys he built for us and the cars he kept running. But there was so much more. For starters, he went to work every day to help provide a comfortable living for our family. I'd like to say he never complained about it, and often he didn't express his weariness verbally. But even when he didn't speak his disdain, his body language showed it when he walked through the door. Most days after work, the house was met by dad's heavy sigh, a deep breath, slowly blown out as he removed his boots and eased into the kitchen.

Many of my fondest childhood memories are of fishing with my dad. Because of his flexible work schedule, he was usually the one designated to take me to dentist or doctor appointments. If it was a school day, almost without exception, we hauled the small fishing boat along and played hooky, heading for one of the local lakes and a day of jigging for crappie. On occasion we'd take along one of his friends. But I was his little fishin' buddy. I know that for a fact because he told everyone we saw from the friend to the bait shop owner. Although he didn't call me "special" like mom did, he made me feel that way every time he called me his little buddy. Those moments are priceless to me.

We didn't always talk a lot on those trips. You would think those days would have been excellent opportunities for my dad to talk to me about God and the afterlife. It never came up; not once. All these stories and descriptions of my dad were painted to give you some idea of the spiritual influence he had on me. In short, I received only brief glimpses of my dad's view on things spiritual.

He was the son of a Southern Pentecostal Preacher and was raised in the deep south of Texas. Dad grew up near Beaumont, Silsby and Vidor, near the Big Thicket across the state line in Louisiana where Bonnie and Clyde were gunned down by law enforcement officers in 1934. Although unusual for the time, his parents divorced at a young age and dad spent much of his time with his Grandpa, camping and fishing on the Sabine River. I always loved hearing stories from those days.

Dad grew up tough, poor, lonely, bigoted and angry. He made it through the eighth grade in school before dropping out and surviving however he could. He eventually got a job on the shipyard until he could join the Navy at age seventeen. After one marriage which lasted less than a year (I didn't learn about that until I was 20), dad met mom. The rest about that is history.

Whatever dad learned from HIS father about Christianity either didn't sink in or he didn't want it. Besides being exposed to racial slurs dad picked up in the deep South, the only biblical wisdom he passed on to me was in the form of things he'd obviously heard his dad mention. "The last perfect man died over 2000 years ago" or "In the end the world will be ruled by a race of small yellow people." To this day I have NO idea what the hell he was talking about. I've read the Bible cover-to-cover and I still can't find a reference to yellow people. Dad heard it and believed it as gospel even if he himself didn't know what it meant. It was his way of departing wisdom to his son.

On one occasion, the parents of one of my friends came to our house to invite my parents to a church they were starting. Dad barely let them get started with the invitation before he told them, "I was a Pentecostal Preachers kid and I grew up in the church. I'll go BACK to church when I am goddamn good and ready." I think it was the last time the two couples spoke. Clearly, dad harbored some resentment about his spiritual upbringing. But even so, on special occasions like Thanksgiving and Christmas, we always said a prayer before eating. "God is great. God is good. Let us thank him for our food. Amen." That was the only praying I ever heard at my house.

For all dad's qualities, good or bad, I can say this without hesitation. He believed in his three boys. He believed in me. I've told more than one person through the years that I or any of my brothers could have killed a man on the front steps of our house, and dad's first reaction would have been, "There must have been a damn good reason." We were his boys and I never doubted for one second he would have died for any one of us without delay. He may not have had a clear understanding of his belief in God, but he believed in me. Did then. Does now. Always will.

Lesson Six:

EVERYTHING AND EVERYONE ARE COMPLETELY CONNECTED

"Life is as dear to the mute creature as it is to a man. Just as one wants happiness and fears pain, just as one wants to live and not to die, so do other creatures."

~His Holiness, The Dalai Lama

Human body-sized bergs of ice floated gingerly down Salt Creek, occasionally coming up for air, as my brother and I waded carefully downstream donned in our heavy coats, rubber gloves and hip waders. Barren elm trees towered over our heads along opposing banks, disrobed by yet another brisk fall and frigid early winter.

My brother and I were winter fur trappers and traders. It fit in nicely with the fantasy I'd developed of being a mountain man. It also helped supplement my allowance and put gas in my car. During some seasons I pocketed as much as $400, which was a small fortune to a teenager.

It was like this most every winter before the hard freeze. Just before the creek froze solid, finally succumbing to sub-zero temperatures, chunks of ice would begin to form and drift along, bumping my brother and I in the back of the legs as we waded along checking our muskrat traps which lined both sides of a creek that varied in depth from ankle to chest. Although we were familiar with the layout of the river, a wrong step would mean filling your waders with icy fluid which at worst could pull you under and drown you. At best, the temperature of your entire lower torso would begin to plummet and the pain and discomfort of approaching frostbite made a usually peaceful outing excruciating. Stepping in a hole and filling our hip waders had happened to each of us at least once and it was NOT a feat we cared to repeat.

On this particular sunny, yet frosty Saturday morning, we were moving our traps downriver to a place where we hadn't yet depleted the population of muskrat. Adding to the intrigue of the ice formations trying to drag us under was the small detail of reports a man had drowned upstream in Lincoln a few days before. No body had been recovered and the search spanned a portion of the river we explored. In other words, every time we were bumped by a chunk of ice, we were sure we had just been discovered by the ghost of Salt Creek. We were both pretty spooky in those days and watching us jump and gasp must have made a hilarious spectacle. In fact, hearing my brother and I share those tales back home was another thing that actually made my dad smile.

We had just completed checking our traps along "Old Salt Run," a stagnate body of moss-layered filthy water which ran from the local cesspool westerly until in dumped into Salt Creek. It was rich with muskrat and we chose to leave those traps where they were for the time being and concentrate on moving the torturous metal objects that lined both sides of the larger creek.

Now would probably be a good time to offer a little background on the "art" of trapping muskrat. You may not like it, but at least it will offer a glimpse in to how we captured the furry prey on a shallow river. Our basic premise was to watch the creek banks for signs of activity in the form of muskrat tracks or dens that were dug into the side of the river. Once a suitable spot was chosen, we would place a steel trap just below water level right against the bank. The end or chain of the trap was then tied to a stake which we placed away from the bank in deeper water. Once the unsuspecting rodent found his leg embraced by the unforgiving steel, the current would pull him into deeper water where he would then drown. We knew we had a catch when there was no trap visible along the bank. A lone stake with no visible trap meant we had added one to our bag of goods. On rare occasions we would find empty traps where larger muskrat had chewed off a leg in order to escape. As gruesome and unforgiving as it sounds now, it was just normal fare back then. I seldom gave it a second thought.

During the previous week we had noticed that raccoon had burrowed a large den under a large tree directly across the river from one of our traps. Although raccoon pelts brought substantially more money than muskrat, we just weren't rigged for trapping them so we stuck to larger numbers of pelts with lesser value. We had discussed trying to trap some of the raccoon family, but collectively decided it just wasn't worth the retooling.

As we approached the trap directly across from the raccoon den, we made a discovery that caught us both by surprise. Although our intent was to merely check the trap and move it downstream, what we found stopped us knee-deep in frigid water. We looked at each other in amazement. An unsuspecting raccoon, while walking down the riverbank looking for food, had stepped in our muskrat trap. Apparently the coon's extra weight and size made it possible for him to step up higher on the bank rather than being pulled into the deeper water. There he stood, firmly grasped by the cold steel, glaring in amazement now at the two men responsible for his predicament.

I have to admit our first response was to count money since a raccoon pelt meant $35 as opposed to just the $4 or $5 we received for a good muskrat. The raccoon's pitiful predicament quickly created a second response from both of us, which was that we should just release him to be reunited with his family across the river. We just stared at each other and shook our head. How on earth were we supposed to approach an angry, cornered raccoon and just let him go? There was no way on earth this bandit-faced rascal was going to let us anywhere near him. He hissed, and glared and pulled back on the trap, reminding us of the cruelty of his plight.

We discussed several options, all of which eventually led to one of us being face-to-face with the angry critter while we tried to loosen the trap. Try as we might to muster a solution that didn't require such close quarters, neither of us could come up with a thing. And even if we could, we wondered, how would he fair in the wild with a broken leg? It seemed the raccoon's fate was determined by a power higher than ours and we clearly couldn't just leave him.

My dad owned a small, .22 caliber revolver which my brother and I almost always carried with us while trapping, just to be on the safe side. Many times we brought along a semi-automatic rifle, but since we were moving traps, we opted to reduce our load and leave it at home. Strapped to my side in a hand-made leather holster rested the revolver. I pulled it from its supple container and pondered my next assignment. I raised the pistol toward the waiting raccoon and pulled back the hammer. What happened then is something I never would have guessed. I couldn't pull the trigger. With the raccoon in close range and clearly in my sites, I just couldn't do it. I eased the hammer back into its resting position and handed the pistol to my brother.

It was now his turn to carry out the task I couldn't bring myself to do. My brother quivered with the same level of regret, but there just didn't seem a better option. As my brother pulled back the hammer in preparation for squeezing off a round into the raccoons skull, something happened even more astounding than the fact that I had been unable to do it. The raccoon pressed his body firmly into the bank, cocked his head slightly and closed one eye, showing without a doubt in all this universe that he knew what was coming. He knew. He knew death was coming and he knew from where…and from whom.

With a deep sigh my brother slowly squeezed the trigger, igniting the gun powder that launched the small pebble of lead into the raccoon, ending his innocent life. He lowered the weapon to his side as the wisp of smoke and smell of gun powder circled our heads. We stood there in stunned silence as I eased the pistol from his hand and slid it back into the holster. The deed was done.

We pulled the now-lifeless wildlife from the trap and placed him in the gunny sack already brimming with muskrat. We exchanged more glances and spoke only briefly of the raccoon's last-minute behavior. We finished moving the rest of our trap line without speaking a word. We were both moved and shaken. Nearly thirty-five years later, my brother and I still often talk about the behavior of that raccoon. His face is clearer to me than that of the deer OR the rabbit. It was as if we had shot a higher being.

There is a reasonable amount of debate in the religious world about the soul of animals. Do they have souls? Do they reason? Do they have a concept of time and do they ponder their mortality? Well, you may certainly feel free to debate that issue all you want. I was there. I saw the face of that petrified creature and I can assure you animals reason. They have feelings and they are, indeed, aware of their mortality. You may ask any person that owns a horse, cat or faithful dog and they'll tell you the same thing. We took the life of another being with a soul that day. It was as if we'd killed a human. It makes me ache for the soldiers that have been forced to do that very thing for centuries.

Although I didn't fully realize it at the time, that day was another huge step in my spiritual journey. It was another reminder of the futility of hunting for sport. Hunting to provide food is one thing. Hunting for profit or for fun is quite another. The desire to hunt or trap took another few years to leave me completely, but a seed had been planted and a doubt sprouted I could not deny. I hadn't the means to put it into words back then, but I certainly can now. We are all the same. We are all made of the same matter. You can call it energy or stardust or spirit or whatever you'd like, but we're all connected. From the smallest caterpillar to the largest mammal, we are all related. Nothing happens to one with affecting all. With all my might, I shall determine to never kill anything again.

Lesson Seven:

CHURCH ISN'T THE PLACE FOR A CHILD TO FIND ANSWERS

"The great awareness comes slowly, piece by piece. The path of spiritual growth is a path of lifelong learning. The experience of spiritual power is basically a joyful one."

~M. Scott Peck

The Methodist church I attended as a child was located across town on the corner of Main and Maple. It was down the street from the Legion Hall, both grocery stores and the local bar. A two-story brick structure, it adorned a large bell mounted on two tall poles on the west and a ground-level marquee in front that announced the service times and name of the current pastor. A narrow set of concrete steps ascended to heavy wooden front doors complete with thick brass handles.

Once inside the foyer, you could trot down the stairs to the basement where Bible School, Boy Scout meetings and the annual Thanksgiving feast were held. There was an open area, two small classrooms and a kitchen. The interior foyer doors opened to a sanctuary filled with dark-stained pews arranged in an open semi-circle with two aisles. Two small steps led up to the raised pulpit overlooked by the large brass tubes of the pipe-organ. The organ itself was situated to the left of the pulpit. The same local lady played that organ for as long as I attended. The windows were typical stained works of art, and depicted the usual scenes of Jesus holding a lamb, Jesus praying by a boulder and various angels. The sanctuary hinted the scent of a library and carried the same ambience.

In addition to the reliable organ player, there was a trio of women who sang nearly every Sunday. (At least every Sunday I was there. We didn't go every Sunday. In fact, we didn't go a lot of Sundays!) Although today I admire the dedication to their church, back then it just seemed they sang the same ole worn out songs. In fact, the hymns the entire congregation sang were slow and boring. Singing those old hymns was like scraping your fingers on the chalkboard. It was almost more than I could bear.

The Methodist church in Greenwood seemed like a landing strip for wayward and worn out ministers. Today I can see that most were either ready for retirement or in some kind of trouble with the Methodist organization, so they were shipped off to a small town where they could be largely invisible. I can't believe any of them actually ASKED for the assignment! Each pastor was responsible for two parishes. They ministered to the flock in Greenwood and also to a lesser population at a country church outside town. Back then, there was no such thing as an Associate Pastor, Youth Minister or Choir director. One person did it all. Yes, one person. We even had female pastors!

I first heard the term "Chreaster" as a young adult. Upon hearing the definition, I was able to attach a label to my religious upbringing and the philosophy of my family. We were, indeed, Chreasters. Except on rare occasions where mom felt the need to drag us to church, we basically attended services on two major holidays; Christmas and Easter. If you're a Christian, it should be easy to identify the importance of these two holidays. Christmas, of course, celebrates the birth of Jesus.

Easter celebrates the death and resurrection of Jesus, whereby he conquered death in payment for our sins and set us all free.

Christmas services were merely an obligatory event we attended after we got bored playing with our new toys. Christmas, for me, was never about the birth of the Christ Child, it was about being good so Santa would bring me lots of toys. Christmas was a colossal event at our house. Christmas Eve was a dress-up event with a "formal" dinner. I can still see the dining room table draped with mom's best lace tablecloth, the clean china, and the smell of Oyster stew. In later years, the Oyster stew was replaced with Prime Rib, thank God (no pun intended), but it was still a feast followed by the opening of ONE gift. I was always in a rush for everyone to choke down the aromatic feast so we could get to the gifts. Except for the singing of an occasional Christmas carol and the usual "God is great, God is good" prayer, Jesus was never mentioned as part of our Christmas.

Easter was an even MORE puzzling event. I'll get into this in more depth later in the book, but it bears mentioning here. If you are a Christian, Easter should be the day that stands out among all the rest. I didn't understand this until years later, but it's hard to believe it got past me. Briefly, (and I'll paraphrase here), Jesus was sent by God to pay for our sins. That payment was to be in the form of Jesus's death and resurrection. On Easter (listen carefully here) Jesus was resurrected. According to scripture, HE ROSE FROM THE DEAD!! Do you understand the thing I never did as a child? THIS day is about the fulfillment of prophesy. THIS day is about the good news. THIS day is the basis for the entirety of Christianity. I hunted eggs the Easter Bunny had hidden.

Easter Sunday meant getting up early for Sunrise Service. It meant putting on a suit I wore for NO other occasion. It meant hunting eggs and eating candy. Then it meant a formal lunch complete with ham, scalloped potatoes and "God is great, God is good." Except for that lame prayer and what little I may have caught at the morning service, Jesus wasn't part of our Easter. That starring role belonged to the Easter Bunny.

I don't blame my parents for this important oversight. They either didn't understand the truth either or, like a lot of people, were just too embarrassed to talk about it. I don't blame the church entirely. I'm sure the message was there somewhere, but without some guidance outside the pews, it was a message lost on a child.

It would be unfair to say that Christmas and Easter were the only times I attended church. According to a schedule I didn't fully understand, I randomly attended Sunday school. I can't recall whether or not my parents attended church while I was in the basement. I just know I saw the same faces and colored the same pictures of Jesus over and over again. You'd have thought they'd taught us SOMETHING about Easter.

I also regularly attended Bible School in June. It was a one-week affair that my mother thought would be good for me. As a parent, I now understand how having your child busy for a week in the summer can also be good for the parent. Regardless of the reason, Bible School was always an extension of the same Sunday school I attended once in a while on Sunday mornings. I colored the same pictures, sang the same dry child-versions of the same worn out hymns, and saw the same teachers. Still, I don't recall anything about the Christmas or Easter stories. I find that odd. In many ways I actually find that disturbing. To this day I haven't received a clear answer of why you would call something "school" and then learn nothing about the subject involved.

There was actually one event held at our church every year that I looked forward to attending. Next to the Volunteer Fire Department Pancake Breakfast, the Thanksgiving feast at the Methodist church was nothing short of spectacular. We never missed it. The same ladies that sang in the trio and taught

Sunday school also prepared a wonderful feast from the small kitchen in the basement. Aided by some of the church men, they prepared turkey, mashed potatoes, sage dressing (I hadn't even heard of cornbread dressing until I moved to Texas), vegetables and a host of different pies. It was all served buffet style by apron-draped, smiling faces. The line to reach the food always extended out the front door of the church. I always looked forward to seeing familiar faces and hanging with some friends I didn't see all the time since I wasn't at Sunday school every week. I wonder to this day if the pastor of the church ever questioned why this many people didn't show up on Sundays.

At the tender age of twelve, someone, and I have NO idea who, decided it was time for me to be baptized. I've since been exposed to traditions from various churches that lead to baptism. It is truly amazing all I had to go through to be prepared for baptism at the Greenwood Methodist Church. First, I had to—well, ok, I had to do nothing. That's the truth. In preparation for my being washed in the blood of Jesus, accepting him as my personal savior and being blessed in the name of the Father, the Son and the Holy Spirit, I did nothing in terms of preparation with the church. I realize now that some preparation of my heart may have been in order, but there was none. I had NO idea what baptism was about. I was told it was something people do and so I did it. And so did my dad. I'm not sure he understood what it was all about either.

On that infamous of Sunday mornings, we all got dressed in our Easter best and trekked across town to church. After a ceremony that was completely like all the rest I ever attended, those to be baptized were lined up in the front of the pulpit and then "sprinkled" by the damp hand of the minister who "baptized thee in the name of the Father, the Son and the Holy Spirit. Amen." No bright lights. No feeling Jesus enter my heart. I was the same kid after that I was before, only wetter.

I just did not get it. But then again, no one explained it to me either. Now I ask you, did the church fail or my parents?

Looking back now I can see that all this wasn't for nothing. What little bit of church I did attend, when combined with the profound teachings of Sunday/Bible school and those of my father taught me some important things. First, there were ten commandments God delivered to Moses and they were strict. Follow them or spend eternity in Hell. Second, I was good at coloring between the lines of Jesus pictures. And finally, the world was going to be ruled by a race of small yellow people.

As sad as that may seem to you, that is what I remember about my childhood religious upbringing from the church. I knew very early that I could never live up to those commandments, so I resigned myself to eternity in hell and got on about living.

Lesson Eight:

GRIEVING THE DEAD IS NORMAL AND OUR SPIRITS LIVE ON

"Every puppy should have a boy."

~Erma Bombeck

Small bundles of liver and white fur balls littered the crushed rock driveway of our Greenwood acreage. The grunting, warm-breathed pups were the latest from the womb of our Springer Spaniel, Tammy. I don't recall exactly how many were in this litter, but I do know that Tammy brought forth sixty-three puppies in her lifetime.

Sitting firmly on its wheel-wells, directly east of our large detached garage was the back of an old insulated milk truck which had long since been painted white. Although clearly a piece of landscaping you would only hear about in a "you might be a redneck if" joke, it then served as a combination "tool storage and dog shed." The front of the "shed" served as a spider web-invested place of rest for old lawn mower and mini-bike parts. The back, set apart from the front with old snow fence was where our dogs stayed in a large pile of fresh straw. As ugly as the old shed was, it was perfect insulation for the animals from the cold Nebraska winters.

Tammy, somewhat of a neighborhood "rounder" as dogs go, was an incredible mother. She mated with a variety of breeds throughout the area, but on occasion we did actually come up with some pure Springer Spaniels. This was one of those litters. As cozy as our milk truck shed was, more often than not, Tammy would sneak off somewhere more remote to have her puppies. She had one batch in the neighbor's shed and another underneath our clubhouse, but up until now, Tammy had never lost a pup. Like I said, Tammy was a great mother.

Baseball season was in full bloom during the spring and my brothers were both stars of the local baseball team. As it turns out, the front of our garage made a perfect backstop for two guys wanting to play a little game of catch. More specifically, Ron would play the part of pitcher while Geary would squat down low and catch. If a ball got by him, the garage made the stop. With a full acre of open field behind us, you'd think playing ball in the driveway wouldn't be necessary, but as kids we used every part of the two acres at our disposal at one time or another. Besides, the field didn't have a backstop.

It was a perfect Norman Rockwell scene that played out that day. I was playing with some toy cars on the back patio. Ron and Geary were playing the pitch and catch game in front of the garage. Dad was working on something in the garage while mom made dinner in the kitchen. The older dogs lounged around in the warm sun as the barely-weaned puppies grunted and waddled their way around the front of the dog shed, right next to the garage. You could not have written, planned or painted a more perfect day. It was as if Contentment and Peace had settled over the Leatherwood Acreage.

The "thud" was so faint that at first I didn't realize what had happened. The event was brought into focus by the screams from my brother of, "Oh no! Oh no! Oh my god, I'm so sorry! No!"

My dad ran from the garage and my mother from the house, but I just sat and stared as the rest of the family knelt around the puppy now seizing from high-speed head trauma. It was the kind of accident that left you sleepless at night. Ron had a pitch slip prematurely from his hand and wildly, yet randomly, the baseball connected with the frontal lobe of a small puppy instead of Geary's glove. There was no fault. There is no blame to be placed. It was an accident where too many objects occupied the same space and the puppy lost the battle where the rules are so clearly defined by physics. The small wobbly pup seized for only a moment and then died. It was my first experience with the bluntness of mortality. First you're here. Then you're gone.

I finally rose to be with the rest of my family who were already crying and surrounding the pup. I too was sobbing uncontrollably and whispering the same "no, no, no" under my breath. The puppies were still too young for me to have actually bonded with one of them. Instead, I bonded with them all. I loved the feel of their fur and the warmth and sweetness of their breath. I couldn't bring myself to believe that one of them was dead. Dead! What does that mean exactly? The only schooling I'd received about death and dying was the typical "When you die you go to heaven" story. And that's what I was told now. The puppy was in a "better place." I have to tell you, I didn't find a great deal of comfort in that. It seems to me the place that puppy was occupying just moments ago was just fine and dandy. Better? And where the hell IS this better place? Heaven? Ok so where IS heaven? What is heaven? Dogs can go too?

This little scene has played out in my head over a period of forty years. No, it isn't a real tragedy in the overall scheme of things, but it was a devastating blow for me then. I can only imagine how my brother must have felt. And as you might guess, it has raised a myriad of questions about the afterlife. It's raised even more questions about why parents are so reluctant to discuss death with their children. Death is part of life. Despite all the questions, the answers would probably encompass a book all their own. We won't bother with it now. But this entire event was a definite marker in my spiritual development.

My dad retreated to the machine shed (different than the milk truck) and grabbed a rounded, rusty shovel from where it was hanging by two small nails on the back wall. His shoulders slumped as his boots shuffled across the crushed rock. He approached the limp animal and with me by his side, scooped the lifeless animal into his arms.

I have absolutely no recollection of where the rest of the family went at that time. I only remember my dad and I carrying the puppy shovel in hand to the east edge of our property where a half acre of Kentucky bluegrass met a small field of alfalfa. Dad placed the puppy gently on the ground as he turned over the first load of dirt. I cried in disbelief, knelt to caress the soft fur and waited as dad finished the small grave where we lay the puppy to final rest. Once he was covered, dad placed his hand on my shoulder and we walked away. No words were spoken, but within the hour I was back at the side of the puppy's grave, on my knees and crying. I wasn't sure what prayer amounted to outside of "God is great" and "Now I lay me down to sleep," but even then I remember thinking something should be said over the grave of this small animal. So I did the best I could. I prayed whatever prayer a young boy prays for the loss of something so precious.

The giant elm tree where I liked to go to be alone was about a hundred feet directly south of where we buried the puppy. It towered over a secluded area behind our machine shed and was graced with a magnificent "tire swing" where I would sit for hours at a time. Up and down. Up and down. Feet in front. Feet behind. Drag to stop. Spin and spin. Unwind until you're dizzy. Repeat. It was my place of solitude and it was there the idea of my pet cemetery was launched. I think it's entirely possible my grown-up fascination with cemeteries was born in the same location.

Within the week following the accidental death of Tammy's offspring, I measured off an area surrounding the grave. It wasn't big, but it was probably enough to make it irritating for my dad to mow around. He never said a word. I drove wooden stakes on each of the corners and stretched a nylon string around each to fashion a fence. On the small mound where the puppy was buried, I placed a small wooden cross I made from some spare wood laying around dad's garage. It was a proper place of rest for the fallen and it was there I went nearly every day to kneel and talk to the small mound of dirt. Strange as it may seem, it was also my small cemetery where I would bring some of my neighborhood friends to pray with me as well. I can't remember a single time anyone ever balked at joining me in prayer at the pet cemetery. What they said after they left may be a different story entirely. I had loyal friends and this book will help you get to know some of them.

There were other pets that earned their place in the Leatherwood Pet Cemetery, but for the life of me I don't remember them all. The first is the one that sticks. The first puppy that I ever truly called my own, Tonka Wakon (The Great One), was run over at my brother's place several blocks down the road and although he wasn't buried in my cemetery, I did use a hot branding iron to emblazon his name across the top of a wooden cross and place it on his grave at my brother's place. He kindly left the marker there for years even though I'm sure it was in the way.

I had no idea at the time these experiences with pets were helping to shape me spiritually. I know today I've felt some connection with almost every animal I've been near. I've even gone so far as to feel sadness over trading a car, or selling a certain lamp at a garage sale. I think all these animals, and even things, have taught me we're all connected. Of that I am certain. And I've marked the grave of every pet I've ever owned.

Lesson Nine:

YOUR BEST FRIENDS AREN'T NECESSARILY THE MOST OBVIOUS

"My heart is warm with the friends I make,
and better friends I'll not be knowing;
Yet there isn't a train I wouldn't take,
No matter where it's going."

~Edna St. Vincent Millay

The pungent aroma of salmon patties filled the kitchen and dining area as my stomach began to churn at the thought of kindly choking down the meal so warmly laid before me by Lonnie's mom. I'm sure she must have prepared other meals when I had dinner with my best friend and his family, but salmon patties is the one that sticks in my memory. It may have been only once, but it seems every time I was there, salmon patties were on the menu and I always did my best to eat them.

Lonnie's dad was pastor of one of our local churches; the Greenwood Christian Church. He was a warm, inviting and humorous man that I admired a great deal. As I slid my chair closer to the table, facing the window that peered out to the open field that was my back yard and home to many baseball and football games, Gail began to pray.

What was a "God is great, God is good" episode at my home on holidays, was a regular event for every meal at Lonnie's house. As Lonnie, his brother, sister, mom and dad and I bowed our heads, Gail would begin with a "Dear Lord," or "Heavenly Father" which was only the beginning of a long dissertation which usually involved thanking God for just about everything you can imagine. His prayers went on forever! Each time Gail took a breath, I would sheepishly glance up from my folded hands, expecting an "amen." It never came as fast I thought it might. If the food was too hot, by the time prayer was over, it was as right as Momma Bear's porridge.

Lonnie was my best friend and neighbor. As very young kids, we spent hours together. His mom watched me during the time my mom worked days at the factory. Along with the salmon patties, his mom made the best afternoon snacks. They always included some kind of peanuts, marshmallows and chocolate chips. Those days are a little fuzzy to me, but I can picture the stairs leading to his basement and the black and white tile floor like I was on it yesterday.

Lonnie's life revolved around church. His dad was the pastor and the entire family sang at church and surrounding as the "Singing Portenier Family"; sort of a gospel singing group. Gail played a Wurlitzer 12-string hollow-body guitar. Lonnie played piano and his younger brother the drums. I don't remember what his mom and sister did. They sounded great the one time I heard them. Today I find that odd. I only heard them sing once.

On occasion, Lonnie and I went to visit his dad at the train depot. In addition to his duties at the church, Gail was a full-time employee of Burlington Northern Railroad. He worked at the local depot which sat along the tracks that ran through town. Today it sits in the City Park as a museum. It makes me feel kind of old to think I used to play in a museum.

There's a point to all this background information. My best friend was part of a devoted Christian family. His dad was pastor of the local church. They prayed at every meal. They HAD to know my family was practically heathenistic. And except for the one time I actually attended vacation Bible school at their church instead of mine, and maybe one or two occasions where I attended some function at their church, they never discussed Jesus or the concept of God with me. Not once. And it isn't as though Lonnie and I moved away from each other. We started Kindergarten and graduated from high school…together.

To be clear, I don't blame them. It isn't something I even realized as a kid. I didn't walk around asking myself why the local pastor didn't try to save my soul. I didn't even know what that meant. But as a grown-up, I now find that odd. As a man who has now BEEN a Christian, I don't understand how people that are don't spend their days saving souls from eternal damnation. But I think we're going to get to that a little later on in the book. I know we are.

Lonnie and I ran with another boy named Randy. He too, was musically talented, but came from a different home than Lonnie or me. His parents were divorced. He seemed to have a little more "freedom" and wasn't watched over much. He seemed like a normal kid, but clearly had greater struggles than me. When he was young he was already playing lead guitar in his dad's band. I'm sure he saw things I couldn't even imagine. He was confident and tough. He moved away before we went to Junior High and was killed in his early twenties by accidental electrocution. I still think about Randy on occasion and remember how he showed me I could run faster by keeping my hands flat instead of clenching my fists. He was ahead of his time.

I had yet another "friend" that inadvertently taught me to question the rules of religion. He came from a staunch Catholic family and as far as I know, they all went to mass every Sunday. He is serving time for murder at this moment and I can recall a time when he got angry while several of us were playing, went home for a knife and came back pointing it at all of us, ranting and raving. This same person, after ordering a burger from a local joint in Ashland where I went to Junior High said, "I can't eat this. I can't eat meat on Fridays." You can't tell me Catholicism isn't a powerful religion. But we'll get to that.

Like just about any small-town kid growing up in the 1970s I had lots of neighborhood friends and Greenwood was our playground. We rode bikes all over town. We hiked and played Ditchem (hide-and-seek in the dark), played football and baseball in the back yard, rode mini-bikes and even got into some mischief. All of it was misdemeanor type stuff and caused no real harm. We fished and hunted and even trick-or-treated together. It was a story book existence. But despite all we did together, I don't recall ever talking to a single friend about God, except for one particular night.

Right next to the machine shed where dad parked his Farm-All tractor and parked the family cars was the neighborhood clubhouse. It sat on the edge of our large back field and was the remains of what was once a chicken coop. It had a rounded roof, a wooden bench that ran the length of the floor, and a trap door which led to an earthen hideaway only a foot below where curious boys could stash a stolen copy of the latest centerfold. It didn't require a setup like a tent and was a haven for me and many of my friends on long summer nights. I lost count of the times we all camped out in the clubhouse.

I don't recall the night we decided to do it nor do I recall the participants except for Lonnie, but on one occasion we decided it would be a night to get spiritual and pray. I remember there being four or five of us. We lit candles and knelt and prayed and chanted and whatever else we could think of that might be pleasing to "God." The actual event is fuzzy, but what I do remember is how "connected" I felt to something or someone. We all professed our love of Jesus even though none of us, save Lonnie had a clue who we were praying to. It just felt good to be spiritual. There may not be a time since when I've felt a deeper connection with God. After a night of prayer and sleep, I awoke the next morning to status quo. The previous night had only been a passing fancy. Everyone went their separate ways and another prayer campout never took place.

I could write chapter after chapter of childhood exploits involving my friends. Winters were a wonderland and the summer days were endless. It was paradise on earth. But all those experiences aren't the point of this narrative. Even as a child I was seeking. I was looking for answers. I was looking for spirit. I was looking for God. I was looking for a way to fit in to our universe before I even knew I was looking. Not my parents, or my friends or even leaders of the local church could provide what I was looking for. You see, they were all involved in their own search just as I was. And although I identified myself as a Christian, it was only because others had given me that label. It meant nothing to me then. I believed in God because I was told God existed. My trouble-free youth was only the beginning of a long and arduous search for answers. They came. But they came ever so slowly. And they came with effort. I had so much to see and experience. There is much unexplained.

Lesson Ten:

THERE ARE FORCES AT WORK WE DON'T UNDERSTAND

"In Witchcraft, each of us must reveal our own truth."

~STARHAWK, Spiral Dance

The eight-foot long, solid oak table levitated off the tile floor as I stood in total disbelief. Six people sat evenly around the edges of the heavy oval table, their fingertips lying lightly on the surface. "Up table, up. Up table, up. UP table, up! UP table, UP! UP TABLE UP!! UP TABLE, UP!!!!" They chanted over and over, louder and louder until the entire table rose gently from the floor. As I gazed in total amazement, the table floated in full suspension only three inches off the floor. With permission, I checked the tension in every hand and forearm. I examined the underside of the table and confirmed there were no knees lifting the piece of furniture. There were no strings, mirrors or ropes. There was no doubt that before me was a two hundred pound table, floating in midair, unassisted by human means.

Mark was one of my best friends during Junior High and High School. He arrived in Greenwood from nearby Lincoln. Mark was a fiery redhead and a great baseball player. He blended well with my other good friend, Mike and collectively we became known as the three M's or "Matthew, Mark and Luke." It's true getting from Mike to Luke was a stretch, but it was a local identifier that stuck. The three of us were practically inseparable. Mark was just like all the rest of us except for one little detail. His mom was a witch. I'm not insinuating that she was grouchy. I mean, according to Mark, she was a bonafide, practicing witch.

Mark's mom was deathly afraid of the most basic superstitions like crossing the path of a black cat or walking under a ladder, breaking a mirror, etc. According to her red-headed son, she would not, under any circumstance, cross the path of a black cat. Mark told of times where his mother had taken a complete detour to avoid such a happening. Mark's mom was one of the sweetest ladies I'd ever met so I found her quirkiness endearing. I think Mark was a little embarrassed. He was a believer in her perceived powers.

On the night I witnessed the game of "Up Table Up," I was spending the night at Mark's house where his mom and dad were entertaining some friends and family. None of what I saw was new to any of them, but to me, it was something from the Twilight Zone. Apparently, according to those playing the game, the table had accurately predicted significant events in family history such as relative's deaths, and so on. In response to simple questions, the table would tap out numbers on the floor…dates, times, etc. It would even allegedly answer yes-or-no questions by tapping once for no, twice for yes. When asked if I was allowed to examine the underside of the table, two solid legs from one side tapped twice clearly on the floor. It then continued to levitate as I examined every possible angle my teenaged mind could imagine. I found absolutely nothing to explain the phenomenon of the floating table.

"Table, is it ok if Matt replaces one of the members at the table?" Mark's mom inquired. Two taps. As one of the family stood up from the table, I slid behind them to the empty chair and placed my fingertips gently on the oak. It continued to float. I don't even remember now the types of questions that were asked. I only remember that there was a response from the table for each. I was told they no longer asked questions about when death would come for certain family members because, so far, the table had been completely accurate and they no longer wanted to know such answers. I just sat in dumbfounded disbelief. Yet as unbelievable as this all was, I was never afraid. I didn't feel the presence of evil spirits or feel the slightest discomfort. I felt only wonder. Mark and I never spoke of the event again. That is, not until nearly twenty-five years later.

In high school, the three amigos befriended a fourth…Dan. Dan was a country kid that came to our school in 9th grade. Over time, he and Mark became inseparable. They were the best of friends and eventually became college roommates. For many years after high school and college, Mark put together a pheasant hunt back in Greenwood and Dan was usually invited. After some good-natured prodding, I was eventually honored with an invitation to the annual hunt as well.

I made a special trip from Texas to spend a day hunting with my old friends. I had seen Dan in recent years, but I hadn't been in touch with Mark in well over a decade. He looked only slightly older than I remembered as we shook hands and hugged. Introductions were made all around and all the members of the annual hunt loaded in the trucks to make our way to open fields of prairie. The landscape was filled with the remains of a magnificent Nebraska fall and I was in heaven. It just didn't get any better than pheasant hunting in Nebraska. The air was crisp and cool as I walked along through harvested fields, gun abreast and ready for action.

After a successful day of hunting, everyone returned to the home of our host, Gary, to clean birds and relive the day's events. It was a wonderful time of laughter and story-telling. When the last bird was cleaned and bagged for later consumption, we all sat around Gary's table and had a beer…or two…or three. Ok, it was a lot of beer, interspersed with shots of Hot Damn, a sort of cinnamon schnapps concoction. The alcohol and stories flowed into the night, yet I had a 6:00 a.m. flight back to Texas to catch the next morning. It wasn't a brilliant move, but certainly a fellowship opportunity that couldn't be disregarded. I had to indulge.

At some point during the evening, Mark, Dan and I decided to hop in Mark's Scout and go for a country drive and have a few more beers. Yes, it was unsafe, but it was great to relive the nights of our youth. We left Dan's truck at the local bar, parked on the sidewalk and nearly through the front door of the grocery store. We piled in Mark's vehicle and headed for rural terrain. (It was after 2:00 a.m. before we remembered where we'd left Dan's truck.)

While driving down remote gravel roads outside of Greenwood, swapping stories and laughing about our mischievous youth, I asked Mark about the night at his home and "Up Table Up." I had not seen or talked to Mark in years so didn't know what his belief system was like. What I do know is that the laughter turned to instant quiet and Mark answered my question in the following manner. "That shit was real. It will never, EVER happen in my house, and I don't want to talk about it anymore." Silence continued to blanket the 4x4 International Scout as we slowly inched our way back to Greenwood. That one question changed the dynamic of the entire day. Apparently I won't ever get details of the table phenomenon. But I've always known Mark to be a man of character and if he says it was real, I believe him.

Many years later, I still think often of the night with the table and the ensuing night with Mark where he refused to elaborate on the event. I don't know if Mark thought there were dark forces at work, or the devil himself come to call.

I only know I felt no fear or the slightest hint of evil when I participated. Not until I heard Mark's answer to my question all those years later. Now I just don't know. I believe in spirit. Yet, I'm not so sure I put stock in pure evil. For all I know, the table levitation was an elaborate illusion that intrigued a child. I'll never know for sure.

What that incident DID do was subconsciously place doubt in a seeking mind about the one-sided view of our universe. There WAS more than meets the eye. There had to be. It was a small, gentle seed that started to take root. Over the years, my view of our universe has changed for the grand, all starting with the wonder of a floating oak table. We're all connected. We're all made of the same stuff…energy.

Lesson Eleven:

CHILDREN NEED MENTORS

"If you're a Boy Scout on Mars with a compass, you're lost."

~Jack Connerney

The small ripples of crystal clear water quietly slapped the sides of my red, canvass kayak as I pushed my way down the drought-ridden trickle of water that was once a swollen Niobrara River. On previous years where spring rains were more abundant, you could easily paddle your way down the scenic wonderland which ran east from the Rockies where it eventually found its way to the Missouri River along the eastern boundary of Nebraska. But not this year. A lack of adequate rain had left the Niobrara River, a popular canoeing venue, shallow and difficult to navigate. I opted for a single-man kayak for this venture and literally had to push the blades of my double-headed paddle against the rocky river bottom in order to make progress. It was grueling work, even for a fourteen year old boy and by day's end, I was completely spent. In ten hours' time, our entire troop had covered only eight miles of river. I drug my kayak to the bank, pitched my tent, denied an offer to eat, and slept through the night.

Trustworthy, loyal, helpful, friendly, courteous, kind, obedient, cheerful, thrifty, brave, clean, and reverent. Those were the twelve words you were to live by as a Boy Scout. The Scout Motto: Be Prepared. And our oath? "On my honor, I will do my best to do my duty to God and my country and to obey the Scout Law; to help other people at all times; to keep myself physically strong, mentally awake, and morally straight." This was the code set before me as a member of Boy Scout Troop 34. It was the closest I ever came as a kid to having a moral code by which to live. The Methodist Church had already made their code seem unobtainable.

Unlike a lot of Boy Scout troops that spent hours and days and months working on a variety of merit badges, ours concentrated on camping and canoeing. We did attend local "Camporees" and even went to Summer Camp a couple of times, but many from our troop never rose above the rank of Tenderfoot. It's not that the many skills you obtained from earning merit badges wasn't important. It's just that our selfless leader felt other lessons were more important; lessons about life. That wonderful, caring, selfless leader was Wayne Howard.

Wayne was a life-long resident of Greenwood. He was an iconic member of the community and there were numerous tales of his exploits as a child. And although he was known by most of the community as the rural mail carrier, to the boys of Troop 34 he was a mentor. His postal code of, "neither rain, nor snow, nor gloom of night" carried over to his caring as a Scoutmaster. Rarely will you find a boy from Greenwood from that era that wasn't influenced in some way by the love of Wayne Howard.

With Wayne there were always consequences for your actions. My brother told me of one fabled story where he had ruthlessly pestered Wayne on a weekend campout. Wayne, although many years older, assured my brother he could not outrun him and that if he kept it up, he would be caught and made to do KP for the rest of the weekend. Some people learn things the hard way and such is the story of my brother. Upon ignoring the repeated warnings of his Scoutmaster, Ron doused Wayne with a bucket of ice water and sprinted for the woods. Wayne followed. Like the tortoise and the hare, Ron sprinted from his consequences and Wayne ran steadily behind him. And just as predicted, Wayne caught my brother and led him back to camp where he did, indeed, do KP for the weekend in order to eat.

On yet another occasion that I witnessed personally, a fellow scout stuck his radio in Wayne's tent as he slept one cold morning. When he got no response from Wayne, he repeated the gesture several times and then finally gave up. About thirty minutes later, Wayne slowly emerged from the canvass hut, stretched and addressed Darrell.

"I'll need a 3x3x3 latrine dug right under this tree. When you're finished, you can eat," he averted with a sheepish grin.

There was no doubting Wayne's resolve and Darrell did as he was told. I can still see Darrell, who was rather large, standing ankle-deep in the hole he had started, ruthlessly chopping away at roots that hindered his progress from a delicious campfire breakfast. It took him well over an hour. But as promised, with the task complete, his breakfast was waiting. Above all Wayne was fair.

For years and years Wayne put aside other duties he may have at home, loaded boys and gear in a pickup truck and went camping or canoeing. And although in the early years two of those boys were Wayne's own sons, he continued long after they left the nest as grown men. Several other local dads took turns chaperoning camping events, but Wayne didn't miss a trip. We camped all over the state, canoed the Platte, Missouri, Niobrara and Snake Rivers, and even spent a night in the woods, nestled in coal-lined shallow grave lean-to's north of Greenwood when the wind chill index reached 25 degrees BELOW zero. In addition to all that, Wayne forfeited his garage every Tuesday night for our Scout meetings. Wayne trusted us, and ornery as many of us were, he always knew we'd do the right thing in the end.

Wayne believed in making memories. On every trip he carried along an 8mm movie camera and recorded movies of our trips. There was no sound to go with the clips, thank God, but every year in the basement of the Methodist Church, Wayne would hold an awards ceremony and show all the local parent's footage of our yearlong exploits. At that ceremony, Wayne had a series of candles lit that represented our twelve principles. He turned out the lights so that only the candles lit the room as he explained what each of those principles represented. With each explanation, he would lick his fingers and snuff out the representing candle to demonstrate how much darker it got with one missing candle. He repeated it with each principle until the room was completely dark, demonstrating what our lives would be like without a code to live by. Even as a restless teen, I always found that display moving. Wayne wanted the best for each of us. For ALL of us.

As I pushed my red kayak along the Niobrara, one of many kayaks engineered by Wayne and hand-made by members of our troop, I'd often catch a glimpse of Wayne on the riverbank melting tar and cutting canvass patches to place on the torn bottom of another victim of the shallow river. I, too, was in need at least once during that day of Wayne's expert kayak repair. The river was tearing up our boats and pressing on meant patching up. Wayne always brought up the rear in his kayak so he could render aid to anyone stranded along the bank. Wayne took responsibility for our safety.

On one of our many river trips, my friend and fellow scout Mark, was treated to a homemade birthday cake made in a Dutch oven right on the bank of the Niobrara River. That cake was prepared and even decorated by our faithful

Assistant Scout Master, Leroy Tinnean. He was as loyal to us as Wayne and rarely missed an excursion. Leroy was jolly and round and his quaking belly was the target of many bouts of endless laughter around a campfire. Wayne and Leroy both cared enough to see that we had home-like experiences even on the river.

If I had a moral compass as a child, I got it from Wayne Howard. The church didn't show me the way. My parents didn't know any better. My friends wouldn't talk about it. But Wayne…Wayne had a code that he lived and taught others. Wayne jogged daily into his eighties. He lost a leg to diabetes and died before I had a chance to tell him what an influence he had on my life and the lives of countless others. But here's the thing about Wayne. I think he knows. And although I no longer believe in an actual place called heaven, if there were such a place, Wayne would be king. Rest in Peace.

I think by now it's clear my childhood was storybook. I had great friends, a wonderful place to grow up and spread my wings. I had two loving parents who saw to it I had everything I ever needed. In short, I had it all. Maybe I had it too good. I had no hardship to sharpen my life skills against. It took adulthood to show me that everything isn't always so rosy. It also took adulthood to lead me to spiritual understanding. It's time to explore that adult life. Come join me, won't you?

PART TWO:
COLLEGE YEARS/AGNOSTICISM

W. C. Fields, a lifetime agnostic, was discovered reading a Bible on his deathbed. "I'm looking for a loop-hole," he explained.

Lesson Twelve:

THERE CAN BE GREAT NEWS IN THE BIGGEST DISAPPOINTMENT

"Nobody has milked one performance better than me—and I'm damned proud of it."

~Bruce Jenner

The bleachers were filled with the spattering of blue and white jerseys, sweats, parents and cheerleaders, all of whom were peering directly at the pinked-hued surface of the University of Nebraska's outdoor track. The uniqueness of the higher-quality surface gave peacefully under the soles of my narrow track spikes as I warmed up for the high hurdle finals of the Nebraska District Track and Field Championships. As a small town athlete, I was used to cinder or asphalt surfaces. This felt like the Olympics and I was center stage.

The carefree days of Junior High and High School were nearing a close. Before me was a summer of work and fun before heading off to college on the campus where I was now preparing to run over 39-inch obstacles for 110 meters. The only business unfinished was securing a gold medal from a major event. To this point, despite years of hard work, silver had been the best I could muster. Today, I knew, would be different. Today I would carry the gold. Today I would earn my place at the State Tournament. Today was my day.

It's difficult to describe the anticipation of entering the starting blocks for a sprint. I'd been there once that day already, but that was simply a qualifying race. This one really counted. I took my place behind the blocks in Lane 2, peeled off my sweats and bent over for one last stretch of my quivering hamstrings. As my pulse quickened and the sweat broke from my brow, I glanced to my right and left at the seven other young men to qualify for this final. I'd seen them all before. I knew their talents. I knew where they were fastest. I knew where they might falter. I knew I'd never beaten any of them. Today was my day. As the crowd and the shimmering sun looked on, the starter called us forward. How could it be possible I had to pee? Hadn't I just gone five minutes earlier? Nerves are a funny thing.

"RUNNERS!!!! COME TO YOUR MARKS!!"

I stepped carefully over the blocks I had previously adjusted to my specifications, shook out my arms and legs, and knelt into position. Right knee forward. Left leg back. Tips of my shoes just making contact with the surface. Fingertips placed closely behind the starting line. Settle in. Focus. Lean forward to bring the right knee to ninety degrees. Focus. Breathe. Listen.

"SET!!"

Weight slightly forward, resting on my fingertips. Head hanging heavy. Butt in the air. Breathe. Listen.

BANG!! BANG!!

False start. Thanks to quivering nerves and a no-false-start rule, the competition was narrowed to six. Today was my day. Today was MY day!

I tried my best to extinguish the sparks firing in every muscle, took a deep breath and returned to my place behind the blocks. Time to do this again. The tension palpable. The heat rising. The pulse racing. The muscles firing. "Don't let 'em see you sweat! This is YOUR day!"

"RUNNERS!!! COME TO YOUR MARKS!!!!"

"SET!!!!!"

The rest is really just a blur of bodies, hurdles and passing track. In just under fifteen seconds, four bodies crossed the finish line in one fluid motion. Then whoosh, whoosh, whoosh!!—the other three. Officials met in a huddle, comparing time pieces, discussing, hashing, rehashing and deciding. It truly had been a perfect race for me. It had been flawless. Yet it seems others had a flawless day as well. I didn't finish first. I didn't finish second or even third. I finished fourth. Four hundredths of a second separated four runners. A virtual tie divided by micro-ticks of a clock. While trying to keep my head up, I returned to the starting line to slide on my sweats. Not only had I not finished first; I hadn't qualified for the State Meet. Or had I?

I made my way to the bleachers where I found my place next to my most staunch supporters; my parents.

"Great race, son! We're proud of you!"

Even to this day it puzzles me I didn't find solace amongst friends or fellow athletes. It brings tears to my eyes to remember the way my parents found no blame in what I considered failure. They found no fault just as future friends would tell me God did.

"God loves you without condition. He is your Father. Through the blood of Jesus He sees no sin in you," they'd say.

On this day I found no comfort in friends or athletes or a God I didn't know. I found it in my parents. As we sat there quietly, acknowledging congratulations from other parents, the announcer tested the loudspeakers in preparation for an announcement.

"We have the results of the 110 Meter High Hurdle Finals."

The names and times of the first three finishers echoed off the opposing walls of the sports complex. There were no surprises.

"In fourth place, with a time of 14.84 seconds, Matt Leatherwood!"

Time stood still as my vision tunneled and my jaw dropped. Everyone in that stadium, including my parents, heard only that I had finished 4th. As I stood in amazement, I found the silhouette of my coach, also standing and searching the crowd for my glowing face. My coach and I heard, not the placement, but the time. A record that had stood at our high school for seventeen years had fallen. I was the new High-Hurdle Record holder for Ashland-Greenwood High School. To be clear, I realize that time isn't blinding speed in most places around the globe, but in my little pond, it was glory. It's a record that still stands today, almost thirty-two years later.

The following days were filled with euphoria of preparation for graduation and the parties that followed. What seemed an eternity in elementary school had arrived in the blink of an eye. I was finishing high school. A guy could write a book about all that happened in those thirteen years. (wink.)

During my last week roaming the halls of our high school I received a bit of puzzling news. Apparently there wouldn't be any parties for me following the graduation ceremony. I needed to be in bed early that night. I was expected in Omaha for the State Track Meet to run the 110 meter high hurdles. I stood before my coach in utter disbelief as he explained to me that my 4th place time just happened to be faster than ANY other FIRST place time throughout the state and as such, I had to be accepted to the State Meet. In other words, in any other district I'd have been wearing the gold. Or would I?

There is an extremely valuable life-lesson in this story that I didn't learn for many more years. The lesson is only in looking back. It's a great dichotomy because not looking back is yet ANOTHER life lesson that took me years to grasp. It wasn't a lesson about working hard or persevering. It wasn't some lame quip like "nice guys finish last" or "you can be anything you want to be." The lesson is this: Nothing happens by mistake. You can spin it how you like. There are no accidents.

Everything happens for a reason. Everything in our universe works in perfect harmony. There IS a reason for everything and understanding it isn't part of the equation. Things just simply are as they are… period.

Simply put, had I actually been in some other district, things would have been altogether different. Maybe I'd have fallen. Maybe I'd have died in a bus crash on the way to the meet. Perhaps I'd have been the one with a false start and therefore disqualified. It doesn't matter. It isn't for me to understand. I WAS at that particular meet in THAT particular district for a reason I may never understand. It doesn't even matter if I understand. It could be as simple as Spirit needed me in Omaha for the State Meet. It's entirely possible something more powerful than I knew I'd be writing a book someday and I'd need a story about Natural Order.

Here's all I really know. Every single thing that happened before that day led up to it. And every single second of activity SINCE that day has been because of it. And the part that'll make your head hurt is that every single second of every single minute of every single day is just like that. We have now. And now sets the stage for what happens next.

There is one more little thing I know. These stories thus far, although seemingly just stories, are setting the stage for something more. There's a lesson in all of them if you look. But there is more. There is much, much more. You'll see. Turn the page.

Lesson Thirteen:

SOMETIMES THE ANSWER TO A PROBLEM LIES IN STEPPING FURTHER AWAY

"The past cannot be changed, but the future is within our reach."

~AGHS Class of 1979 Motto

There is precious little I remember about my high school graduation. In fact, I only remember being there. I don't remember who I escorted or who I sat next to. I had to reference my senior annual to remember who the Valedictorian was of our class. Even the class motto, although swirling around in gray matter somewhere, had to be recalled by the hard-backed book. I couldn't tell you who our keynote speaker was or even remotely recall what he said. Although I'm sure the speeches given by my classmates were equally inspiring, I remember not one word uttered across the microphone and echoed into the bleachers at Memorial Stadium. Nothing beyond the constant drone of Pomp and Circumstance and a prayer with no meaning remains. Perhaps it was the wind. Maybe it was my lack of attention. Or maybe none of their words really mattered to a young man who knew nothing yet felt he knew it all.

That's the essence of the saying, "youth is wasted on the young," isn't it? All over the country; all over the world; year after year, ceremony after ceremony, young people cast out to a world with a false sense of knowledge that high school and a few drinking experiences with their friends have prepared them for what lies ahead. There are, perhaps, some more prepared than others. One may have mastered college physics at fifteen, while yet another may have endured an excruciating childhood of abusive parents or even malnutrition… or both. The point is, being eighteen doesn't qualify you for what lies ahead. LIFE qualifies you for what lies ahead and you haven't lived nearly enough of it at eighteen to have a clue what's about to happen. At least, that's how it was for me. But then again, my experience was somewhat unique; or so I'm told.

I had a storybook upbringing. In a world full of ever-increasing divorce, domestic disturbance and urban takeover, I was nurtured by two loving parents who rarely even quarreled. I hardly even knew of kids in single-parent households. My nearest lessons of death and dying came at the hands of a couple pets and two grandparents who I hardly knew. My biggest challenges were two older brothers who occasionally picked on me and deciding what part of the great outdoors I was going to explore on a daily basis. I lacked for nothing. I was seemingly popular in my school, had plenty of dates, and drove a nice car for a teenager. I was Athlete of the Year during my senior year in high school and had known what I wanted to do for a career since the age of twelve. I had it all, knew it all, and wanted it all. There was just one teensy-weensy little problem with that scenario. I hadn't learned about conflict. I hadn't learned struggle or pain and least of all… patience. What I knew was that if you wanted something you got it. I had no real code. I had no belief system. I had nothing to believe in greater than myself.

After yet another stream of lazy, hazy, crazy days of summer, armed with only my positive outlook on life, I set off for the University of Nebraska only seventeen miles from my parent's house. I had no desire to venture from the comforts of that home so commuted to class for my first semester under the comfortable blanket of my parental support. Without actually having to spread my wings and fly, I ventured forth into the world of Animal Science and a career as a veterinarian. Enter face slap number one.

As naïve as it may seem, it hadn't occurred to me during all my years of "college prep" in high school that to be a veterinarian you needed to be good at science. I thought you just had to love animals. You needed to actually LIKE science and have a basic understanding of things like Biology and Chemistry. Through charm and luck, I had somehow managed to escape high school with NO understanding of basic science or even the slightest remnants of things like Calculus. Hell. I hadn't even taken Ag in high school so I knew nothing of animals except how to feed and pet them. I'd like to blame that on my guidance counselor or my teachers, and back then I probably did. But the truth is, the responsibility was mine and I'd failed miserably at seriously preparing for a life of advanced academics. I had no study habits. I had no clue.

I remember entering the auditorium for my first Chemistry class which actually held nearly five times more students than were in my graduating class. I was lost from the start. I may as well have been taking a physics class taught in French. Even during the labs downtown, I was completely lost as to how different pieces of equipment worked. I didn't know if my experiments were right or wrong. The same was true of my Biology and Animal Science classes.

In Animal Science I was surrounded by Ag kids who knew a lot about livestock and judging. I'd never even set foot in an arena. I tried to maintain a low profile and hope my professor never called on me to openly judge a class of cows. I was somehow able to dodge that bullet and actually got good at judging, of all things... pigs! The entire experience was pointless and stressful.

Because I commuted to class, my evenings were much as they were in high school. I came home with buckets of homework, set out to study, then became distracted by television or an invitation to party by a friend and the work didn't get done. I was totally disconnected from the world of academia and felt like I was engulfed in a world I didn't understand. When was I going to learn about animals? When did the part about being a veterinarian start? I still had charm going for me. Maybe I could slide through college on that alone.

We could beleaguer my lack of preparation and understanding forever, but the bottom line was this: College and pre-vet wasn't what I expected. Not only did I not care much for science, my lack of understanding was teaching me to hate it. I managed to skate through my first semester with a C average, barely a 2.0 on a 4.0 scale. Even my naïve little brain knew I would never make it to vet school with grades like that. My parents, of course, were so proud of me because I had passed classes way outside their understanding. They were way outside of mine too! But the damage was being done. I hated school, yet had absolutely no backup plan whatsoever. Being a vet was all I ever wanted to do. My second semester began with a hodgepodge of education, business and coaching classes in a feeble attempt to redirect my career goals. It didn't work. I'd never learned to stand up to resistance so I did what all spoiled kids tend to do who have no direction and no god to lean on; I dropped out.

Lesson Fourteen:

SOMETIMES YOU HAVE TO GET DIRTY

> *"Work is the refuge of people who have nothing better to do."*
>
> ~Oscar Wilde

Microscopic shards of fiberglass dust soaked through my clothes and skin like the realization that I was now part of the working class. I was dressed in long pants and boots, a long-sleeve shirt, a doo rag and paper face mask. In my right hand I held an air-driven, diamond-tipped, open-faced router I was to use in trimming the rough edges from fiberglass tub/showers. Surrounded by unfinished product, lined up in rows like soldiers going to battle, I gingerly placed the whirling tool along the jagged edges of shower after shower, filling the stifled inside air and my lungs with microscopic dust. This, I realized, I had traded for a life of academics.

Upon breaking the news to my disappointed parents that I had withdrawn from university, I ventured forth to find work. It didn't take me long. A small factory that manufactured plastic agricultural tanks and fiberglass reinforced bathroom fixtures was looking for an able body to work in their trim booth. I was that able body. The work was hot, uncomfortable and physically demanding. Round after round of products came through my booth that needed to be finished for shipping. That meant trimming, drilling and bracing each and every shower before it went to final inspection for shipping. After each round I was able to blow the dust from my clothes as best I could, but the small particles always permeated the open pores beneath. Work was always followed, not by a warm, comforting shower, but by running water as cold as I could stand so as not to open my pores further. Nights of sleep were interrupted by the feeling of pins and needles caused by the tiny shards of fiberglass. In short, working was miserable.

Because I had more time than money, I added a second job to my repertoire on nights and weekends. As much as possible, I pumped gas at a local truck stop only three miles from my childhood home. It was the first time I can remember filling an emotional void with the art of keeping busy. The more I worked, the less I could dwell upon the decision I had made to give up on school. It was the tactic of a young man with no direction. I was missing one of the most important elements of life. I had nothing to believe in.

I've often called my job at the fiberglass factory the best job I ever had. There is no doubt it was miserable, low-paying work, but it taught me an important lesson about the inner soul of Matt. I didn't want to use sweat and labor to make a living. That job taught me in VERY short order that I needed to get back to school at the first opportunity. When I withdrew, that's how I had justified it.

"Oh, you can always go back next fall," I told myself. "This is just a temporary setback."

All the naysayers around me had already made it clear how rare it was for someone to quit school, get a job, and then re-enroll. Because I had parents who continued to support my immaturity, going back was easy. But that all-important element was still missing. I still had no goal. There was no "eye on the prize." I had no god and frankly, I didn't ever give it much thought. Something out there was going to fill that little hole I had in my gut and I simply needed to find it. When I look back on my life, it's the first time I see the makings of a seeker. We're all looking for something aren't we? We look for answers to the meaning of life or the definition of God. We turn over stone after stone in search of the one thing that will give our life meaning. That's what I was doing now; seeking. I hadn't actively thought about my purpose in life as a child, but as a young adult, the rest of my life was unfolding before me and I wanted answers. I wasn't sure where to look so I did what most people with no direction do. I walked forward. I took one baby step at a time hoping the next step would provide answers. No, I had indeed not been actively seeking. But I was about to in a big way.

As I made my way to wash the windshield of yet another 18-wheeler after a long day of trimming tub/showers, the notion hit me like a tsunami. Track and Field was my ticket in high school. I could make it my ticket again. Without the foggiest notion of what it would take to walk on to an NCAA Division I track team, I set my plan in action. Beginning the next day, I started getting back in shape for my reentry plan. I was going to walk on to the University of Nebraska Track Team.

I had no idea how to prepare or even where to go to ask permission. I just started running. I bought shorts and headbands that matched (it WAS the 1980s!), weights to wear on my wrists and ankles and good running shoes. I ran every day either 2 or 4 miles. Some days I wore weights. Some days not. But EVERY day I wore matching clothes. I had to look GOOD while I was training. I reduced the calories I ate every day and ate higher quality foods. I dropped to an all-time training weight of 155 pounds. I was lean and in the best aerobic shape of my life. I never missed a day of training. I kept my eye on the prize. I enrolled in classes for the fall and registered to live on campus this time. Everything was going to be different.

A month before classes were to begin, I sheepishly approached my supervisor at the fiberglass plant. (I'd been fired from my truck stop job.) I'd never quit a job before and I thought he might look down on me for leaving them without a shower trimmer. Even then I guess I felt responsible for how my actions influenced others. I wondered what they'd do without me.

It was warm and rainy and I was actually outside in the factory yard working with my supervisor the day I gave him my two-week's notice. I simply told him I had decided to go back to college. Marv didn't get angry or fire me on the spot. He looked at me, and for the first time in the six months I'd worked there, he smiled.

Marv had a big bushy mustache and his teeth showed for the first time from beneath his woolly facial hair. His eyes even sparkled a little. He placed his big hand firmly on my shoulder and said, "Good for you, Matt. Good for you."

I can't be completely sure, but I think I saw a hint of remorse in Marv's eyes. It was similar to the one I often saw in my brother's eye. Because of a back injury, Geary was unable to play football his senior year which probably cost him a scholarship to a small college. So instead, he impregnated his girlfriend, got married, and spent thirty years working in a rubber factory sixty to eighty hours a week. I saw that look in Marv's eye. It was a clear look of, "I'm glad you're getting out kid. I'm glad you're getting out."

Lesson Fifteen:

DREAM BIG. THE UNIVERSE WILL PROVIDE YOU THE OPPORTUNITY TO FULFILL IT.

"I can accept failure. Everyone fails at something. But I can't accept not trying."

~Michael Jordan

Frank sat behind his small cluttered desk, smoking a cigarette, a window overlooking a back-alley of campus at his back.

"Yeah?" he asked without even looking up over the rim of his stained glasses.

"My name is Matt Leatherwood and I'm interested in walking on to your track team sir," I said as my insides did their best to remain within the walls of my skin.

"Yeah? Whaddya run?"

"I'm a hurdler, sir."

"What kinda time you got?"

"Well, sir, I ran a 14.8 in high school, which I realize is not terribly fast, but I think with proper training and hard work I could…."

"Here kid. Take this piece of paper down to property and they'll set you up with some clothes. We'll run some of that extra weight off of you and see what you got. It's up to you," he said as he cut me off mid-sentence.

Frank was clearly a no-BS kind of guy. I just stood there with my mouth gaping open.

"What are you waiting for kid? Be here Monday at 3:00 ready to work. Now go!"

I hadn't made a phone call. I hadn't looked into the process of what it took to be a walk-on. I simply trained and envisioned my life as a member of UNL's track team. Then on that fated day, I pulled into a parking spot near the athletic department, walked in and asked if I could speak to the track coach. Someone whom I have no recollection of told me where the office was upstairs. I simply walked in unannounced, stated my intentions, and walked BACK out with a piece of paper that said I was in.

To be fair, Frank and his Assistant Coach Dick had nothing to lose except what little it cost to wash my daily workout clothes. They didn't supply me with fancy running shoes. I had to provide my own. There was no scholarship money. My parents provided that. All they did was give me a golden opportunity with little inquiry. Considering the fact I hadn't done my homework and just showed up on the doorstep, I'd say that was incredibly generous. And I didn't realize it at the time, but this was perhaps one of the first examples of the universe providing what I envisioned.

I showed up at 3:00 p.m. on Monday, the first day of classes and was introduced to two other young men who were freshman hurdlers. One was a scholarship athlete. The other, like me, was a virtual unknown. He hadn't been visited by college scouts or offered scholarship money. He walked on. Let the games begin.

It would be girlish of me to say the three of us sized each other up on a daily basis, but in reality, that's exactly what was happening. Every afternoon we'd meet up (none of the established team members were even thinking about working out yet), don our ugly gray sweats and run at least 5 miles.

We always cheered each other on, of course, but in reality we were seeing who could run the fastest... the farthest. Who was winded? Who was wavering? We followed our runs with grueling weight workouts and the same comparisons always subliminally ensued.

I was knee-deep in homework and classes which consisted of subjects I slept through in high school. I had switched majors to business for lack of any other direction, which meant I had to study Accounting, Computer Science and Calculus! I knew absolutely nothing about any of those subjects so I studied late into the night, got up for breakfast, went to class, ate lunch, took a nap and then trotted off to track practice. Then it was supper, homework and bed. It was the same routine every day. I loved it.

The first semester was tough from an academic standpoint and uneventful in terms of my sport. Every day it was running and lifting. I hadn't so much as looked at a hurdle in almost two years. But by the time Christmas break was over, things began to change. The outdoor running stopped and we moved indoors to the track. We ran intervals around a 176 yard oval that was grueling on my joints. Ole Frank would just stand on the sidelines smoking like a chimney screaming, "Ya gotta pick it up!" I never did understand the concept of interval training because frankly, I never intended to run more than 110 meters. The indoor hurdles were only 60 meters! Who couldn't do that?

It was while we were beginning preparation for the indoor season that I began to get a first-hand look at the world-class athletes I was running with. I was awed at the raw talent. In my heart I knew I'd never be that caliber of athlete, but I was grateful to be in their presence. I think those athletes from all over the globe are the first things I held in awe. The first things I idolized.

I finally got to spend a great deal of time working on my specialty. It turns out college hurdles are three inches higher than high school hurdles. Who knew? It was just one more thing a little planning would have revealed. Despite the change in height, I was able to quickly make the adjustment and was soon in old form. For starters I was in WAY better shape than high school. Secondly, I was being much better trained.

As we neared the start of the indoor season we were told that Saturdays would be "all out" days. In other words, we were going to run our event one time as if we were competing. Thousands of butterflies flittered through my bowels just to think about easing my feet into starting blocks again after two years. I knew that these Saturday runs were to reduce the roster and it was time to show my stuff. Remember, I was yet to see my competition run in the actual event and the fact that they were scholarship athletes did nothing to boost my confidence. I was intimidated to say the least.

The dim neon lights high above the indoor track hummed quietly as the team prepared for "all-out Saturday." The high hurdles, looming a full 3 inches higher than two years before, stood as mighty barriers for sixty yards before me. For reasons that took me some time to understand, athletes that had already proven their worth weren't required to run. For reasons I'll NEVER understand, the other walk-on hurdler was a no-show for the Saturday run. Behind the blocks stood me and the new scholarship hurdler whose times in high school were far superior to mine. The little trial was really just a duel to be run just like an actual event.

"Runners!!! Come to your marks!!" (I threw up in my throat just a little.)

Like I'd never stepped away from the cast aluminum braces riveted firmly to the spongy track, I took my place in front of the blocks, knelt down and positioned my feet exactly as I'd done a hundred times.

"Get... SET!!"

In high school my strength had always been the last half of the race. Despite my efforts at improving my explosiveness, I had never been one of the quickest from the blocks. In high school I had 110 meters to accelerate. Today I would have only sixty. But then again, I'd been training a little harder this time around.

BOOM!!!!

The starter pistol sounded and I shot from the blocks like a missile aimed at space. My opponent did the same. I could carry on about every little nuance of the race, but sixty meters passes in the blink of an eye. When this sixty meters passed, I was neck-and-neck with the superstar. It was a dead heat. No. I didn't win. But neither did he.

Even above the "thud" of running into the pad at the end of the track to kill momentum I could begin to hear the buzz. The star hurdler from our team was talking to the coach about how well I had run. It was then I learned something I'd never considered.

"I know. I know," I could hear Frank explain. "But he's academically ineligible."

In a microsecond it came clear to me that "he" was me and several people were amazed I had kept pace with the new guy. Yet I had no idea what the talk of eligibility had to do with anything. No one had exactly explained it to me. Frank stepped over and did just that... finally.

"That was a great run, kid, but we can't put you on the team yet. NCAA rules state you have to complete two successive semesters before you're eligible to compete and since you sat out last semester, we can't run you until next year."

"Wha... What... WHAT?"

Some lessons simply come the hard way and that's the way I learned this one. I had clearly run well enough to make the team, yet a life decision from over a year prior was going to delay my dream one more year. As I continued to gasp for air from the recent sprint, I was overcome with disappointment.

AND pride. In the overall scheme of things, I had done what I set out to do. I just couldn't do it yet.

The remainder of the year was spent doing what I'd been doing for weeks. I went to class, ate lunch, took a nap, went to practice, then studied. Rinse and repeat. It was a comfortable routine and I looked forward to working hard every day in anticipation of the coming year. And then something I hadn't expected happened. I got hurt.

To say I "got hurt" probably isn't completely accurate. The more precise statement would be that I "developed an injury" from running tight curves on the indoor track. Severe tendonitis reared its ugly head in my right foot; the foot I used to "push off" while accelerating over a hurdle. My running time was impeded dramatically and I spent an hour before practice in the training room receiving ultrasound treatments. After practice was another hour of hot and cold whirlpools and more therapy. In such a session is where I first had a trainer tall me that "I just wasn't built for running." But I'd get better. I knew I would.

Winter gave way to Spring and the outdoor season. Spring gave way to summer and a break from track. I had three months to relax and heal. I spent that summer working. I didn't train. I ate. And I got heavier. And I got slower.

When I reported for practice in the fall the Assistant Coach took one look at me and told me not to worry about the weight. He'd run it off of me. And he did. Like the fall a year before, I spent every day running and lifting weights until the extra padding was gone. My foot felt great and I was finally eligible to take my place on the team.

And then we moved indoors for interval training. The very first time I took a curve during a workout, my tendonitis returned at full strength. This was bad. At a time when I didn't yet understand that there is no good or bad, there's just what is, this was bad. After four months of healing, one lap on the track set me back almost a year. From day one it was back to the training room before practice and after. I was only able to run at practice on rare occasions. Frank and Dick were looking at me less. The other hurdlers were way ahead of me in training and my foot just wasn't getting better.

Letting go of a dream never comes easy. I had dreamed of being a veterinarian and the reality of things like, uh, SCIENCE had required I let it go. I dreamed of making the University of Nebraska Track Team and had it not been for the shock of giving up becoming a vet, I probably would have. It was the confusion of changing career paths that had made me decide to take a semester off. The truth is, it doesn't matter *why* anymore. An injury I couldn't shake and the reality of countless hours at the track cutting into the mounting class load made stepping away from track an easy decision. It wasn't easy to do. It was easy to see what the smart thing to do was.

And so it went. I turned in my clothes to the coaches, shook their hand and thanked them for the opportunity and walked away. Some may call me a quitter. Some would say I should have stayed the course through the injury. Maybe. But the reality of my talent and the waning of my passion made it the decision best for my spirit. It was a great opportunity. It isn't what the universe had in mind for me.

Lesson Sixteen:

LIFE PASSES AT AN EXPONENTIAL RATE AND WILL CONTROL YOU IF YOU LET IT

"The truly important things in life—love, beauty, and one's own uniqueness—are constantly being overlooked."

~Pablo Casals

Life away from the track gave me the opportunity to focus on what I came to school to do… get an education. Studying was something I NEVER did in high school and although I had worked hard at my studies so far, my true focus had been trying to make the track team. With that behind me, there was much to learn about normal life on campus.

I lived in a dorm with an awesome roommate, ate dorm food, studied with friends and spent a lot of time with my girlfriend. Janet and I had dated since high school and we lived in adjacent dorms before she pledged a sorority. But even then, the house where she lived was close to my dorm. Our living quarters were close. It took me years to learn that our life paths were miles apart. But there will be more on that later.

Living in the dorms taught me one of my first lessons in tolerance. I took pot-luck on my first roommate selection and drew a young man from Tennessee who actually believed he wrote the words to Saginaw, Michigan. In fact, within the first ten minutes of our meeting he insisted he play the song he'd written on his guitar. His playing and his singing were atrocious (not to mention the fact he was singing a song written decades before that he claimed to own), but I nodded and smiled, telling him how good he sounded. He didn't care for bathing much and had a nasty habit of setting his alarm for a 6:00 a.m. J.R. Tolkien class which he rarely attended. I should have gone because I was usually wide awake after that while Wade snoozed peacefully.

On more than one occasion I found Wade sitting at his desk sobbing. Both times I asked him what was wrong and was told "so-and-so" had been killed. I took a sympathetic posture and told him I was so sorry to hear about the loss of his family member or friend only to find out that the loss he was grieving was of a character from his Dungeons and Dragons game. I took a lot of deep cleansing breaths during that semester. And although I do give myself some credit for surviving as long as I did, one semester was all I could take of dear Wade.

While sitting in a giant auditorium filled with lost Accounting students, I met my new roommate, Ted. His roommate was moving off campus and we seemed like a good match. We were. Ted was a tall, blonde, handsome Irish boy who hailed from the most Irish of all Nebraska towns, O'Neill. He was a pre-med/business/whatever major and had an inviting wit and charm that helped change everything about my life at university. And the boy was smart! In fact, he's the only person I ever knew that actually buffaloed his way through Organic Chemistry exams, which for most is where dreams of Med School end.

Ted drank up life and we spent hours playing backgammon in the lobby, holding impromptu parties in our dorm room (which were strictly forbidden, by the way) and on more than one occasion, skipped Friday classes to play a round of golf at one of the lush green courses of Lincoln. Ted was a natural at just about everything. He made me smile on a regular basis and seemed to let nothing bother him. Even when he spoke of his alcoholic father who had drank up most of the family fortune, he did so with a twinkle in his eye. Ted was a faithful friend and was Best Man at my first wedding. Yes, I said first. As I said, there's way more to come about all that. The Lincoln Town Car I had rented for the special occasion went completely undecorated because Ted spent most of the night of the reception guarding it. He was loyal and meticulous. He was also great at holding his liquor and on the few times I tried to compete, Ted always saw that I made it back to the dorm in one piece.

I had other friends on the dorm floor as well, and was invited to take part in such youthful rituals as "Pearl Harbor Let's Get Bombed" night and events of hypnotism put on by one of the guys whose dad used hypnosis in his dental practice. I had no idea the fire we were playing with at the time, but I learned a valuable lesson that took me years to grasp about the power of the subconscious. Risky as it may seem, I willingly took part in the little game and was stunned to find out that under the power of suggestion I was unable to do the simplest things like removing my hand from a wall or lifting my foot off the floor. And although I learned that lesson years ago, it took a gentle reminder from the love of my life to remind me that we can accomplish great things through our subconscious mind.

One of my favorite activities while attending UNL was going to football games. As a student I could buy a season pass to see one of the country's premier teams for only $35. Many of the games I scantly remember because they were always preceded by a "beer breakfast."

By 9:00 a.m. on football Saturdays you could expect to hear the William Tell Overture blasting from enormous stereo speakers placed at the end of each hallway, powered by wires that were somehow miraculously run OUTSIDE the building from one corner to the next. The music was so loud it literally vibrated you from your bed and even the deepest sleeper, suffering the worst hangover couldn't avoid its power.

After a quick shower (or not) and a glance in the mirror, carloads of us would venture to a house off-campus (usually owned by someone we'd never met), tap a keg, drink beer and eat donuts until it was time to pile back in the cars and head to the game. Even after a morning of beer and sugar, you could still count on several people sneaking bottles of booze into the game in their sock to be mixed with soft drinks served by vendors. As I mentioned, there are many games I don't remember so well. What I do remember is joy, wonder, fun and the feeling of time spinning away uncontrollably.

This was college. It was studies and friendship and parties and learning. I actually did learn a lot at college, but the most valuable lessons didn't come from a textbook. They came from social interaction and learning to be independent. This was living. This was just the beginning of an independent life as wondrous as my childhood. Mine was a charmed life. Nothing else could ever trouble me. Life was wonderful. Or was it?

Lesson Seventeen:

BABY STEPS AREN'T ALL THAT RISKY AND RUNNING WON'T FILL THE HOLE

"The willingness to accept responsibility for one's own life is the source from which self-respect springs."

~Joan Didion

He had a reddish, sandy-blond, Fu Manchu mustache with short, slightly balding, curly hair to match. Around his neck was a red silk tie which didn't match his polyester shirt which just so happened to be tucked in to faded and worn blue jeans. A shirt and tie were required for his job. Slacks were not. On his feet were tan hiking boots laced to the top. And… he was my new boss.

Joe was the Resident Director at the dorm where I took a new "job" as Student Assistant on a dorm floor. Although I'd held jobs in high school, this was my first real attempt at taking at least a little responsibility for my life and finances. Ted had decided to move off-campus after two years as roommates. He invited me to come along, but I thought it might be a burden for my parents who were footing the bill for college. Besides, I loved life in the dorms. Where else can you get three meals cooked for you every day and never do dishes? It's like living at home without the parents to nag.

As a Student Assistant I began to feel a part of something. I was one of a large staff responsible for the behavior, counseling and questions of hundreds of college students. I was held to a higher standard and regarded as something of an authority figure. It felt good. I liked the feeling of being in charge. It was probably my first real glimpse at finding peace in the feeling of being in control, although it was years before I recognized that trait as something that could be challenging as well as rewarding.

Perhaps the greatest perk of being on staff was having a large private room. I set my dorm up like a small apartment, complete with nasty second-hand furniture and settled in as the "go to" guy on Abel 5. Because the floor I lived on was so populated, I shared responsibilities with another Student Assistant who lived at the other end of the hall. Together we tackled the challenges of dorm life on Abel 5 and basked in the thrill of being two of Joe's staff at Abel/Sandoz.

Jim, my partner, was a tall, somewhat shy character with an easy style and demeanor. I liked him from the start. He was an engineering student so he was as concise as he was mellow. He liked things to run smoothly and if they didn't, he got a little edgy. I, on the other hand, was rapidly developing into a young man who liked the feel of "power" and never minded taking control of a situation or going the extra mile for one of the other students. My door was always open. Jim and I made a good team. Being an S.A. was one of the most rewarding times of my life. I was made for it.

Stories from that year on Abel Hall could fill a book all its own. There was the time I opened my door early one Saturday morning after being rousted from a deep, youthful slumber to find Jim standing there with a bath towel around his neck. His coke-bottle glasses with dark frames were pushed back against his face and he had a rare look of disgust.

"Ah, Matt! Ah, geez, Matt! You gotta come see this!" he nearly pouted as I stood in the door with my mouth gaped open.

I mean, what in the HELL was he doing pounding on my door at this time of morning on Saturday? Sadly, it didn't take me long to find out. I followed Jim down the hall, having still not spoken a word, and then into the common dorm bathroom where I couldn't believe my eyes. Inside one stall and through much of the entire room, feces covered the walls. The stench itself was enough to bring you to your knees, but the sight of it was beyond belief. We backed out of the room and walked down the hall to the common lounge area where we accidentally found the culprit. Passed out from a long night of drinking was clearly the man who had plastered the bathroom with human excrement. How we knew isn't worth mentioning.

I recognized immediately that the man was a resident from Jim's end of the hallway. In a rare moment of disunity, I smiled at Jim, told him good luck, turned and went to my room where I locked the door and buried myself under the covers. I prayed the vision would go away. To this day it hasn't.

Jim seemed to have the worst luck between the two of us, and on yet another occasion I found him at my door beckoning me to follow him down the hall. This time what I saw almost made me proud. It still makes me smile.

Living in the dorm room that was immediately to your right as you exited the elevator were two young, burgeoning rock stars attending college for no other reason than to party. And party they did. It was nothing for Jim to have to confront them on a regular basis regarding loud music or after-hour visitors, etc. This must have been a particularly rough night for the two lads because they forgot to shut their door before they passed out for the night. In the middle of their floor, in plain sight, was the largest bottle of empty vodka I have EVER seen. On the beds, easily visible from the public lobby, lied each of the residents… naked. Next to each of them... a naked coed. It was hard to feel so proud, envious and responsible all at the same time. I hope those two fellows made a go of it, because that memory still makes me smile.

In what was becoming an occurrence less rare, I smiled at Jim, wished him luck and returned to my room. It got to be kind of a joke. He knew I had his back.

Jim became more than just my partner in herding students. He became my friend. And he introduced me to something I didn't think I would ever care to wrap my mind, heart or soul around. Jim introduced me to long-distance running. I was a sprinter after all. The Universe blessed me with more fast-twitch than slow-twitch muscles. I was built for speed. I always had been. But going the distance, although it started as a simmer, began to boil in my blood and rush through my veins.

I had consistently run three to five miles while training during my time with the track team and had also done interval training on numerous occasions; most often until I puked. But this "jogging" thing was different. I started slowly, but soon was running six to eight miles a day regularly and then upped the ante to ten miles at least once a week. I always ran alone and learned to love the solitude, the battle within, and the sheer will to finish what I started. I experienced "runner's high" and became edgy when I didn't get to run. It became a big part of my campus life.

As Jim watched my progress which included losing the bulk that came from weights and sprinting, he encouraged me to consider running the Lincoln Marathon. I was already logging 50-60 miles a week running so the idea seemed completely feasible. By late winter, I began to focus on running 26.2 miles in early May. I didn't have a plan, as such. I simply followed the "Forrest Gump" program and just kept running.

It bears mentioning that in the midst of all this school and Student Assistant work and running, I had become engaged to the girl I dated in High School. The wedding was planned for the third week in May. I wasn't really part of the planning committee. I was simply told what day to show up. That should have been a yellow flag at the very least, but I overlooked it and just kept running.

In March, there was a half-marathon locally that I thought would be an excellent warm-up for the full run in May. It was an enormous eye-opener. I'd love to give you a colorful commentary of every step of that race, but I just don't remember details about that day and creative license seems unnecessary. What I DO remember quite clearly is that, although I had run ten miles on dozens of occasions, thirteen miles was a bit farther. I wasn't prepared mentally or emotionally and clearly didn't take the days prior to race time seriously enough. I finished, but I finished poorly. And more importantly, I finished emotionally drained. When I crossed the finish line I simply broke down and cried. It wasn't the thrill of finishing or the glory of accomplishment. I was exhausted and in pain.

Right then and within twenty feet of the finish-line, I decided not to run a full marathon only two weeks before my wedding day. I had heard the marathon horror stories about people seizing up with cramps, defecating themselves and taking weeks to recover. I thought the responsible thing to do would be to withdraw. Reflecting, it was just the excuse I needed to bow out.

Just recently, nearly thirty years and three marriages from quitting on my first marathon (I never even considered running another), I decided I should finish what I started. And like the first time around, running or the planning of running or the thinking about running pushed out other things in my life I found more rewarding (like writing this book, for example) and with some reluctance, I once again decided the marathon just wasn't something I was meant to do. It didn't feed my spirit.

There is much within this chapter that seems mostly about nothing. And to some it will be. But for me this was truly a time of starting to spread my wings with a safety net by way of working in the dorm. And it was my first conscious attempt to fill that burning hole I had with "something." I'd done it before, but only subconsciously. This time I thought running far enough or fast enough or finishing a marathon might make me feel whole. It didn't. Not by a long shot. And working in a dorm while attending college isn't all that risky. The risk was just around the corner. And I wasn't ready.

Lesson Eighteen:

CHOOSE WISELY AND BE MAN ENOUGH TO ADMIT IT WHEN YOU HAVEN'T

"The first and worst of all frauds is to cheat one's self. All sin is easy after that."

~Pearl Bailey

Like the sound of crackers being crushed into a soup bowl, the tires of my Torino ground slowly over the crushed rock of my high school parking lot. I eased to a halt at the front sidewalk to let my girlfriend out for school, because I was ditching for "skip day." We were arguing about her best friend and my recent indiscretions in that regard when she pulled the ring off her finger and hurled it at me across the front seat of the car. It was over.

I had purchased the shiny pearl ring, adorned with two small diamond flakes and presented it to Lori for Christmas. It was a "Promise Ring." You remember those, don't you? We had been dating for quite some time and my class ring just didn't seem a sufficient sign of my "love." So I gave her the ring, insinuating a promise that we would one day be engaged and married. I did a lousy job of keeping that promise. In fact, it was the first of what became a life-long pattern of not keeping promises where relationships were concerned.

Lori and I met at the country club swimming pool when I was fifteen and she fourteen. We became fast friends and began to "date," which meant we got to double occasionally with her sister and I often walked the two miles to her country home from my house in Greenwood for us to spend time together. It was probably what most would call "young love," but we managed to maintain a relationship for a long time. We fit well together, but I found her to be closed and a little puzzling. She had two older brothers, a sister, an enabling mother and (in my opinion only) an overbearing alcoholic father who behaved unpredictably. Even so, I was accepted warmly by her family and her by mine. We spent holidays together and truly became a local item. She was "the one." Yet I still had that nagging feeling of not really knowing her. She was good at keeping people at arm's length. And yet I continued to maintain a relationship with her. It was another first perhaps in that I had an early addiction to relationships and maybe even adrenaline.

They say you never forget your first time and the same holds true for me. At a dangerously early age (16 and 15) Lori and I became each other's "first." I wish I could tell you it was a magical moment filled with love and commitment, but as a young man with teenaged hormones, the truth is, it was probably more of a conquest. Admitting that is painful.

After two full years together our relationship began to stale a bit. We argued more and frankly I began to feel bored. I tried breaking things off with Lori one time, but by the time I was home I was a complete wreck, crying uncontrollably and sobbing in my mother's arms. (Admitting that is REALLY painful.) Within the hour I was back in my car on the way to Lori's house to patch things up. To this day I'm not sure whether it was Lori I missed or the fear of not being in a relationship. I believe it was probably the latter, due mostly to what I did next.

Lori had a lifelong friend named Janet. They did almost everything together as kids even though they lived six miles apart. Janet was our "friend" as well and was always supportive of Lori's relationship with me. Janet was also flirtatious and cute... and she knew it. Can you spell "red flag"?

When things began to lose steam with Lori, I did what any young, warm-blooded American boy with no sense or character would do. Rather than openly discuss my feelings with Lori and consider the longevity of our relationship, I began to consult with Janet about her friend and the things I was feeling. It was completely covert and was not without a hidden agenda. Admitting THAT is painful as well.

It doesn't take an advanced degree in Teen Psychology to guess what happened next. Janet and I secretly decided to go on a date. As an adult I see clearly the rude, senseless and just plain mean path of that decision. How on earth could one human being treat another with such disrespect? All I know is I was able to justify it in some unexplainable way. I wanted to know if there was something with Janet before I broke things off with Lori. I was acting cowardly and looking for a safety net in which to land when things with Lori were over. It's pitiful, really, but it's what I did. And if you remember from Part I, we lived and schooled in VERY small towns. The rest is easy. Janet and I went to see a movie in Lincoln and Lori found out. I don't even remember how and it doesn't matter. The simple fact is I violated the trust of someone who cared about me. I didn't even give her the courtesy of my honesty. I betrayed her and myself. That's what led to the ring-throwing and school parking lot breakup. At a mere seventeen years old, I had completed my first round of "cheating." Like lying, after you've broken the seal, the next time is easier.

Lesson Nineteen:
IF YOU FIND YOURSELF INTERESTED IN ANYONE OTHER THAN THE ONE YOU'RE DATING, THE ONE YOU'RE DATING ISN'T THE ONE FOR YOU

"My boyfriend used to ask his mother, 'How can I find the right woman for me?' and she would answer, 'Don't worry about finding the right woman—concentrate on becoming the right man.'"

~Unknown

As with many things from that era, details are a bit sketchy. Or at the very least, my memory is selective. Either way, I don't remember the exact order of things, but I do know that I wasn't the only one cheating when Janet and I had our first "date." She was also dating someone so even after the breakup with Lori I didn't fall immediately into a safety net. I actually spent the summer before my senior year of high school… single! Oddly, it was one of the most pleasant and trouble-free summers of my young life.

I had a great little job at the local gas station. I basked in the sun, washed and waxed my muscle car and did more things with my friends. I even caught the fancy of another local girl who practically stalked me. I wasn't interested, but the attention was nice. It was a summer of bliss. I found a way to compartmentalize the betrayal with Lori and deal with the fact that Lori's now EX-friend was unavailable. The brain is a powerful, wondrous and frightening tool.

In typical, small-town, mega-drama fashion, Janet and I did began to date near the beginning of my senior year in high school. And even knowing now that Janet was a poor choice for me, by far the largest mistake was dating someone "steady" at all. I'd been perfectly happy without a relationship through the summer. Why on earth would a young boy yoke himself to one wagon when there was so much to experience? Was it status? Insecurity? I realize now it was a little of both. But more than that, it was ignorance.

The first thing on the agenda for my new "girlfriend" and I was to deal with her emotionally injured, persistent, wealthy farmer of an ex-boyfriend. He drove by her house constantly. He called her. He called her parents. He came by the house to SEE her parents when she wasn't there. He cried on their shoulder and spoke poorly of their daughter's new Gear Head from Greenwood. (The truth is I was more a Jock than a Gear Head, but that's immaterial.) He talked himself up while talking me down. It was an uphill climb. I suspect Janet still continued to have contact with him when I wasn't around which is most likely why he felt so compelled to keep trying, but at the time, I just thought he was a jerk.

At a high school basketball game in Waverly one winter night, Janet's ex was there in what I considered "stalker" fashion. He lingered behind us and was always glaring at us. When I walked by he made some snide remark followed by flipping me off which led me to invite him outside. He wasn't interested in doing so at the time. (Oh my God, this is SO high school!!!!) After the game I spotted him in the parking lot. I told Janet to wait in the car as I began walking towards him. My testosterone levels soared beyond their usual astronomical limits and I seethed with anger. The thought of setting things straight with this pest made it hard for me to see straight.

I wanted him to go away. And I was ready to do just about anything to make that happen.

He was already seated in his ride and apparently thought I was there to talk. He rolled down his window as I approached the car in a lame gesture of comradeship, assuming I wanted to chat. In one lightening display of teenaged fury, I delivered an unanticipated, yet on-target cheap shot directly to his jaw sending him stunned to the other side of the front seat. In one more fluid motion, I yanked open the front door and climbed on top of him, delivering blow after blow as I released pent up frustration. As I began coming to my senses, I realized his face was swollen and bloodied. His eyes were stunned, yet panicked. My thumb throbbed from the chipped bone which resulted from my initial punch glancing off his door frame. I climbed off, stepped outside the car and screamed at him like a crazy, panting animal.

"Stay away from us and stay away from her parents!!! I mean it!! Stay away!"

It was the last time we had issues with Leon. He stopped calling and stopped driving by. In immaturity, that incident led me to believe that sometimes violence is the only way to resolve issues. I didn't make it a habit, but it wasn't the only time I resorted to it either. Now I'll be the first to admit, that even in adulthood, there are times when you just have to get someone's attention. I'm not condoning violence necessarily, but sometimes in the heat of being taken advantage of, when other means have failed, you have to set a firm boundary. I adhere to a principle now that love is the solution to most everything. But the first issue is to love yourself. If that means PROTECTING your interests in the process, then everyone's best interests are served in the long run. Love wins. Doing what's best for me, ultimately serves what's best for you.

I'm not proud of the fact I beat a guy up over a girl. In fact, it should have been another red flag where Janet was concerned. Most of the tension was probably caused by her manipulation, but I bought in to it. I have no one to blame, but me. And for reasons I'm yet to understand, getting Leon's attention served a higher purpose. I'm glad he didn't have me arrested for aggravated assault!

There doesn't seem to be a lot of spiritual significance attached to my senior year of high school. It was a blur of what I considered to be "normal" stuff. I went to Homecoming, Prom and graduation. In between I played a little football, went on dates with Janet and ran track. Those topics we've already covered. But now I was heading off to the next stage of life with a girl that clearly wasn't good for me. She was arm candy. She was status. Nothing more.

The beige rotary telephone hung on the wall between the two long windows of my dorm room. Ted was stretched out on his upper bunk as I stood looking out the window at the tennis courts ten floors below. The cord was stretched to its maximum length as I struggled to keep the handset of the phone pressed between my shoulder and my ear. My eyes rolled in exasperation. It was then I remember muttering the words EVERY man should avoid, "What's the problem? Don't you trust me?"

I had just spent the better part of my Saturday working on a term paper that was due the following week. In those days we didn't have laptops. To script a term paper meant researching in the library instead of on the internet. It meant pouring over blank sheets of paper as you wrote longhand, and then typed it on some old typewriter. It was grueling.

To celebrate completing the hand-written portion of my term paper, Ted and I had decided to head out to a local pub later that evening. Janet had plans to spend the evening with her dad at her sorority's Father/Daughter Banquet. She apparently didn't like the idea of me drinking without her within arm's length and began to make a big deal about it. It was then I muttered the words I'd come to regret.

After pleading my case and putting my foot down, I told Janet to enjoy her evening and Ted and I left for Horsefeathers, a local college hangout. It was there I was introduced to a new concoction called a Long Island Iced Tea. It's a smooth and delicious drink made of nearly everything in the liquor cabinet.

Once we arrived at the bar and ordered our first round, Ted realized he was short on cash and left for the nearest ATM. By the time he returned, I had downed my third tea. The rest of the story gets fuzzy in a hurry. I excused myself to the restroom where some time later Ted found me actually passed out standing up over the urinal. After less than an hour at the club, he dragged me toward the dorm. While on the way I managed to fall in the street, scrape the side of my face, fall again in a large shrub where I was pummeled with snowballs and break out a window on ground level of the girl's dorm. I was a drunken mess.

Once safely back on the tenth floor of Cather Hall, the alcohol, mixed with as sundry other gastric items, began making their way violently back up my esophagus and into the dorm toilet. It was a long trip from our room to the bathroom, so I eventually landed, semi-conscious in the lounge, hanging limply over a trash can. I was cheap amusement for a few of the guys that had stuck around for the weekend and, of course, Ted stayed close to make sure I didn't die of alcohol poisoning.

I have no idea how much time passed between the bar and what happened next, but it must have been much longer than I imagined. In my drunken stupor I heard the elevator doors open as young college men scattered like rats from a spotlight. "Hello, Janet," I muttered without even looking up. And there she stood in all her "high society, greater-than-thou" glory, making sure everyone saw who wore the pants in that relationship. I simply giggled.

We hardly spoke for nearly a week. Janet was angry that I had betrayed her trust and I bought in to the entire drama. I apologized endlessly, swearing I'd never do it again, etc. etc. etc. But here's the thing I've come to realize. I didn't do anything wrong! Yet because someone made me feel as though I had, I began backpedaling and saying I was sorry. The entire issue was never about what I had done. It was about how Janet thought it made her look. I wasn't mad then, but it angers me now to think about how I cowered before her. It was always about her. It was always about how she looked, either in the mirror or in the eyes of others. I was simply some poor sap from a small town who should feel blessed to be in her presence. There's a little self-esteem lesson there I believe.

As if that little fiasco wasn't enough of a glaring red flag where Janet was concerned, others followed. Not all of them I consider her fault.

After leaving the track team I continued to work out at the sports complex on the north end of campus. It was there I met Carly (name changed to protect the innocent.) Carly was a scholarship tennis player who just happened to also be one of Janet's sorority sisters. On numerous early mornings, I'd find Carly at the gym and we'd strike up a conversation. At other times I would run in to her on campus and we'd stop and talk by the fountain in front of the Student Union. I'd like to state clearly for the record that at no time did any of our conversations ever become inappropriate. We never touched and we never met privately. Yet it was clear that Carly and I had an attraction to each other. Even so, we kept it casual, because I did have a girlfriend after all.

On one of our rare "encounters" on a campus sidewalk, Carly asked me if Janet and I were going to the sorority dance the following Saturday. After I answered in the affirmative,

Carly asked if I might save her a dance. Innocently, I told her I would. There's nothing wrong with a friendly dance with my girlfriend's sorority sister, right? I had come to regard Carly as merely a friend. I had no intention of it ever going beyond that. And it didn't.

On that Saturday evening, I did my best to dress in a way Janet wouldn't find embarrassing to her sorority sisters and off we went to the dance. The evening was completely uneventful until Janet and I prepared to leave. Carly took notice of our exit and came up to remind me I'd promised her a dance. As Janet was slipping on her coat, I told her I'd be right back after a quick dance with Carly. As I slipped back into the dance hall for a quick dance with Carly, Janet left in stunned silence without me. After the groveling I did after the drunken escapade, you can imagine how it went for days after this event. To tell you the truth, I don't remember now how or when I caught up with Janet to explain. What I do know is how painfully clear it is now that Janet was insecure and controlling. And I was insecure and weak. But things improved once more and life went on.

Throughout our remaining college years, Janet and I spent our summers working for her brother in Texas. The first summer we stayed with my grandparents so our alone time was "supervised" and therefore okay with her parents. The next summer we lied about our marital status so the people in Tilden, Texas would rent us their trailer for the summer. Her parents believed we were living under separate roofs. It was all a lie. All of it. I didn't stand up to Janet OR her parents so we lived a sneaky life of lies in order to do what we wanted. At the time, I didn't think a thing of it, but there are lessons upon lessons to be learned from all of this.

It may be a bit puzzling why I would interlace such intricate stories about my relationship with Janet, but I'm here to tell you, the theme of the lesson is posted at the top of the chapter and it took me nearly a lifetime to learn it. Throughout our relationship, I had an inner voice telling me it was a mistake. It started wrong and it wasn't healthy. I wasn't my true self and I didn't like the "true self" Janet turned out to be. Yet I kept pushing forward under the cloak of "love." Learning what love is took me years longer to find out. And although I know now that everything about that relationship from beginning to end was wrong and unhealthy, I was about to push it to the next level. Some things you just have to learn the hard way.

Lesson Twenty:
MARRIAGE IS SOMETHING YOU REALLY SHOULD UNDERSTAND BEFORE YOU ENTER INTO IT. AND IT BETTER BE WITH THE ONE YOU LOVE.

"A man doesn't know what happiness is until he's married. By then it's too late."

~Frank Sinatra

I've been planted before this keyboard for some time now, trying to recall a romantic, tear-creating, heart-throbbing story of the day I proposed to Janet. Sadly, I can't do it. I don't remember. If there ever was a romantic place and time where I got on one knee and asked for Janet's hand in marriage, the memory is erased from my consciousness. It simply isn't there. I don't recall asking her parents (which I'm sure I did strictly because I'm old fashioned that way) and I don't remember what the ring looked like. To be truthful, details of the wedding day itself are even sketchy.

Whether or not I remember details of the event are far less important than the lessons I learned and the way I see things now. Getting married to Janet was strictly part of the natural order of things. I wasn't absorbed with the love of my soul mate or dying to stand before God and pledge my undying faithfulness. We dated a long time. We went to college together. Our families crossed paths during holidays. I was friends with her brother. The only thing left to do was get married. That's what is supposed to happen next, right? I was told by a wise man some years later that if you don't know what to do, just do the next thing; like brushing your teeth for instance… or getting married.

The thought of breaking up with Janet through dating and the stories I related from college never occurred to me. We were just together and that was that. I didn't consider my happiness, our compatibility, our backgrounds, our faith or any of the things you would think to consider before taking such a step. I just asked, she said yes, and the fiasco began. I just sat back and watched.

Janet was raised as a Methodist like me. I guess that meant picking a church was easy. But the thing is, I had no earthly clue what it meant to be a Methodist. I had no idea what it even meant to be a Christian. It seems through my experience in college I had learned a valuable yet troubling skill. I learned to ask questions. My college years are where I began to question the existence of God and proudly labeled myself an Atheist, or at the very least, Agnostic. I had plenty of questions beginning to surface about the entire story of Jesus and I engaged plenty of other people just as ignorant as I was in conversations regarding faith. I got nowhere. But we're going to get WAY off into that later. Hold on to your seat.

So here I was, a young Christian Methodist in the eyes of those planning the event, ready to stand in a church and profess my undying love and loyalty in front of a god I didn't believe in. But when you get married you always do it in a church because that's what you're supposed to do. That's what people expect. So that's what I did. I stood before 300 people I hardly knew, in front of some minister who thought he knew who I was, and before "God" and made a long list of promises I already knew I couldn't keep. To this day I'm not sure whether you should marry at fifteen, have kids, then start enjoying your life at thirty-five, or simply wait until you're fifty and BEGIN to have the curtain removed from your narrow vision.

I learned about being a faithful groom almost immediately after the proposal (whenever that was!). What SHOULD be a sacred moment between two people in love (which I wasn't) immediately turned in to a small town media event orchestrated by my future mother-in-law. There are things that happen after a formal engagement that I never even dreamed of!

Apparently first on the list is a formal engagement picture and announcement in the local gazette, which means you have to pick out just the right outfit and photographer. Let's be clear. I didn't pick either. Of course, I was accompanied to the local men's shop to pick out the perfect wool suit which cost a ridiculous amount of money. The photographer was chosen by Janet and her parents and an actual shoot took place. Once the announcement was actually published, there was an ENGAGEMENT DINNER!! Are you kidding me? The wedding was months away and the money was already flowing like Niagara Falls just to announce the engagement. What I should have bought was a good pair of running shoes.

I won't pretend to list all the things that go in to planning a wedding, but it's lengthy. Colors, a theme, music, the guest list, a dress, a tux, the wedding party and the reception plans are but a tiny fraction of the details that have to be worked out. Oh, and if you're going to have guests bringing gifts, then you have to register for things like China and Silverware. I wouldn't know what ours looked like. I didn't help pick it out. I may have had an opinion about invitations and I did have to get fitted for a tuxedo. I chose my half of the wedding party and rented a car for the day of the event. Other than that, I was merely required to show up. The rest was all being handled by Janet and her mother, the quintessential social director. This day wasn't for Janet and me. It was for her mother. It was the Titanic of local weddings in more ways than one and Janet's mom was at the helm.

Now it may sound as if I'm complaining, but I'm not. Today I can clearly see the event for what it was, but at twenty-two years old, I simply thought it's the way things were done. I remember thinking it a colossal waste of money, but it wasn't mine that was being spent. It was our parents'.

Stresses ran high for several months, but the fateful day did finally arrive along with over 300 guests, most of whom I did not know. So as to be out of the way, I played golf with my Best Man that morning, then picked up the Lincoln Town Car, dressed and arrived at the church for pre-wedding pictures. Janet and I were not to see each other until the ceremony because it's bad luck to do otherwise. Just typing that statement makes me laugh out loud as the full force of its audacity slaps me in the face. Who comes up with these silly rules anyway? It's a little like the "white dress" rule. Her mother actually caught us having sex so virginity wasn't in question, yet anything other than a white dress was never considered because the neighbors might know. It just occurred to me. Young people should not get married. In fact, no one should.

I stood at the altar, burdened under the watchful glare of a sanctuary of people, half of which were dabbing their eyes because "it was just so beautiful." As I stood there, also being watched by the stained-glass version of Jesus holding a lamb, listening to solo after duet from Miss Nebraska herself and then one of UNL's Scarlett and Cream singers, my mind just went blank.

"Listen to the music. Smile. Just say the damn words. Smile. Shake some hands. It'll all be over soon and we can party at the reception," were just some of the things I can imagine thinking at the time. It was hot. It was expensive. It was a circus act. The pastor couldn't even pronounce the word "love." I heard the usual passage from Corinthians. I had a ring slipped on my finger. And then it was done. After months of planning, the ceremony itself took less than thirty minutes and that's including the musical performances from some of Nebraska's biggest stars.

From the church we paraded hundreds of folks out to the country club for the reception. I don't remember what we ate. I don't remember our first dance. I don't remember cutting the cake. I don't care. We came, we ate, we danced, we left. That's how I remember it. From there we went to the hotel and the awesome honeymoon suite where we just went to sleep because we were exhausted. The next morning it was up and at 'em early to get dressed for the gift opening party which required ANOTHER damn special outfit. Everything was side-show. And I just went along.

All of this is just to drive home the point about marriage. Young people are by their nature, naïve. I was no exception. Yet it's in our youth we decide we're in love with some person we hardly know and then ask the state and God to rubber stamp their approval on a lifetime of commitment. We spend (or our parents spend) an enormous amount of money for an event that lasts under an hour just so we have a piece of paper that says we're married. I'll tell you something. I no longer need a piece of paper OR God to define my level of love and commitment. But that's what society brainwashes us in to thinking we need.

I'm still not complaining about the events of the day. It's easy to arm-chair quarterback looking back twenty-eight years. But I know this. It never should have happened. I should have been smarter. I should have read the signs and I should have spoken up. A wedding is not the place to start establishing boundaries. But life has a way of teaching us about that doesn't it?

Lesson Twenty-One:

YOU HAVE TO MAKE TIME FOR FUN. IT FUELS THE SOUL.

> *"We should come home from adventures, and perils, and discoveries every day with new experience and character."*
>
> ~Henry David Thoreau

"Ahem. Pssst! Psssst!! MATT!"

"What?"

"Hop in the truck. We have some paperwork to finish in the office," Jim said.

"We do?"

"Yes, we do. These other guys can finish up here. I need you back in the office."

Once inside Jim's pickup, he just smiled at me as we steered a course southwest for Texarkana, Texas, some thirty miles from our current location in Arkansas.

"We're out of beer," he grinned.

So that was our code. When Jim needed me back in the office, we were out of beer and needed some male bonding time, cruising back roads of Arkansas looking for mischief. They were some amazing days of living carefree.

One of the few benefits of my relationship with Janet (besides the birth of our daughter of course) was becoming friends and eventually an employee of her brother, Jim. Although three years my senior, Jim was the first to really demonstrate for me a life of fearlessness.

Although his parents dreamed of him being a doctor, Jim sat in pre-med classes dreaming of owning his own business. Once he earned his degree, that's exactly what he did. He moved to Texas with his wife Donna and started his own utility construction business. Although he started small, his business eventually grew to near $2.5 million in annual revenue. And then he went bankrupt. From that financial hurdle Jim emerged at the top with yet another business venture with two partners in Indiana. It went great for years and when that business failed he started another... and another. In between, if Jim didn't have an income stream, he took up sales of some kind or another. He never considered how he was going to do things. He just did them. There were times in my younger days I had a hard time understanding his method, but it's crystal clear to me today. He lived in the moment.

I also considered Jim's wife Donna as a close friend and she was equally fearless. She "followed" Jim wherever his dreams led and always seemed to support him. I can't be sure, but I suspect there were times the risks caused tension in their marriage, but they always seemed to thrive.

Donna, herself, went to medical school and earned her M.D. while raising their two children and moving around the country with Jim. Since that time, she has rarely actually practiced medicine to any great degree which again always made me pause and wonder why someone would to that. Today I see her quest and applaud the fact that she did it. It's not a question of why, but why not? She's a doctor! Who cares if she owns her own clinic!

On another occasion, Donna spent two weeks in the mountains cross-country skiing, living in igloos, completely out of contact with civilization. It was enormously adventurous and no-doubt, dangerous. I had vast respect for them both, although as I've stated, I didn't always understand their motives when I was younger.

Jim and Donna were the first two people with whom I remember discussing religion. Jim obviously grew up in the same Methodist family as his sister and Donna was raised in a house of staunch Catholics. Yet somehow, they seemed more open-minded; more forward-thinking. We would sit around the campfire on little campouts and discuss the vastness of our universe, or the presence of God. We discussed the silliest things like whether or not saying "Goddammit" was taking the Lord's name in vain since you didn't really MEAN that you wanted God to "damn" someone or something. We discussed heaven and hell, the contents of the Bible and much, much more. Beer will do that for you!

Texarkana was a curious town. Set fully in the heart of the "Bible belt," Texarkana is split down the middle between Texas and Arkansas. The Texas side of Main Street was lined with Liquor stores since that particular Texas county was "wet." The Arkansas side of Main Street was lined with laundry mats because THAT particular county in Arkansas was "dry." I could write an entire book about the ridiculous liquor laws spattered across the Bible belt, but suffice it to say, if we wanted alcohol in Arkansas, we went to Texas to get it. (Or to the little drive-thru trailer house where a guy sold bootleg beer.) In theory, you had to be careful not to buy too much lest you be arrested for bootlegging while crossing Main Street back into Arkansas. Like I said, ridiculous.

The case of Bud Light was iced down and well within reach as Jim and I began our long, winding trek back to Hope via the back roads of eastern Arkansas. It was frosty cold and flowed freely down the backs of our parched throats as we took turn after unmapped turn down gravel roads, discussing the state of the world, how we wanted his business to grow, how I fit in to that plan, and how we were going to spend all our money in the lap of luxury. The more we drank, the wealthier we became. Those were great days.

The lightly asphalted "farm-to-market" road began to veer a bit to the left and expose the tall sand embankment of a crystal-clear gravel pit. The deep pool of man-made water was surrounded on all sides by tall mounds of sand, nearly fifty feet high in some places and littered with dry brush trying to take root and flourish. We cruised by slowly, our fifth or sixth beer on the way to our stomach, and shared the same thought at the same time. "Should we?"

Jim had recently purchased a new 4x4 truck that was just begging to be tested. Without saying a word, Jim turned the truck perpendicular to the small road and faced the overshadowing mound of sand. From our drunken vantage point, it looked straight up. His foot hit the floor as he drove the accelerator forward and the truck sped the short distance to the enormous sand pile. "Woo hoo!!!" I screamed.

The front wheels of the monster truck sunk in the sand and then grabbed ever so slightly as we pointed skyward and began to inch our way up the sand.

"Vvvvvvvvvvvvvvvvvvvvvvvvvvvv," you could hear the tires saying as they spun and tossed sand and sticks everywhere as they inched us toward the top! And then just as we neared the crest, the sand defeated us in the first battle of this war and we slid back down until our bumper scraped the road. By maneuvering until we nearly tipped over, we were able to free the bumper, back across the road and take another run. Same result. At least four times we tried to pound, claw and grind our way to the top of the sand with Jim's fancy truck, but it just wasn't to be. Gravity and the slippery sand won every time.

Giggling like schoolgirls, yet defeated, we parked the truck and "walked" to the top of the sand. From the apex of the mound we stared, mouths gaped open, over the deep, cold, clear water and realized our fortune. Had we succeeded in conquering the mound, we would have plunged immediately into the watery abyss! There are a couple lessons there I'm sure.

One, don't drink and drive. Two, a little planning never hurt anything. Three, it wasn't gravity and sand that "defeated" us, but the universe saving us for another day. Everything happens for the right reason at the right time and two drunken boys drowning in Arkansas wasn't meant to happen that day. But we weren't quite finished!

As we attempted to stand upright, slapping each other on the back while staring in amazement at our cheated fate, yet another interesting artifact caught our eye. Apparently others as adventurous as us had stretched a long metal cable from one side of the lake to the other. On our side, merely thirty yards to our right, hung the T-bar by which you could hang and "ride" out to the middle of the lake. Again, the look and the thought, "Should we?"

Jim got a head start as we stumbled and stripped to our skivvies in route to the rock just below the T-bar. The platform where we were able to stand and grasp the bar was, in fact, an enormous gray rock with jagged edges, yet smooth as silk on top. It was only ten feet to the edge which gave way to a thirty foot drop to yet more rocks that lined the edge of the pool. How those rocks got there in the middle of a giant sand pit is anyone's guess, but they were there, nonetheless.

Jim grabbed the bar in his usual fearless way, gave me a huge grin and lifted his legs to put the ride in motion. "Squeaky squeaker squeaky squeak!" The bar ground slowly over the cable until Jim was poised about halfway across the lake. It was there the cable sagged to its lowest point and the ride was over. Jim let go and plunged the ten feet or so, barefoot and half naked into the icy clear water. I held my breath until he resurfaced. He popped up wearing that same half-drunk grin and let out a blood-curdling "WOO HOO!!"

"How was it?" I hollered at the small head bobbing in the middle of the lake.

"It was AWESOME! A little slow, though. You need to get a RUN at it!" was Jim's reply.

I began to pull the T-bar back by the recovery rope as Jim swam back toward shore. "Get a run at it, huh? I'M a runner, by God!" was running through my alcohol-influenced brain. "Wait until you see THIS run!"

I had the T-bar in my hand as Jim was reaching shore. I back up along the top of the platform rock until the bar was difficult to grasp. I stood twenty feet from the edge of the rock, poised for speed. I sprinted the short distance with all I could muster, reaching top speed in a flash. If you'll recall, one of the lessons learned from the sand climbing was "plan ahead." It would seem I overlooked that little lesson yet again as I launched myself from the edge of the rock, thirty feet off the ground and another thirty from the water's edge.

I slept a lot during Physics class in High School. I should have paid attention. There has to be some law about momentum, speed, etc, but I forget what it is now. My speed and therefore, momentum, FAR surpassed the ability of that rusty cable to absorb the thrust and deliver me on a smooth, speedy ride to the cold plunge. No sir. My body launched straight out until I was parallel to the cable. The pulley squeaked slowly behind as I began to swing like a drunken pendulum on the end of a half-rotted wooden T-bar. I immediately lost my firm grip and now hung by the last digit of my right ring finger. It's truly amazing what adrenalin can do for you. Still swinging, I glanced down to measure my distance to the water's edge. With one final "whip" I lost my meager grip on the T-bar and shot straight to the edge of the shoreline where my impact was absorbed by a mere six inches of water.

"WHAM! SPLAAAAASH!!!"

I hit the water and smaller rocks like a sack of potatoes. Although alive, I wasn't sure about the extent of my injuries. Then I heard it. It was faint at first, like the scenes in war movies where a bomb has just gone off near the victim. Then it became louder and clearer. It became MUCH louder and MUCH clearer. Jim was laughing. In fact he was laughing so hard I thought HE was going to fall off the rock and join me on the shore.

"Are you okay?" I could barely make out above the roaring laughter and the ringing in my ears.

"I... I don't know! I think so!"

More laughter. "That was AWESOME!" Still more laughter.

As I pulled myself slowly to my feet, I realized I was injured, but only slightly. After an afternoon of drinking, trying to climb high sand dunes and swinging from a rusty cable out into depths unknown, the worst of it was a pulled tendon in my right arm making it difficult to use hand tools for over a week. I'd say that's a small price to pay for an afternoon of adventure.

On the way "home," Jim and I nearly finished our case of beer. We were wet, filthy, drunk and happy. We were going to have some major explaining to do with our spouses. And no, they didn't believe a word of the story we made up. Over time, the truth was a lot more fun anyway.

Lesson Twenty-Two:

SOME THINGS JUST SHOULDN'T COME SO EASY

"The only job where you start at the top is digging a hole."

~Unknown

In many ways, Jim's generosity towards me was a blessing that I'll never be able to repay. His heart was definitely in the right place and there isn't anything he wouldn't have done for his sister and me. In other ways, Jim made things easy for me, much in the same way my parents always did. I'm not complaining. I'm eternally grateful. But what I've learned throughout life is that having things given to you without working for them isn't necessarily what's best for you.

Throughout my years in college, Jim always provided me a summer job. I learned a valuable trade as a cable splicer and loved being outdoors and working by the unit. It was good money and the freedom was invigorating. One summer was spent splicing cable just north of Dallas. Another was spent installing rural phone systems south of San Antonio. Still another was spent doing the same near Hope, Arkansas. I loved the work and I didn't take Jim's generosity for granted. I was a diligent worker and made few mistakes. I considered myself an asset to his small company.

I already mentioned that Jim and I considered my role in his company early in our relationship. We spent summers talking about where we would take his company and how the money would pour in. It was a win-win, in that I would have steady employment and Jim would be close to his sister and have someone reliable to help him run his company. Not once in my later years of college did I consider employment with another firm. I was spared the painful process of interviews and research, hoping a Fortune 500 company would scoop me up and pay me top dollar. I just always knew I'd work for Jim.

Janet and I were married in May of 1983 and I graduated the following December. Upon graduation, we packed up the U-Haul and headed for Hope, Arkansas, the current headquarters for Jim's company. Janet was able to complete her final semester of student teaching in nearby Arkadelphia and I was able to sink my teeth in a new career. However, there were some things about this arrangement I hadn't carefully considered. I didn't think the whole thing through and I didn't include Janet in all the decisions.

For starters, I told Jim not to worry about salary as long as he provided our basic needs. Sure, that was a generous offer on my part, but I didn't see the need for money that belonged to me and Janet. If we needed something, it meant asking Jim for it. He never said no. It just wasn't a mature arrangement and Janet grew resentful of always asking her brother. Today, I completely understand that. Then, I just thought she was being difficult.

The second thing I hadn't fully considered was the amount of travel I would be doing, leaving a new bride to basically fend for herself in a strange place. I had a company credit card. She had to ask her brother. After doing some basic office work that needed updating, like making our accounting system operational, I began to do more project-management. But in a small company, managing projects meant also doing the labor.

I'm not afraid of hard work, but my unrealistic expectations were that a BS in Business would eliminate the word "labor" from my vocabulary. Not so.

Not long after our arrival in Arkansas, I began traveling during the week to a project in Norman, Oklahoma. Janet moved to an apartment in Arkadelphia with her sister-in-law and we saw each other on weekends. Because our long range plans were to move our operation to Dallas, Janet and I moved to a Dallas suburb after her graduation in the spring of 1984. We had our own place, but I still traveled during the week while Janet worked beneath her qualifications at a local day care. I had work and co-workers. Janet was now basically on her own until we could get the company moved to Texas. She was miserable. And although I didn't like the arrangement all that much, my ego kept telling me I was working hard for our future and all we had to do was "suck it up" until things got better. It didn't. At least it didn't get better soon enough.

The project in Norman continued to expand as the project moved from one phase to the next and things with Janet were becoming more stressful. Our weekends were nice, but it was clear this wasn't the place for her and I wasn't feeling as though my "talents" were truly being utilized by a small company. I was impatient. I had a place with Jim's company. It just wasn't the right time and I didn't really care for that "place."

After a long summer that kept me on the road most of the time, we discovered Janet was pregnant. That sealed the deal. Together we determined our place was being close to relatives in Nebraska where our new baby could be close to grandparents. My dad came to Texas late one night to help us move from our apartment under the cover of darkness. We left no forwarding address and headed north. We took turns living with my folks and Janet's while I began to look for work. Once again, people that cared about us were keeping us afloat. I was determined to see that didn't continue to happen.

I learned some things about myself when we relocated to Nebraska. I was diligent. I was smart. I was manipulative. Looking for the perfect job became my full time employment and I worked at finding a job eight hours every single day... for SIXTH MONTHS!! Like a job in sales, you have to go through some "no's" to get to a yes and I went through plenty of them. Resume in hand, I began to navigate the world of unemployment while living with relatives.

Although I majored in what amounts to General Business in college, I developed a fondness for Behavioral Science, specifically as it related to Human Resource Management and made up my mind that a future in HR was just what suited me. I wanted to be part of the hiring process for a large company. I wanted to wear a suit and tie and go to power lunches. Again, my expectations were slightly skewed. It's difficult realizing you're going to have to start at the bottom when most of what you have has been given to you.

I learned about networking. I became a master at getting my foot in the door. Everyone I met or knew was a potential contact or employer. I sent résumés, made phone calls, typed cover letters and went to interviews day after day. My problem, as it turned out, was that I kept asking people for a job. What I needed was advice.

Lincoln Telephone and Telegraph was a family-owned, well-respected telecom company in Lincoln, Nebraska. It was a place every blue collar family dreamed their kid would work. They were solid and they had great benefits. The pay wasn't bad either. Sitting in a small office in the Personnel Department of LT&T was a woman named Pam who had the job I was seeking. I had a background in Telecom and a degree in Business that emphasized human behavior. She was the Management Recruiter and I wanted her job. So I did what any young man that wants work would do. I called her and begged.

"Look, Pam," I said. "I know you guys aren't hiring in HR and I'm not asking you for work. All I'm asking is five minutes of your time to get some of your professional advice on how I can make a career LIKE yours somewhere else. I really just need your help."

"Five minutes," she answered as she let out an exasperated breath. "Be here tomorrow at 9:00 a.m. and you can have five minutes. It's all I can offer you."

"I'll be there, Pam. Thanks."

The following morning I showed up at Pam's office wearing the best $100 suit I owned, carrying the brief case I got as a present for my college graduation. It was empty except for the lone résumé I had packed inside which I had no intention of showing Pam unless she asked. We shook hands. She looked busy. We spoke for over an hour. She took my résumé as we laughed and shook hands for my departure. I had no job, but I had a "power person" in the business on my side. It was all going to be fine.

Pam made it clear they had no entry-level jobs in Personnel at LT&T and I wasn't qualified for a lot of their higher tech jobs. But I knew she liked me and would go to bat for me. Still, with no immediate hope of employment there, I took a job at a "Headhunting Firm" for minimum wage. The work was at night and my job was to simply call potential clients and find out if they were interested in the possibility of being farmed out to big companies looking for their talent. The work was lonely (I worked alone in an empty office) and I was completely out of my element, but I did the best I could. I did well enough that the nice Jewish man that owned the company said I might make a good recruiter one day which meant I would basically be a commissioned sales rep. It terrified me.

It was shortly after I was offered the night job that I got a glimpse of how the universe provides when you continue to expect the best while doing what needs to be done. Even though

I had a job of some kind, I continued to work diligently at finding my dream job. Although not usually a fruitful avenue, I checked the professional section of the local newspaper one morning while drinking coffee and saw the following heading; "Management Recruiter." Well, by gosh, that's what I want to do! The ad caught my eye for a couple reasons. I loved the heading, but it was also what I came to know as a "blind ad" which meant you had no idea which company was doing the hiring. Historically, they're a complete dead end. The only way to make contact was to submit a résumé to the published address and hope for the best. I slid my chair up to the typewriter and tapped out my best cover letter, attached it to a résumé and dropped it in the mail, en route to the mysterious P.O. Box. What the hell. I certainly had nothing to lose.

About a week passed from the time I dropped the letter in the mail to the day the phone rang with Pam's voice on the other end. "We're so glad we got your résumé, Matt."

"Um, I'm sorry. What?"

"Matt, I'm going to be taking a job in a different area of the company. It was a move I had no idea was coming when we spoke, but when they offered me the position, I thought immediately of you as my replacement."

"I'm not sure I'm following you, Pam, but go on." I pleaded as Pam continued to explain.

"There are lots of internal candidates within our company that are basically qualified to do my job, but we wanted you. That's why we placed the blind ad in the classifieds. We didn't want to tip off internal people that we were looking and we hoped you would respond to the ad. It was basically bait. It's never been our policy to run blind ads," she continued.

"Pam, what are you saying exactly?"

"If you're still interested, we want to offer you MY job. Be here first thing in the morning and we'll work out details."

"Oh my god. Oh my g… yes! Yes! I'll be there first thing in the morning, Pam! Thank you!! Thank you!!!"

I hung up the phone quivering. The next morning I was offered an entry-level position in Human Resources, recruiting management for Lincoln Telephone. I was going to have a salary (a whopping $16,800 per year), benefits, and a desk! The search for my perfect job was over. But the best part wasn't really about the job itself. The best part was how I landed it.

No one that I knew personally was connected to Pam or anyone on staff in Personnel at LT&T. I did it on my own. No one made a call for me. No one called in a favor. I don't think anyone has ever looked for a job as hard as I looked for those months. Sure, I was living under my parent's roof and had something to eat, but again, I didn't take that for granted. I looked hard for work every day to the best of my ability and it paid off with my dream job. I could hold my head up because I was going to be able to provide for my family. For the first time in my young life, I began to feel like a man. Working hard for something feels good. Working hard isn't to be confused with struggle which we'll discuss in later chapters, but doing what needs done while sending the right signal to our incredible universe and then having it pay off, is one of the most gratifying feelings there is. Some things just shouldn't be given to you before you've earned them.

Lesson Twenty-Three:

GIVING BACK FEELS GOOD

"The greatest good you can do for another is not just share your riches, but reveal to them their own."

~Benjamin Disraeli

"Beep. Beep. Beep," my office (ok cubicle) phone rang indicating I had a call from inside the office area. These were before the days of Caller I.D. so I initially had no idea where the call was coming from. But as I looked up through the door of my cubicle, I could see Laurie, one of our shared receptionists holding her phone and looking desperate that I pick up. I was puzzled in that she usually just walked the few steps from her desk to mine if she had a message of some kind to deliver.

I hadn't noticed until now that a young man was sitting at our common-area conference table feverishly scribbling on a piece of paper.

"Personnel Resources. This is Matt. How can I help you?" I said as I answered the phone in my most professional voice just in case it WASN'T actually Laurie calling.

She began to whisper into the phone and point from behind an open hand meant to hide her pointer finger. "That man at the conference table came here all the way from Kansas to fill out an application. I told him we only accepted résumés at this time and he said if I loaned him a pencil and paper he'd write one!"

I had begun to settle nicely into my new career as Management Recruiter for Lincoln Telephone and Telegraph. I attended a seminar in Chicago designed to help me sharpen my interviewing skills and was making friends with many of my co-workers. I was in the process of finishing an internal data base program designed to qualify internal talent that Pam had started and felt I was already being seen as an able professional. I liked my boss, her boss and her boss's boss. The administrative pool was excellent and I was learning to feel my way around the Wage and Salary division of HR which consisted of a hard-nosed man-and-woman team of pencil pushers. Every offer I made had to be approved through them. In short, I was fitting in.

The phone call from Laurie came as I was reviewing a stack of résumés much like the one I had submitted before Pam had offered me a job. It felt good to know I had actually a little control of the employment situation now. I looked up from my inbox to glance at the unkempt, rather young man that Laurie was referring to and sized up my schedule for the day.

"I don't have anything pressing this morning. When he's finished tell him I'll see him," I said in a way that I thought made me sound infinitely more important than I actually was.

"Really?" she asked in the same whisper. "We don't usually see people up here without an appointment."

"I know," I said. "But the poor guy drove up from Kansas. Let me know when he's ready."

After another beep beep beep from the phone, alerting me that my unannounced visitor was ready, I stood to go offer my hand and introduce myself. "Hi, I'm Matt Leatherwood. Please come in."

The young man introduced himself as he took my hand and we moved for my cubicle where I could review his résumé. He had an eerie confidence. He didn't fidget or ramble. He kept eye contact in a way that made me a little uncomfortable. I finally glanced down to read his pencil-sketched, hand-written résumé. I knew immediately I was in unknown territory.

It was difficult to avoid reacting emotionally as I began reading a very unorganized "letter" that explained how this young man had invented the electric car, but his idea shut down by the federal government and big oil companies. Even with my untrained eye I could see this was a man wrapped in delusion and paranoia as I continued to read account after account of how he'd been targeted by our government. He was seemingly a nice kid, but like a curtain being pulled back from a horrible accident scene, I began to see the reality of what I was dealing with. At first I was afraid. And then something different bubbled to the top… compassion.

One of the things I loved most about my new career was being a recognized, local Human Resources Professional. That meant I was continually asked, by local agencies that served those less fortunate, to sit on panels and share ideas on the best way to get a job. I indirectly had the opportunity to help the unemployed, the underprivileged, the handicapped and the challenged. I loved every opportunity I had to serve on those panels. It felt great to share the secrets I had learned the hard way while I was seeking employment and to also shed a little light on how local HR worked. I was becoming somewhat of an "expert" in résumé and letter writing. And I was developing a long list of appropriate answers to common interview questions.

I told the young man sitting across my desk that we just didn't have any opportunities at Lincoln Telephone for someone with his talents, but promised I would make some contacts with people I knew within the area that might be able to help him find what he was looking for. What I DIDN'T tell him was that the people I would be calling dealt on a daily basis with people facing mental challenges just like his. He seemed to take the news in stride and left me his phone number. I promised him I'd be in touch.

"Hi Sarah, this is Matt Leatherwood over at LT&T," I spoke confidently into the phone.

"Oh. Hi Matt! It's good to hear from you!" she answered politely.

"Listen Sarah," I sighed as I tried to sound caring. "I met a guy this week from Kansas that could really use the help of your agency. I know you're funded by the State of Nebraska, but if there is ANY way we could find a way to get him in to your next workshop, I would REALLY appreciate the favor."

As Sarah politely agreed to bend a rule or two to make room for my guy, I realized there truly were a variety of advantages to serving on so many committees. I also realized that my professional courtesy was appreciated by others in our community and it made me feel good to be able to call in a small favor. I was determined to make a difference in the young man's life.

I was vague when I spoke to the young man's mother by phone the following morning. He was unavailable at that moment so I merely asked her to see he came to my office the following week to meet with me about an opportunity I'd created for him I thought would help. She agreed and so the meeting was set.

On Monday morning, I confirmed with Sarah that she had a spot in her upcoming seminar and reserved some time in our private conference room. Bob (I have NO recollection of what his real name was) showed up on schedule wearing the same tattered jacket he had worn a couple weeks before. I was beaming with the thought of breaking the good news to him. I was making a difference.

"Bob, I have some GREAT news for you," I said softly as we sat across from each other at the long cherry-wood table. "I called in a favor or two with a friend of mine and she's agreed to make you a part of her next workshop beginning next month. It's a great program that helps people gain employment skills. Because you're from Kansas, she had to take considerable risk to get you in. This is a great opportunity for you."

"What's the name of the organization?" he asked.

I gave him the name and his next question surprised me a little. "Who provides the funding for this organization?"

"It's a great program funded by the State of Nebraska," I told him carefully.

Something suddenly didn't look right on Bob. "You know I don't want anything to do with the government."

"But… but this is a great opportunity for you and people have gone to some length to provide it for you," I affirmed as my mouth began to fall open.

"I told you. No way! I am NOT getting involved in anything funded by our government!!"

The emotional explosion started slowly, but it reached an early peak as Bob began ranting uncontrollably about how the government had targeted him. This was all part of some trick or trap or some other scheme.

"Bob. I can ASSURE you that this…"

"NO!!!!!"

The actual fear of dealing with the unknowns of the human psyche began to rise in my throat. I slowly rose to my feet and opened the conference room door. "I'm afraid I'm going to have to ask you to leave."

Thankfully, Bob did as I asked. But the glare I received as he left actually gave me the feeling that I and those in the office weren't safe. He left via the stairs at the edge of our complex of cubicles, screaming the entire way about a variety of things I didn't understand. Security was alerted immediately and everyone kept a watchful eye. We never saw him again.

I explained to everyone in the office what had occurred and returned to my desk in stunned silence. What on earth had just happened? I don't know that I ever really answered that question for myself, but it was a definite wakeup call that there were people... lots of people... who suffered in ways I didn't understand. And although I thought I was becoming a big shot in the ways of human behaviors; I clearly was in way over my head on this one. I called Sarah and explained what had happened and despite her efforts, Bob would not be attending the class. As far as I know she understood and never held it against me. I had so much to learn.

On still another occasion (I won't bore you with minute details) I stuck my neck out for an Iranian citizen who held exactly the kind of computer skills we were looking for. His Visa had expired and needed a person or large company to sponsor him in order to regain temporary work status. I plead my case to the Computer Department and to my boss and because they had faith in me and my ability to assess talent, reluctantly agreed to sponsor this candidate.

Citizenship and work status are complicated matters. With sponsorship, this young Iranian still had to physically leave the United States and reenter via the Canadian Consulate because the U.S. was not accepting Iranians through ours. It was an enormous expense covered in its entirety by LT&T and based on my assessment of this man's talent and trustworthiness. All went smoothly and he became a productive member of our technical team; at least for about six months. At that time, despite all we had done to provide the man with the means to work in the U.S., he left us to work for another local utility company. Again I WAS stunned by the lack of loyalty and appreciation. It's probably important to note that I was a mere twenty-five years old at the time. I was idealistic and saw most things in "black and white." What this guy did was wrong.

There were some enormously valuable lessons to be learned from these encounters and others like them. For starters I learned that people won't always behave the way you expect them to simply because you've helped them. I believe Mother Teresa would say, "Help them anyway." I learned that if you want to feel good about "giving" you have to do it without expecting things in return. The gift is in the giving itself. This may be where I first started to get nudges from the universe, telling me I didn't always know what was best for people. Who was I to decide the man from Kansas needed help in Nebraska?

Fortunately, the episode with the fellow-human from Iran didn't leave much of a black mark on my reputation. My heart was in the right place. I knew better than to stick my neck out like that again anytime soon, however. I think those that knew me at least realized I wasn't afraid to risk the company's money for a good programmer!

Maybe the most important thing I learned was to begin being mindful of other's suffering. I had a great job, a roof over my head, food to eat, a new baby at home, and (thanks to very tight budgeting) a new Oldsmobile in the driveway. Others weren't so lucky. I learned to look past my own ego and ask more questions before I offered help to people. And I began to start listening to my own inner voice. I had far, far to go with that one, but at least it was a beginning.

The winds of change were already beginning to blow... again.

Lesson Twenty-Four:

I AM DRIVEN BY MY RESTLESS SPIRIT

> *"Man hath still either toys or care: But hath no root, nor to one place is tied, but ever restless and irregular, about this earth doth run and ride. He knows he hath a home, but scarce knows where; He says it is so far, that he has quite forgot how to go there."*
>
> ~Henry Vaughan

Life, for me at LT&T continued to go well. I think we've covered that. What I failed to mention adequately, is that my amazing daughter was born in February of 1985. She was beautiful and soft and cuddly and I was totally in love from the moment I laid eyes on her. I love both my daughters that way today.

Having a daughter at home changed things in my life considerably. It meant a feeling of more responsibility. It meant being obligated to provide for another life. It meant (and this probably sounds selfish) that I was no longer living a life of MY choosing, but a life of obligation that comes with parenting. As a child I always dreamed of a yellow house with white shutters, a wife, kids and animals. And that's almost exactly what I had at the tender age of twenty-five.

Before Chelsea was born, Janet and I found a nice one-bedroom house to rent just outside of Ashland, Nebraska. It was on two acres and was truly a cute little place. We had two dogs of our own and a cat named Adolf which apparently came with the house. We added Chelsea to the life of dreams and I had a job everyone envied. We lived near family and saw them all often. As near as I can tell, that's just about everything on the checklist. I had it all. Or did I?

Now, at fifty years of age, I see clearly that it takes tremendous courage to live the life you want as opposed to the life you've been taught you should. I didn't see it then, but the feelings swelling inside my gut were from living a life of "ought to's." Everything about my life was just how I had planned. The problem was I didn't feel the way I thought having all those things would make me feel. Something was amiss. I was restless and unfulfilled. I felt pressure and the urge to do more. It felt like I was always on the verge of missing out on something. I was happy on the outside. I was restless with a capital R on the inside and it grew worse every day.

My restless spirit began to manifest itself in a number of ways. I still had a longing to compete at some level so I began researching the world of Triathlons. And although I really enjoyed my job, I began to watch the clock. When the whistle blew (metaphorically of course) at 5:00 o'clock, I was out the door and to my car as fast as possible to get home, kiss the baby and head out the door for the day's training. I didn't consider the fact that my wife had been home all day with said baby and that SHE may need a release too. It was about me.

Every night was a combination of two events chosen from swimming at the local pool, bicycling and running. I leaned out to 155 pounds and under five percent body fat. I became cranky if I missed a workout and even left family events early to go home and get in a workout. Working out became my drug of choice, chosen to mask the pain of unrest. Nearly one weekend a month, I loaded up the car with wife, baby, bicycle and camping equipment to head for an event anywhere within a three state area. I found it to be adventurous. My wife found it to be a burden. I believe I can see her point now.

The love of triathlons led to an even greater fascination with the world of cycling. I loved bicycles and the intricacies of their mechanics. I loved riding most of all and looked for reasons to work on my bike. It bears mentioning that I added some debt to the family budget by going at lunch to buy a racing bike that I didn't discuss with Janet. I NEEDED a good bike if I was to compete and I DID have the job after all. I was heading down a path of recklessness where it came to my relationships. I just wanted to do what I wanted to do. It was still about me.

An interesting combination of love for cycling and the desire to own a business caused me to consider opening a bike shop. Basic needs such as how to finance such a venture weren't important.

One of my other loves from college was the study of Small Business Administration. Next to human behavior, I found the independence of owning my own business fascinating. I knew nothing about it of course, but that didn't stop me from using time at work to begin writing a feasibility study for my bike shop. There were no big projects to do. All the departments were nearly at full staff; therefore I wasn't screening many candidates. I didn't have a desktop computer in those days so I basically scripted the entire plan for my business, by hand, on lined computer paper. I was sure to keep some work-related paper at hand so I could cover my project if discovered. I became consumed with the plan and sometimes spent an entire workday researching products, marketing schemes, and mechanic schools. The really good ones were in Oregon. How I thought I'd pull that off with a new family is anyone's guess, but I wasn't thinking in those terms.

The next phase of my restlessness began to rear its ugly head in the way of loneliness. I had a wife and child at home. We had friends that we got together with on a regular basis and we lived close to family. Yet it was during this phase of my life where I first began to discover that "alone in a crowded room" feeling. There was only one way I knew to fill it.

I want to state here and now that I did not ever, in any way act inappropriately with Laurie from work. There was never any physical contact and I never even considered her romantically for a single moment. But we did become good friends. And being around Laurie began to plant seeds of further doubt regarding my choice of spouse. Her husband also worked at the same company and I would never have stepped over any boundaries. Every conversation Laurie and I ever had, every lunch or break we went on, either together or with a group from Personnel was always on the up-and-up. That was part of the problem. I never thought to keep any of it secret.

I worked in a department staffed with twenty people. Of those twenty, eighteen were women. The other guy wasn't exactly my type in terms of personality trait, so guess who I talked about when I got home at night?

Self-absorption is a funny thing. You assume others will see things the way you see them. I learned that to be untrue. I'd walk through the door at night and after an obligatory, "How was your day?" would launch into a detailed account of how, "Laurie said this. Dee talked about that. Margaret and her friend did this or that." Every talk I shared with my wife about my life at work included some topic about another woman. I didn't hold back about lunches or breaks. That was just part of the world I worked in. And although I believe Janet trusted me to some extent, I was becoming more and more withdrawn.

"Are you having an affair with Laurie?" she inquired one evening as we shared a cigarette on the front porch after Chelsea had gone to sleep.

"What? Of course I'm not having an affair! What would make you ask such a silly question?" I defended.

"You just talk about her a lot. You just don't seem yourself. You're distant. You're… you're… emotionless!"

"Don't be ridiculous. She's a friend. Nothing more."

That's what it had come to. No attempt at filling the void and calming my restless spirit could even begin to accomplish what my subconscious could. I was shutting down. Nothing phased me. Not Janet's pleading. Not a new cuddly baby at home. There was no thrill in completing a triathlon. There was no joy from the little things. I felt trapped, unappreciated (unreal, right?) and I was beginning to find it hard to breathe. My mind did the only thing left to do. It detached.

There is no doubt the description of my mental state at that time is a bit melodramatic and overstated, but in reality, that's exactly what was happening. I was becoming a robot programmed to feel sorry for myself because other people needed things from me that interfered with my personal agenda. Things had always come easily for me. I believe we've clearly covered that. Having things handed to me on a silver platter had made me spoiled and impatient. And although I had worked hard to land the job of my dreams, after only two years I was bored. It wasn't a challenge. I was ready to do almost anything to regain that feeling of adventure, including leave my wife and child.

The answer to my "suffering" came in the form of a phone call. Universe to the rescue.

Lesson Twenty-Five:

TOUGH TIMES ARE EFFECTIVE TEACHERS

"Adventure without risk is Disneyland."

~Doug Coupland

I lit my second cigarette of the morning and took a long sip of the lukewarm coffee. After a quick flick of the growing ash I rested my forehead in the palm of my hand, careful not to let the ember touch my hair as I flipped to the next page of the long accounting document printed on large, lined computer paper. Cigarette still in hand, I moved over the keyboard of the industrial calculator with lightning speed as I ran yet another calculation meant to shed light on the current financial situation of the company. This was way worse than I thought. It was bad. It was really bad.

Only a month earlier, the phone call that answered all my immediate questions came while I was trying to look busy at Lincoln Telephone. Boredom was reaching a new pinnacle.

"Hello, Matt. This is Jim!" he said enthusiastically as I answered my office phone in the usual professional manner.

It was good to hear his voice and we exchanged pleasantries about his sister, his wife and the state of his business in Texas. Since my departure less than three years prior, Jim's company had begun to double in size nearly every year. He constructed a superb stone office complete with a small shop, hired bookkeeping help and moved the entire operation to Greenville, Texas. I was pleased he was doing so well.

"Listen, Matt," he said. "We're really rocking along down here in Texas and I think we've grown to the point I could use someone with some business savvy to help me run the entire operation. In short, I need someone to run my office and analyze the accounting and personnel. You'd be running the show from the inside. As things are, I don't know from one month to the next which jobs are making money and which aren't. We have no real system in place. I'm up to sixty-five employees and we're still doing payroll manually. Although we're busy, things are a bit of a mess."

My stomach began to churn and my mind raced. With cotton setting up temporary residence in my mouth, I tried to muster a response.

"This definitely sounds like a great opportunity," I started. "But you know we're going to have to do things differently this time if I decide it's something I'd like to do. For starters, I'm not interested in more field work. And we'll have to address an actual salary and benefits. Chelsea is still young so I'm sure we'll have to consider the consequences of moving her away from grandparents and friends. It'd be a big move, but I love the sound of the challenge. I'll talk it over with Janet and get back to you. Thanks for calling."

The above is, of course, a paraphrase of the conversation that took place. My boss was nearby and I needed to stay quiet regarding my intentions, but the adrenaline was already flowing and I knew it was something I wanted to try.

I got home that afternoon and told Janet the news about her brother calling. We were still in the thick of our "emotionless" issue and I think Janet saw this as a new start as well. What I DIDN'T know is that she was looking for a way to escape a situation of her own. We'll get to that.

Within two days we made the decision to give Texas another try. Much to everyone's surprise, I gave my two-weeks' notice at LT&T and by the next week we were packing up the Ryder truck. We were stuffed to the gills with furniture, baby and two dogs. Adolf stayed with the rent house.

I distinctly remember standing in the driveway of my parent's house, truck packed, Chelsea in arm, tearfully saying goodbye. I handed Chelsea to my mother for a last hug and she reluctantly gave her gently back. This was a major turning point for me. My parents have always been enormously supportive. I knew they thought this move was a bad idea, but they supported it, nonetheless. It meant getting to see their granddaughter twice a year as opposed to twice a week, yet they offered nothing but support. I cried as I apologized to my mom for taking her granddaughter so far away. My mother, tears streaming down her face, assured me I was doing what I thought was best for everyone and they would be fine. The turning point for me came in leaving the comfort of those that loved me and gave me things to a life where we'd be on our own.

Now you may think the first time we went to Texas would have carried those same emotions, but they did not. I think we all knew the first time was just an experiment. THIS time we all knew it was for good. To this day, my mother thinks that my move to Texas was her punishment for taking my dad from Texas so many years before. It's not true, of course. It's simply the universe's way of aligning things to a grander plan. We're just here for the ride.

Janet, Chelsea and I moved in to a single-wide trailer (part of the compensation package) right next door to the office. The first couple weeks were spent settling in, catching up with Jim and Donna, and acquainting myself with the staff and the way things had been done while I was away. But as I lit my third cigarette and sipped at my now fresh cup of steaming coffee, the realization of the move I'd made began to become crystal clear. There are financial benchmarks to give you some indication of the financial health of a company. And although Jim's company was already grossing more than a million dollars a year, his company was sick. It was very sick. Two things became evident. I wasn't sure he'd be in business for long which meant I'd be unemployed 650 miles from home. And I wasn't sure I was smart enough to dig him out.

I asked Jim to come into my office after the cigarette smoke had cleared and began to tell him what I now knew.

"Jim, I don't want to be the one to paint a dark picture, but we're in some trouble. For starters you're only turning your receivables twice a year. Industry standard is six so you have a real cash flow problem. Your debt-to-income ratio is way above what it should be. Our line-of-credit is maxed out and we've spent the money on equipment instead of payroll. That type of credit has basically been misappropriated so our interest rate is way too high. There is no means of checks-and-balances so our spending is out of control. Our phone bill was $5,000 last month. On top of that, there is clearly no legal separation between you and your corporation. If it goes down, you're going down with it," was how I painfully began our conversation.

It was then I first heard Jim mutter one of his famous lines. "How can that BE?" he asked.

For the next hour, one item at a time, I went over what I knew based on the hand-kept records I had used for my analysis. Jim seemed stunned and looked a little worried. Controlled growth can be a good thing for a company, but skyrocketing growth like he had experienced the last two years can actually be the kiss of death. It takes a lot of money to operate a growing company and if you don't have the cash to sustain it, you become overburdened with debt and eventually you crumble. Jim's company, although he had worked enormously hard, was well on its way to ruin. But I had a trick or two up my sleeve.

Being young and cocky helped me to do the things I felt I had to do to slash costs. With Jim's blessing we changed our payroll from weekly to biweekly. We cut health insurance to all but supervisory personnel and did away with the one company calling card that everyone was sharing. People that hadn't worked for Jim for years were using his long distance card. We required purchase orders for any items bought at remote sites and established a system of accountability for people's spending. We saved well over $5,000 the first month alone. It was a start, but suffice it to say the "new guy" wasn't so popular in the field. I sent memos and held meetings to explain the need for these drastic cuts, but they still weren't popular moves.

We began to pay Jim and his wife an actual salary. We put away his personal credit cards and gave him company cards to show a separation between his personal finances and his company. We rewrote the company charter and named me Vice President of Finance (big title, small company). We standardized the way we did projections for bonding with his insurance company, thereby eliminating guesswork and turning what was once a two-day project in to one that took an hour or less. Again, just more beginnings.

Jim had purchased a great computer and software system two years earlier. It all sat in the conference room covered in dust. If we were going to run efficiently, tackling that software had to be next on my list. I cleaned and started the computers, downloaded the software and began the process of teaching myself the intricacies of corporate accounting. I established account numbers for everything and with the help of another field manager, developed a Job Cost system to track profit and loss by the job. Within a month we'd be able to tell which jobs were making us money and which weren't… and WHY!

I standardized the payroll system and turned another project that took two to three days into something our bookkeeper could run in a couple hours. The payroll proved to be considerably challenging which meant living right next to the office was a bit too convenient. When I found myself stuck on a particular piece of the software, I'd pop up wide awake at night with an idea, put on my slippers and walk down the sidewalk to the office where I'd experiment with ways to make it run. It was all tedious work that had to be done. I was consumed. I loved it. Harvard Business wouldn't have taught me some of the real-life lessons I was learning. But there was still more.

In order to meet our biweekly demands for payroll, we had to improve our cash position. The first thing I did was start to lean hard on people that owed us money. I became the "heavy" and was relentless in my pursuit of receivables. The next thing I did was schedule a meeting with our bank to increase the limit on our line-of-credit. I placed a call to the loan manager at the bank and told him our intentions. He assured me that wouldn't be a problem and Jim and I should come in next week to sign the papers. We set the appointment assuming our short-term cash problems were solved. Don't you just love the innocence of youth?

Jim and I donned our best business attire and entered the bank on a rainy morning early the next week. The loan officer met us at his desk, gave us wimpy handshakes and avoided eye contact at any cost. Something was wrong. Even with my underdeveloped senses of twenty-seven years I could smell the problem from across the room.

"So we're here to get those papers signed like you asked," I said with confidence. "Let's get started."

"Let's go upstairs and meet with our new V.P. first," he said still acting like a dog with his tail between his legs. Jim and I gave each other a puzzled look,

We were introduced to the V.P. who invited us to sit across from his desk as he began to explain our situation.

"In the last month, we've acquired a new CEO here at this bank. His policy is to eliminate, across the board, all lines of credit secured with accounts receivable."

"I'm sorry," I said as Jim continued to sit quietly and take this all in. "I'm not sure we understand what you're saying. We were told to come in and sign papers to increase our line of credit just last week. Am I missing something?"

"Not only are we not going to increase your line, we're closing it. We're calling your note. We'd be more than happy to keep your secured equipment loans, but you have thirty days to secure new financing for your company."

In stunned disbelief, Jim answered exactly as I hoped he would. "We've been doing business at this bank for a long time. If you're not going to back us with a line-of-credit the size we need, we certainly aren't going to extend our secured loans to you. We'll move it all in thirty days. Thank you, gentlemen. We're done here."

We didn't speak as we left the bank, but the words flowed like a raging river when we hit the car.

"How in the HELL did this happen? How are we going to meet payroll this week? Where will we get the cash for repairs on our dozer?" the list went on and on.

What lay ahead for us was a daunting task in the best of times, but during the banking crisis of the late 1980s, this was going to take a miracle. We decided to let this settle for a day so I dropped Jim off at his house and drove back to the office. I needed to begin to formulate a plan for what we were facing. I needed to do what I learned to love best.

I started my first book.

Lesson Twenty-Six:

TOUGH TIMES DON'T LAST; TOUGH PEOPLE DO

"Life's a tough proposition, and the first hundred years are the hardest."

~Wilson Mizner

In the midst of all that was happening with business, my personal life was becoming more challenging. It was during our financial crisis that I learned why Janet was so interested in making a move to Texas. She was running.

In one of the great examples of poor communication of all time, Janet had developed a jealously regarding my friendship with Laurie at LT&T. We had clarified the fact that it was purely platonic, but in an effort to "get even" Janet had developed a "friendship" of her own back in Nebraska. Her exact words, in fact, were, "If you can have a friend, so can I." Mounting evidence began to clarify that her friend was something more.

Because I was again absorbed in my work, Janet made several trips back to Nebraska to "see her parents." Chelsea always went along. It was during these trips that Janet's relationship with her new friend blossomed. When she was actually in Texas, I continually found her on the phone with her friend. We began to get correspondence addressed to her in the mail. In a complete breach of privacy, I opened one of her cards to find all the evidence I needed that they were WAY more than friends. I was no longer having sex with my wife, but somebody was.

In a tearful confrontation, Janet admitted to the affair and promised to end it. I naively believed her and we began marital counseling to work on our issues. It was the beginning of a year-long fiasco that taxed my patience and commitment, but I was determined to protect the sanctity of a two-parent family for Chelsea. Since that time I've learned there are things much worse than having divorced parents, but at the time I was determined to stick with it. I did my best to forgive Janet and continued to bury myself in the issues at work.

Upon the news of our impending refinancing, Jim and I began to write a professional business plan to present to potential banks. It was a work of art and we labored over it tirelessly between the pressing needs of daily operation and my family problems. A great deal of the work was completed while the rest of the world slept. After several heated discussions about content, financial accuracy and format, we completed a grand work that totaled 150 pages. It was a thorough and optimistic document, professionally bound and printed on the best of company letterhead. We were prepared to present our case to a new bank.

Most of the thirty days our bank had given us to move were spent authoring the business pro forma. We needed to act fast and I began making appointments, first with local banks, to present our company. After exhausting local options, we personally visited with the upper management of the top 25 banks in the state. It was an exhausting endeavor that went well over the limit established by our current bank. They agreed to grant us another thirty days, but our line-of-credit was still frozen and our cash position weakened every day. We were skating on incredibly thin ice. We were given, almost to the word, the same canned speech at every bank.

"This is the best business plan that has ever been presented to us," they always began. "But we can't help you. Please understand that banks are becoming much more conservative and the construction business is risky. We're so sorry."

Day after day, week after week we got the same story. We were nearing the end of our list the day Janet walked into my office in tears. I was right in the middle of muddling through the latest crisis, trying desperately to keep our fledgling company afloat, when she walked in and stood before my desk, tears streaming down her face.

"What is it?" I asked. "I'm swamped here."

Through gasping sobs, she pulled herself together long enough to tell me, "I'm pregnant."

I pushed the documents I was studying to one side, let out a deep sigh of disbelief meant to imply "why me?" and leaned back in my tall leather chair, fingers laced behind my head.

"Are you sure?"

She merely nodded and then began to tell me how sorry she was. I honestly don't remember feeling anger at that moment. What I felt was overwhelmed at how work and marriage were crumbling before my eyes. But I didn't fold. I focused.

This was one of those character-developing moments we all have in life. It reminds me of a story I watched repeatedly on Sunday mornings during the religious cartoon, Davey and Goliath. It went a little like this.

There once lived a very wealthy rancher with a big house, servants and plenty to eat. Next to the rancher lived a poor man whose wife and kids were starving. One day the poor man slipped under the rancher's fence and was caught trying to steal a calf to feed his family. The rancher's cattlemen took the poor man before the rancher and asked what they should do with him. Now, that old rancher could have said a lot of things, but what he did say was, "String him up. It'll teach him a lesson."

That night the rancher dreamed he was standing before his maker. God asked for a complete account of the rancher's deeds throughout life, including the killing of the poor man caught stealing his calf. After hearing all the rancher had to say, the angels asked God what they should do with him. Now, God could have said a lot of things. But what he DID say was, "Forgive him. It'll teach him a lesson."

And now, as Janet stood tearfully before me, I could have said a lot of things. I could have told her I'd raise a baby belonging to another man as my own. I could have told her it'd be ok no matter what. I could have told her most anything to be supportive and encouraging. What I did say was, "Well, it clearly isn't mine so you two decide what you want to do with it and I'll help if I can. Now if you'll excuse me, I'm in the middle of a crisis here."

I've heard experts say, "There are two types of people. There are those that fold under pressure and there are those that focus."

I was focused. Despite the devastating news just delivered, I turned my attention back to the problem at hand. Our business was folding before my eyes. As it turns out, Janet was right. I was absolutely capable of operating without emotion. I understand now that my "emotionless" state was simply a way of hiding from feeling. What I considered to be strength under fire, was really a mask to cover my cowardice.

Jim and I went to every single bank and were turned down every time. We were completely without financing. And as much as we hated it, we had no choice but to allow our present bank to keep our long-term equipment notes. It was a lesson in swallowing my pride. Although not having a bank to secure a line-of-credit should have been the kiss of death, we got more creative. Our creditors became the short-term answer to our cash-poor position.

More jobs continued to come our way. As they did, we began robbing from Peter to pay Paul. Every job we did for the government included a material pre-payment that helped us to operate once our materials arrived at the job site. We always used that pre-payment to pay off the material from the PREVIOUS job. It meant our cable suppliers were kept waiting for their money for two or three months at a time. It also meant that in order to keep up the scheme, every job had to be bigger than the next. And so every job we bid WAS bigger. We got further and further behind with our creditors and our suppliers were getting nervous. Instead of being a relentless pursuer of money owed us, I was now a constant deflector of requests for money FROM us. Every mom-and-pop operation that worked on our machines or supplied small tools and supplies was told that we would never pay faster than ninety days. Without exception, small town businesses throughout Texas and Oklahoma who were suffering like we were, agreed to the terms.

We sought protection under the umbrella of bankruptcy meant to give us time to reorganize our financial structure. We scrimped and saved everywhere we could and were about to land a huge contract with Southwestern Bell. It meant hope for us because it meant the opportunity for daily bidding and work. It meant stability. The day before we were scheduled to supply support documents and sign the contract, our bonding company canceled our policy for non-payment. There was no cash to reopen the account. Like a spear through the ribs, it was the final blow. No insurance, no bidding. No bidding, no work. It was as simple as that.

As much as reading this may lead you to believe this all took place over a short period of time, it took nearly two years to go from "trouble" to "closed." A lot had happened in my personal life prior to the morning I walked into Jim's office and delivered the news.

"Jim. It's time. There isn't anything left we can do. We need to close the doors and walk away. It's over."

"How in the hell can this be?" he whispered almost to himself. He put his head in his hands and I left him to absorb the bad news. It had, indeed, been a valiant fight.

Lesson Twenty-Seven:

BOUNDARIES ARE GOOD; SOMETIMES YOU JUST GOTTA LET 'EM GO

> *"When two people decide to get a divorce, it isn't a sign that they 'don't understand' one another, but a sign that they have, at last, begun to."*
>
> ~Helen Rowland

This chapter begins a gradual transition into the meat of my spiritual development as an adult. Please understand that today I have few if any regrets about my past. I completely understand that things happen for a reason… usually a GOOD reason and we do the best we can with what we know at the time. What I knew during the fall of a business and my marriage was that I was doubtful of a supreme being who cared about me. Saying I was Agnostic was a stretch at best. It was all about me and I was in charge. And I apparently wasn't very good at running things. This chapter isn't full of sunshine and hope. It chronicles the types of things I was capable of during my late twenties.

The universe was setting the stage for an awakening by giving me challenges to face. My Christian friends would say, "The Lord works in mysterious ways." I would say, "We don't always know what's best for us." Either way, MY truth about our universe was about to start being revealed one thin layer at a time.

I don't know whether or not Janet ever shared the news of her pregnancy with her boyfriend. It doesn't matter. I didn't ask then and I don't care now. What I do know is that she approached me a couple days after our little office meeting and told me she wanted to terminate her pregnancy. I told her that decision was hers alone to make and I'd be happy to escort her to the clinic, which I did. The morning we arrived I was in full "shut-down" mode. The clinic was in a small residential neighborhood in Dallas and I sat with Janet in the plush waiting room while she anticipated the "procedure."

As they called her in for her abortion, I turned my thoughts to the problems at work. I refused to let my mind wander to the place that made me acknowledge the fact we were ending a human life. It wasn't my child biologically, but Janet was my wife. My spiritual place today would probably have led me to a different solution, but I justified the decision by removing myself from it. This was Janet's baby. I was strictly there for a shoulder and payment. At the time I thought that was generous. Today I understand that regardless of the biological connection, we are all spiritually connected in a way not so difficult to understand. I believe if faced with the same decision today, I would encourage her to keep it. I can't explain how I know, but the fetus whose life we ended that day was a boy. He would have been twenty-four years old this year. Despite his confused parenting, he would have had a chance at life on earth. Maybe he still did in another form. I'll never know for sure.

Janet came from behind the doors of the clinic clearly shaken. We didn't speak as we walked to the car and made the drive back to Greenville. She went home to "recuperate." I went to work hoping to forget the day's events and secure financing for our dying company.

In between the arguing and my grueling (yet clearly self-inflicted) work schedule, Janet and I found time to attend marriage counseling. Although this was my first experience with professional counseling, it certainly wasn't my last. I found the entire experience somewhat helpful and I thought Janet did too. But one of life's little lessons is learning to trust your instinct and I began to realize that Janet simply wasn't capable of being honest with me, the counselor OR herself. We were wasting our time. Although Janet had agreed to end her relationship, she didn't. And though she agreed to different exercises suggested by the counselor, she was never able to go through with them. I don't judge her for that today, although I certainly did at the time. Life teaches you tolerance. Once the counselor began to clearly cease his impartiality and side with me, the sessions were over. Janet wasn't interested in taking an honest look at herself. Since that time I've been in her shoes myself so I understand how hard the study of self can be. She just wasn't ready.

Chelsea and I waved from the front porch of our trailer as Janet pulled out of the driveway to meet her boyfriend in Dallas. It was Friday and he was boldly flying in to meet with Janet even though he was aware I knew. She assured me she was going to meet him at the airport, permanently end it and return the same evening. She got back Monday afternoon. I guess there had been a change of plans.

While Janet was away on her rendezvous, Chelsea and I played. We built and painted a sandbox and had three great days together. When she slept, I worked. When she was awake, we played. There are two questions frequently asked of me by those who know this story. Why didn't I confront the guy courting my wife and why didn't I leave with Chelsea while her mother abandoned us to meet her guy?

The first question is easy to answer; at least for me. I hadn't taken vows with Janet's boyfriend. I had taken them with her and I held HER accountable to end her relationship, not him. As for why I didn't leave with Chelsea; I have no idea. The thought honestly never occurred to me. I took Janet at her word when she said she'd be back on Friday. Yes, today her stuff would have been on the front lawn. Then, I was young and hopeful. I still thought I could change her.

Janet packed a few things, loaded Chelsea and left for Nebraska the next week. We called it a separation for her to sort things out, but we all know how that goes. I thought it was good that she would have the support of family and Chelsea would get good quality time with her grandparents. I would be free from the stress of a dishonest spouse and could concentrate on my job. My, how easy it is to live in a world of twisted priorities. What Janet really wanted was for me to make her feel "needed." I made it clear that although I "wanted" our marriage, I didn't "need" her to make my life complete. Even if it were true, it probably wasn't smart to say it and she ran to those that could make her feel that way. I shut down the neuro-pathway from my head to my heart and consumed my every waking moment with work.

For the next several weeks I spoke with Janet frequently and made the drive to Nebraska every other weekend to see Chelsea. I sent her money to help with expenses and remained hopeful she would come around. And on one particular trip I thought she had. I left Chelsea with my parents and went to Janet's parents to ask one final time for her to come back to Texas and make a go of it. She had previously assured me her adulterous relationship was over so with naïve hopefulness, I asked her to come home. She agreed.

In two cars, we made the long trip back to Texas where I began to hope we could make our family whole again. On Friday night, we got a babysitter and went to the local dance hall to celebrate. Details aren't important. While there, Janet was asked to dance by a young man. While dancing he asked her to accompany him to his place where he was having some friends over to sit in the hot tub. She actually ASKED me if she could go. She left with him and I went home to be with our daughter. Janet returned the following morning as the sun was coming up.

We took Chelsea to her uncle's house and then went to the local restaurant for breakfast. I got Janet's attention and while looking at her hung-over bloodshot eyes said the following:

"We've been working at this for over a year. I'm done. Either make a decision here and now to stay and be my wife, or pack your stuff and go. I've had enough."

That afternoon, our daughter strapped to her car seat in the back of a 1977 Toyota Corolla Wagon, Janet left for Nebraska for good. At that moment I was overcome with two distinct feelings.

The first was a feeling of intense relief. I don't know if I'd ever loved Janet. I don't think so. Every move we ever made was founded in "what should come next." But I know this with absolutely certainty. I felt NO love for her at that moment and was almost giddy at the thought I was finally done with her. The second feeling was grief that my daughter was moving 650 miles away for good. As a lone tear trickled down my face, I turned to go inside. I lied on our rough green sofa (which is one of the few things I got in the divorce, by the way), covered up, and slept for hours and hours. The worst was bound to be over.

What followed was a long series of trips to Nebraska to see my daughter and a complete lack of tolerance for anything relating to Janet. On the upside, I felt I was doing everything in my power to maintain a loving relationship with a daughter far too young to understand how things were. Every other Friday at 5:00 p.m., I pointed my new, 1987 Ford Taurus north for Nebraska. I usually arrived at 3:00 a.m. and slept for a couple hours before making arrangements to get Chelsea. Because my parents were loving and supportive, more often than not Chelsea was already at their house. It made things much easier for me. I'd spend about thirty-six great hours with Chels, then head back south at 3:00 p.m. on Sunday, arriving back in Greenville sometime after midnight. I'd sleep, go to work, then two weeks later do it all again. I maintained that schedule for a year. I eventually had to start leaving Nebraska at noon and after a year, cut my visits to once a month. I hated to do it, but wear and tear on my body AND my car were making the trips impractical. Imagine, considering the practicality of seeing your own child.

On a more negative note, I was seething with anger over Janet taking our daughter so far away. I had no idea it was possible to limit the distance she could move. After the first few months of our second separation, Janet signed a contract to teach school for a year at an elementary school smack in the middle of a conservative Mennonite community. I took that as a sign she was there for good and began divorce proceedings in Texas to avoid the possibility of paying alimony on top of the child support I was paying. To be cruel, I had Janet served divorce papers AT school where it would be seen by all. It dealt a blow to her that actually made me laugh on the inside. What I didn't realize then, but have learned since, is that my vindictive nature and anger were only serving to make me miserable. Without a spiritual direction to turn, I relied on my killer instinct to make things hard for Janet. It was immature, but all I knew to do at the time. I didn't know it then, but I was going to be taught that lesson later.

After being attacked by Janet's mother for being such a "horrible husband and father," I parlayed with a blow-by-blow account of Janet's abortion and the sexual nature of the cards she received from her boyfriend. Her mother didn't believe me so I backed my story with a credit card receipt and copies of the cards I had made. It was an enormous blow to her AND to Janet. Before it was over, Janet was admitted to a "hospital" for a time for evaluation. I was playing nasty and I bathed in the luxury of inflicting pain. I am NOT proud of what I did and many will even defend my actions as those of a wounded person, but in retrospect, dealing those kinds of low blows to someone who was dealing with her own demons was inhumane. I'm not apologizing for it. I did the best I could with the undeveloped spirit I was nurturing at the time.

In the meantime, Jim's company was edging toward the brink I described previously. I was mentally and physically exhausted. My hours were long, the trips to Nebraska brutal and my pride was wounded. But things got better in a twisted sort of way. They always do.

They say time heals all wounds and I would say that's largely true, but not without some scars. The last sixteen chapters have been quite a journey from college through one of the most "tragic" learning periods of my life. So you must be wondering what all this has to do with the spiritual development of an average "Joe" like me.

By now you're hopefully beginning to see that we all have trials and it was important for me that you read about mine, if for no other reason than to help you see you aren't alone in yours. The spiritual awaking was coming. No, not right away, but in baby steps that allowed me to discover my truth. It's not an easy path and there are more trials to tell you about along the way. But as I got older, those trials became more awakening. Yes, I was still Agnostic, but I was standing in line for the rollercoaster ride of a lifetime. Keep reading. You're going to like this journey.

PART THREE: THE AL ANON YEARS

"There is guidance for each of us, and by lowly listening, we shall hear the right word. Certainly there is a right for you that needs no choice on your part. Place yourself in the middle of the stream of power and wisdom which flows into your life. Then, without effort, you are impelled to truth and to perfect contentment."

~Ralph Waldo Emerson

Lesson Twenty-Eight:

GREAT THINGS CAN COME FROM "BAD" DECISIONS

"Even cats grow lonely and anxious."

~Mason Cooley

The thick grayish haze hung heavily near the ceiling adorned with black-painted duct work. What air you could find was dense with the aroma of stale beer, cigarette smoke and cheap perfume. It's difficult to look cool and smile when you can barely breathe, but single men try to pull it off every night in every bar across the land. We're tougher than we look.

I had my back to the bar closest to the women's restroom and leaned back between two stools and against the polished oak edge. The heel of my left foot rested on the short step which resulted in a knee so slightly bent. My heavily starched Wranglers made it hard to move as I scoured the dimly lit room with cigarette in one hand, cold beer in the other. I was cooooooool, man. Cool.

Here I was, less than a month after Janet's final departure to Nebraska, standing in the same bar where she met her hot tub friend. It was an enormous honky-tonk just outside Greenville with a circular dance floor the size a skating rink. The dance area was separated from the dozens of wobbly tables by a rickety, yet Texas-looking wooden rail. It was Billy Bob's but without the steroids and the only real dance club for miles. All the locals went to Texas Star for the weekend to dance and romance. At least I hoped so.

I truly didn't take notice of her until I began to realize she was being asked to dance on a regular basis by guys other than her apparent date. He looked a bit out of place anyway in his Air Force uniform. Apparently in Texas, asking another guy's girl to dance is acceptable. But where I come from, a repeated stunt like that would have resulted in an ass-whoopin' for somebody.

They were sitting at a round table just to my left. After she got up to dance for the sixth or seventh time with someone else, I approached the airman.

"Is that normal down here?" I asked.

"Is WHAT normal?"

"You know, having other people dance with your girl all night."

"I wouldn't know. I'm not from around here." He said as he glanced over his shoulder to watch her return from her latest spin around the floor.

I politely excused myself from the table as she approached and returned to my position at the bar, this time taking a stool. I continued to watch the bar, afraid to actually speak to anyone, when I saw her get up to dance still another time. On the way back she walked directly up to me, put her hands on my knees, and with eyes I later learned reflected drunkenness said, "Hi. My name's Rita and you can dance with me any time you'd like." Then she walked away. Well, ok then!

I eventually mustered the nerve to ask her to dance, ignoring my Nebraska manners after a few beers of my own. It was there I learned that her date wasn't necessarily romantic, albeit most likely sexual. He was simply on a visit to the local government contractor's factory where she worked and she was "showing him a good time." I was beginning to get the picture.

In what was an enormously awkward moment, Rita asked me to join them for something to eat after the bar closed down. It was clear her "date" wasn't thrilled about the invitation, but with young, cocky hormones, I accepted and met them at the restaurant which ironically was the same where I issued Janet her ultimatum. Isn't life odd?

I don't recall the content of our three-sided conversation, but I do know I was cutting into this guy's play time. I finally excused myself and went home once I learned Rita was also freshly divorced for the 5th time and her date was married. I should have changed my name and left no forwarding address. I didn't see Rita again for several months.

What led to our first date is lost to memory, but what I do remember is how it ended up. It was my first real introduction to two things; partying and alcoholism. After dinner we stuck around to listen to a live band and we both began to drink. And as it turns out, Rita could drink A LOT! Rita was completely uninhibited and by the end of the evening the singer was asking to have some of "whatever she's on"! During the ride back to her place, she passed out. I had to physically remove her from the car and carry her inside where I put her to bed. (And NO, I did not take advantage of her.)

A normal guy would already be leaving a smoke trail behind the vehicle getting away from any further contact with someone like that. But except for the passing out part, I actually had a good time. After all, she was the only real "friend" I had in a strange place. I chocked it up to one night of excess alcohol and put it behind me.

And thus began a chapter in my life that revolved around partying. Rita was smart, open and fun to be around. She was also thirteen years older than me. Her kids were basically grown and mine was in another state. We were free to party at will. And we did. Rita was VERY well known by the local bar owners. Every Friday night (and sometimes Monday through

Thursday as well), we would head to the local pub for Happy Hour where we were sure to find a large reserved table with placards that said "Rita." Not only did Rita like to party, but people followed her around to party. There's no telling how much money she earned for local clubs. She was an icon.

After a very short period of time, Rita and I moved in together and rented a high-end condo on the lake in Rockwall. We bought a boat to put in the marina and continued to party. We drank at the clubs; we drank with friends at the lake and we drank at home. And by "we" I mean I had a couple and Rita drank until she had what I learned to recognize as the "the lights are on, but no one is home" look. That look was always followed by unreasonable gibberish and morning-memory-lapse. I was beginning to suspect Rita might have a drinking problem. Hey, no one said I was fast!

Interspersed with our life of partying were monthly trips to Nebraska and, of course, our jobs; mine with Jim's fledgling company and hers with a large local government contractor. I always looked forward to the trips to see Chelsea, and Rita became somewhat of a tolerated but not-so-well-liked addition to the long trips. My mother didn't like her for a variety of reasons, most of which are probably another story for another time. Two important things were about to happen that changed the course of my life entirely.

First, (and this you already know about) Jim's company finally went completely bankrupt which meant I was unemployed. Second, I decided being unemployed was a perfect reason to move back to Nebraska. Although Rita and I had lived together for some time now, the thought of her pulling up roots to move to Nebraska never entered my consciousness. I didn't ask. I simply came home after a long day of closing up shop for good to tell her that although our time had been fun, it was time for me to move home. There wasn't much discussion and in the following days, I packed my bags to go look for work. I was heading home.

The night before I was to leave, Rita and I took the boat out to do some fishing and to, more or less, say goodbye. It was during that outing that a conversation similar to this took place.

"I guess this will be our last trip on the boat," I said, breaking the silence.

"You know," Rita said. "You didn't even ask me to go along."

"Your family and job are here. It didn't occur to me that you'd want to."

"My kids are grown," she went on. "I'd be more than happy to move to Nebraska with you, but not without some type of commitment."

"What are you saying?" I asked. "You mean marriage?"

"That's exactly what I'm saying. I'd go, but not unless you marry me first."

As I write this, my entire being is screaming at the man I was back then. Don't do it you fool! Don't do it! Run! Ruuuuuuunnn!! I delayed my trip for a week and the following Saturday we were "married" by some pastor that just wanted the fee. I absolutely chose to get married to avoid the pin-prick of saying goodbye.

Now I'm not saying Rita was a bad person, because at her core she was a fair and decent human being. But she was thirteen years my senior and in a completely different place in life than I. The decision to marry Rita is as close as I've ever come to having a regret in life. But as I've learned, it's difficult for us to judge whether events are "bad" or "good," for good does come from a seemingly bad decision. Had I not married Rita, I may have missed my first real spiritual lesson. But even before the spiritual training began, I learned a more valuable lesson that took me years to comprehend. The Universe/God/Spirit/Mother Earth moves in perfect harmony. We're all going somewhere and becoming something. Great things can easily come disguised in the form of a bad decision.

The following week I left for Nebraska to look for work and share the "news" with my family. "Hello, Mom. Yeah, isn't it great! I'm moving back to Nebraska! Yes ma'am I'm here to look for work now. Yep. It's gonna be wonderful. Oh yeah, Rita and I got married."

Mom didn't look at me, but I saw the tears instantly begin to stream down her face. "That's great, Matt. That's great," Was all she said.

You see, for no other reason than the fact she thought it was better for Chelsea, Mom harbored the hope that Janet and I would reconcile. I understand her sentiment and her reaction was based on wanting what was best for me. But I knew from the beginning that Rita and I were never going to have the full support of my family. That, also, was a lesson in doing what you have to do regardless of what those closest to you might think.

The week I was back in Nebraska looking for work was fruitful in many ways. It didn't take long to reestablish my contacts at LT&T and within a few days I was told they'd find a place for me somewhere in the network of personnel professionals upon my permanent return. It also didn't take long for me to realize living in Nebraska meant dealing with misinformed and judgmental former in-laws on a daily basis. In addition, there was my mother to deal with. Don't get me wrong. She wasn't hateful. She was just disappointed. Within a week I determined finding employment would be easy, but living in Nebraska under the circumstances would be difficult at best.

I headed back south to announce to my new "wife" that I wouldn't be moving. In what may count as my second "regret," I decided that I could be a better father from 650 miles away than I could be from across town. Had I possessed the tools then I do now, my decision would likely have been different. And although the long trips to Nebraska on a monthly basis continued and I maintained a relationship with Chelsea, there was much I still missed. In later years it became an area of resentment for Chelsea which I now fully understand. Still in my late twenties, I chose a life of convenience over a life close to my daughter. We all do the best we can with what we know at the time.

What happened over the next several months was nothing short of a whirlwind of activity. Because I had no income we were forced to move from our expensive condo to a small rent house. We bought a great Labrador Retriever named Winston and he became my trusted companion. In what I see now as the Universe telling me to resist putting down deeper roots, I dabbled in work that didn't amount to much. Thanks to another lead from Jim, I took a commissioned job in sales which I hated. Each and every morning I woke up nauseated at the thought of making cold calls and having people tell me no. I clearly had the wrong mind-set for a career in sales.

I purposely left out information about Jim's new business venture in Indianapolis for a variety of reasons, but on the wings of yet another favor from Jim, I was flown up for an interview and subsequently offered a job. I turned it down. Once I'd returned from Indianapolis, Rita basically supported my idea of starting my OWN business in career planning and placement. It was what I loved to do anyway.

Although I was making absolutely NO money, I dove headfirst into a business plan for Career Impressions: "Helping People Help Themselves." I was never able to secure outside financing, but I was eventually able to secure enough clients to rent a small office in Dallas where I became heavily involved in the Chamber of Commerce and other "business clubs." In what I consider to be a minor success, I secured contracts with a state agency and a major university, both of which threw me enough seminar activity to pay the rent. I had a few individual clients who hired me to write their résumé and coach them in interviewing techniques. It was all a great deal of fun, but it just wasn't paying the bills. After a year and only $5,000 in gross sales, I closed up shop. It was an enormous disappointment.

If you've been following along at all, you can probably hear the winds of change beginning to get a head of steam. It's said the only constant in life is change. And for me it was coming fast... again.

Lesson Twenty-nine:

DESPERATE PEOPLE DO DESPERATE THINGS

"Desperation is the raw material of drastic change. Only those who can leave behind everything they have ever believed in can hope to escape."

~William S. Burroughs

"I can't drink Wild Turkey," she said. "Turkey makes me crazy."

"Apparently I'm becoming intolerant to Weller," came the response a month later. "I guess I'd better stick to beer."

Within the next month, "Maybe I'd better just stick to wine."

The next month it was wine coolers. And so it went. After moving into the run-down rent house, Rita and I began a game of negotiation. I'd suggest she cut back and she'd suggest a way to do it that avoided leaving alcohol alone altogether. I'd agree and the cycle would start over. In pure enabler fashion I justified her alcohol consumption and continually gave her the benefit of the doubt. It was miserable.

The true wake-up call came for me in two stages. The first came when I entered the house on a hot summer afternoon after mowing the lawn to find a tall glass of "iced tea" on the kitchen counter. I was dying of thirst and tipped the tall plastic container back to quench my thirst. It took two giant gulps for my brain to register the foreign taste and I spat the last mouthful all over the kitchen counter.

"What the HELL is this?" I choked. "Are you freakin' kidding me?" I yelled.

"I like the way it tastes," she said as I slammed the cup back to the faded yellow countertop.

"You... put... EVERCLEAR in a glass of tea? You put pure grain alcohol into a glass of tea and you're telling me you like how it tastes?" I pressed as I glared at this woman in stunned disbelief. "Rita. You have a problem."

And so the hiding or disguising of booze had begun. As the monthly negotiations became harder for her to accept and my disapproval became apparent, Rita began to do what most alcoholics do at one time or another. She continued to "function" while keeping the level of her consumption a secret.

Yet another level of our negotiation came when Rita suggested she not drink while traveling for work, which was something she did quite often. I agreed, naively believing she could choose to not drink. The next stage of my awakening was next.

"Where the hell WERE you last night?" she screamed into the phone from her hotel room in California.

"I was right here at our house in Texas," I said as I led her to slaughter.

"We were supposed to talk last night at 10:00!" Where the hell were you?" she repeated.

"I was right here... on the phone with you. Don't you remember?"

Silence fell on the other side of the phone as I recanted how we had, indeed, talked on the phone the previous night. I recalled for her the content of the conversation she couldn't remember during her alcoholic blackout, having clearly fallen short of her promise to not drink while traveling on business.

"But I only had two glasses of wine," Was all she could muster.

"We'll discuss it when you get home," I said, and hung up the phone.

The clarity of Rita's drinking problem and my mistake in marrying her hit me like a freight train. I was again legally bound by the state and in the eyes of "God" to a woman with issues. I'm not suggesting I didn't have issues of my own, but at this very moment, the issue was with her and I made up my mind to end it when she got home. And I should have.

I stood sternly in the kitchen as I watched Rita arrive two hours late, riding in the Corvette convertible of a man she'd "been on business" with. I was loaded for bear. When she hit the house I unloaded on her immediately. I was no longer angry, but I was firm and explicitly direct.

I didn't give her time to say a word. "We agreed you would not drink while on business. You violated that agreement. And I don't care how much you think you drank. It was enough to cause a black out (I later learned alcoholics can experience blackout without drinking at all) and I want you to know I'm through. You have a drinking problem. It's just that simple. Not long ago, I told someone to get out of my life for good and if you think I won't do it with you, think again. You either get help right now, this night, or tomorrow I'm leaving."

"I'll call someone tomorrow," she said.

"You didn't hear me. You do it now, or I leave tomorrow. Period."

I left the house and took Winston across the street to let him swim in the lake. He loved to chase sticks in the water. It was all I knew to do. As soon as Rita had assessed her situation, she actually called a co-worker who she knew had recently given up alcohol with the help of Alcoholics Anonymous. I don't know the exact content of that phone call and it doesn't matter. My foot was more than halfway out the door already.

There was just no way Rita was ever going to give up alcohol. I was wrong. The last I knew, which was probably five years ago, Rita was eighteen-years sober and still active in AA. Why she chose the path of sobriety over just letting me go is a question I can't answer. She had been married on five previous occasions, so I didn't see where one more would bother her. She chose sobriety, but it was a long time before I accepted the fact she was serious about it.

We drove almost thirty miles to the basement of a church in Greenville, Texas, where the smoke was thicker than the bar where I'd met Rita. As I cleared the last step from the staircase leading to the basement, I knew something was different about these people. For starters, there were only two people in that entire room that weren't smiling… Rita and me. Despite the heavy smoke, there was something light and airy about the room. It wasn't packed full of people from skid row. Surrounding a very long, wobbly table sat men and women from every imaginable walk of life bubbling with hope. For the first time in a long time, I began to feel a little hope myself.

Lesson Thirty:

THERE IS MUCH YOU CAN LEARN FROM THOSE WHO HAVE BEEN TO THE ABYSS

"Rarely have we seen a person fail who has thoroughly followed our path. Those who do not recover are people who cannot or will not completely give themselves to this simple program...."

~The Big Book

"Hi. My name is Paul and I AM an alcoholic."

"HI PAUL!" The group bellowed.

"Thanks to the 12 Steps, the grace of God and good people like you, I haven't found it necessary to drink or do cocaine today." (There were many in groups like this who had dual or even multiple addictions rooted in excessive alcohol use.)

Paul was a no-bullshit kind of guy and although the truth was he hadn't had a drink or done cocaine in well over seven years, he didn't take his sobriety for granted. He lived one day at a time. I once heard Paul tell a new guy that if he was ready to give up alcohol, Paul was more than ready to help. But if he WASN'T ready, Paul said he'd go buy him enough booze to get him to his "bottom" so he WAS ready. He went on to tell him that if he wasn't serious about his sobriety, he shouldn't waste Paul's time. His sobriety was all that mattered and he wouldn't risk it on someone who wasn't serious.

Rita and I only visited the group in Greenville one time. It was there they encouraged us to find a group close to home, because they highly recommended someone ready to give up alcohol make "90 meetings in 90 days." It was at our new group in Rockwall where we met Paul, his wife, and many just like them.

And that's how it went for the next three months. Rita and I made a meeting of some kind, somewhere every night during that time period. If circumstances prevented us making a meeting on any particular night, we made two on Saturday and Sunday. (There was usually a noon meeting and an evening meeting most places.) Although Rita was brought up in the Catholic Church, she was what I learned to call "Catholic Light." She used the title, but never practiced the religion. We didn't go to mass on Sunday. We went to AA.

Not long after discovering the world of AA, I was personally introduced to a little gathering that took place in the back room… Al Anon. Al Anon is the AA equivalent 12-step program for family and friends of Alcoholics. It was in Al Anon that I began to discover the root of my own "disease" which was Control. I had always believed I could manipulate the world around me with enough hard work or just plain will. These groups were made up primarily of the wives of alcoholics so as a man, I was somewhat of a minority. Within the walls of these little back rooms sat either those whose spouses were sober or those still out there drinking. We learned about taking care of our own issues and not concerning ourselves with the behaviors of the drunk. Their sobriety was their issue to deal with, not ours.

It bears mentioning that Rita was, indeed, one of the lucky ones that began to take responsibility for her sobriety. She wasn't still out there "practicing." She was in a smoky meeting every night working her program. She quickly found a sponsor and dove, head-first, into the world of the 12 Steps. I didn't drag her to meetings. She dragged me. If I was going to keep up, I was going to have to practice this way of life myself and I already liked what I saw in those that worked it.

Although I did find SOME comfort within the bounds of Al Anon, I began to see the people most serious about working their 12 Steps, those whose lives depended on a guide for living, sat around the table in AA meetings. They lived more in the Solution and less in the Problem. It wasn't true in every single case, but I often found Al Anon to be a session of griping wives who still didn't get that they couldn't fix their alcoholic spouse or boyfriend. For that reason alone, I often opted to sit through "open" AA meetings. Being "open" meant they could be attended by anyone. There were also "closed" meetings reserved for those trying to beat alcohol and on those nights I attended Al Anon. Otherwise, you'd find me around a smoky table of people trying to get serious about making a change in their life. It's where I finally began to get a grip on the concept of God, or in AA's words, Higher Power.

I purchased a Big Book (AA's "Bible") and began to read vigorously about how the program worked. As I write, my leather-bound copy sits beside me, hi-lighted, dog-eared and noted from heavy use. To this day, although no longer active in the program, I occasionally look to this awesome guide for living when I'm feeling lack of direction.

Like the quote above, it really is a simple program, but it is NOT easy. The entire notion is based on cleaning up your past, learning to relinquish control of your life to a higher power, and then sharing that information with others. It's about rigorous honesty and it's about service. Sound familiar? To give you some background, following is the complete excerpt from Chapter 5 of *The Big Book of Alcoholics Anonymous*.

RARELY HAVE we seen a person fail who has thoroughly followed our path. Those who do not recover are people who cannot or will not completely give themselves to this simple program, usually men and women who are constitutionally incapable of being honest with themselves. There are such unfortunates. They are not at fault; they seem to have been born that way. They are naturally incapable of grasping and developing a manner of living which demands rigorous honesty. Their chances are less than average. There are those, too, who suffer from grave emotional and mental disorders, but many of them do recover if they have the capacity to be honest.

Our stories disclose in a general way what we used to be like, what happened, and what we are like now. If you have decided that you want what we have and are willing to go to any length to get it—then you are ready to take certain steps.

At some of these we balked. We thought that we could find an easier, softer way. But we could not. With all the earnestness at our command, we beg of you to be fearless and thorough from the start. Some of us have tried to hold on to our old ideas and the result was nil until we let go absolutely.

Remember that we deal with alcohol—cunning, baffling, powerful! Without help it is too much for us. But there is One who has all power—that One is God. May you find him now.

Half measures availed us nothing. We stood at the turning point. We asked His protection and care with complete abandon.

Here are the steps we took, which are suggested as a program of recovery:

1. *We admitted we were powerless over alcohol—that our lives had become unmanageable.*

2. *Came to believe that a Power greater than ourselves could restore us to sanity.*

3. *Made a decision to turn our will and our lives over to the care of God as we understood Him.*

4. *Made a searching and fearless moral inventory of ourselves.*

5. *Admitted to God, to ourselves, and to another human being the exact nature of our wrongs.*

6. *Were entirely ready to have God remove all these defects of character.*

7. *Humbly asked Him to remove our shortcomings.*

8. *Made a list of all persons we had harmed, and became willing to make amends to them all.*

9. *Made direct amends to such people wherever possible, except when to do so would injure them or others.*

10. *Continued to take personal inventory and when we were wrong promptly admitted it.*

11. *Sought through prayer and meditation to improve our conscious contact with God as we understood Him, praying only for knowledge of His will for us and the power to carry that out.*

12. *Having had a spiritual awakening as the result of these steps, we tried to carry this message to alcoholics, and to practice these principles in all our affairs.*

Many of us exclaimed, "What an order! I can't go through with it." Do not be discouraged. No one among us has been able to maintain anything like perfect adherence to these principles. We are not saints. The point is, that we were willing to grow along spiritual lines. The principles we have set down are guides to progress. We claim spiritual progress rather than spiritual perfection.

Our description of the alcoholic, the chapter of the agnostic, and our personal adventures "before and after" make clear three pertinent ideas:

a) That we were alcoholic and could not manage our own lives.

b) That probably no human power could have relieved our alcoholism.

c) That God could and would if He were sought.

How It Works was read at the beginning of every meeting and it was an honor to be asked by the person chairing the meeting to read from this sacred chapter. How It Works is where the foundation is laid for the entire program. The rest of the book is filled with HOW you do each step, when and with whom. There are also wonderful stories written by Bill Wilson, the founder of AA himself, and others who "recovered" from the grips of alcoholism by diligently working this program. The entire book represented for me, for the very FIRST time, an actual guide for living my life. And I was surrounded by people whose sobriety depended upon teaching me how to do it. I wasn't an alcoholic, but I suffered from the effects of alcoholism and various other "ism's" nonetheless. I had no code by which to live. I had no moral compass. I had no guide. Right there in the rooms of AA and Al Anon is where I intended to find those things. And these great folks who had cheated death one last time were going to help me.

Lesson Thirty-One:

"GOD" IS A GOD OF MY OWN UNDERSTANDING AND THINGS ARE IN NUMERICAL ORDER FOR A REASON

"Lack of power, that was our dilemma. We had to find a power by which we could live, and it had to be a Power greater than ourselves. Obviously. But where and how were we to find this Power?"

~We Agnostics, *The Big Book*

The "ism's" I talked about in Lesson 30 could all be boiled down to one thing: Lack of Power. Oh, I felt powerful alright, but it was clear that despite my best efforts, the way I had been running the show called "my life" wasn't working out as planned. I was still in my twenties, once divorced, married to an alcoholic, basically unemployed and 650 miles from my home and child. Looking back through the clarity of life's looking-glass, I can see just how wonderful all those experiences were. They're what molded me. Not many people can say they've been where I've been or done the things I've done. And I'm certainly not complaining. My life wasn't bad. Lack of perspective and maturity made it FEEL bad. It just wasn't what I expected and I felt as though it was spinning out of control. Lack of power. That was my true dilemma.

As a practicing Agnostic, I found it a particular challenge to come to grips with the first three steps.

1. We admitted we were powerless over alcohol (I chose to replace "alcohol" with "alcoholism")—that our lives had become unmanageable.
2. Came to believe that a Power greater than ourselves could restore us to sanity.
3. Made a decision to turn our will and our lives over to the care of God as we understood Him.

To be honest, the first step wasn't so bad. I knew I wanted some guidance and in my mind, life had clearly become unmanageable. But that next step stuck in my throat like a fish bone. I wasn't well-versed in the ways of "God" and what little I DID know was laced with influence from those who only knew a Christian perspective. I always pictured God as a white-bearded man, sitting on a throne, floating on a cloud, judging the "quick and the dead." Like Santa Clause, the Easter Bunny and the Tooth Fairy, it just didn't hold water with my spirit. I knew on a deep level that this whole god fairytale just wasn't true. Since you can't take Step Three without "completing" Step Two, this posed an issue for me.

"I don't care if your god is a goddamn doorknob! It isn't about WHO he is or WHAT he is! The point is, something or someone is running the show and it ain't you! God is of your choosing and YOUR understanding and no one else's. Accept that and you've completed the Second Step." Paul boomed at an open AA meeting after I shared about having issues with the concept of God. Like I said, Paul was a no-bullshit kinda guy.

"Ok," I said to Paul after the meeting. "So let's assume for the sake of argument that my Higher Power is a dust speck or whatever it is. How exactly am I supposed to go about turning my life over to this higher power? I'm not sure I can do it."

Paul only smiled. It had to be difficult for him to listen to the whining of some kid who was merely divorced and a little low on money. He had nearly died from cocaine and alcohol addiction. He had lost absolutely everything, including his job, family and self-respect and yet had found his way back. My petty concerns paled in comparison, yet I think he understood I had the troubled mind of an alcoholic. Alcohol just wasn't my thing.

"You gotta start paying more attention, Matt. There is NOTHING in the Third Step that says you have to turn your life over to anything. Read it again. It doesn't say you turn your life over. It says you become WILLING to turn your life over. If you can say you're ready to accept the fact there is a power greater than yourself and are willing to turn it over to 'Him' through the process, you are at Step Three. You're ready to go on. See, dumbass? You don't know anything." Paul hugged me and walked away to share with someone else.

"Oh," was all I could say before Paul left me with my thoughts. I had so much to learn.

Like Organic Chemistry to the pre-med student, Step Four is the great divide between staying where you are and moving toward your goal. And just like the chemistry student, it's unlikely you'll succeed without the help of those that have gone before you. I needed a sponsor.

Finding a sponsor in AA, it turns out, is less than a scientific formula. All you're told is "Find someone that has something you want and ask them to give it to you." By asking someone to share their "sobriety" with you, you're actually benefitting them by allowing them to share what they know. "You can't keep what you don't give away." In the end, sharing what you know with someone else is how you keep what you've worked for... sanity.

To be truthful, there wasn't anyone I knew from the Al Anon side of things who had the kind of peace and serenity I came to find from the recovering drunks on the AA side. Besides, most of them were women and they discourage sponsorship relations with those of the opposite sex. Things were about to get intimate in a non-sexual way and it's best to share it with someone who sees things from the same perspective.

So I asked Paul. Again, he gave me that big, goofy, patient smile and told me NO! For starters, he was Rita's temporary sponsor (clearly against the grain of the opposite sex rule) and he had someone else in mind for me. Paul recommended that I ask HIS sponsor to be mine, as well. I met Larry at an open AA meeting on a Saturday night when he was there to address the group as a guest. Saturday nights were often "guest speaker" night. Today, I would compare it to someone addressing a church service with their "testimony." I asked Larry after the meeting and he agreed... sort of.

If Paul was serious about his sobriety, he learned it from Larry. Because I wasn't really recovering from alcoholism, Larry was unsure how well he could relate, but agreed to be my temporary sponsor and get me through the next couple steps as long as I played by his rules and his rules alone. I was required to check in with him at least once a day to let him know how I was doing. And I was to diligently move forward with Step Four or he'd drop me like a hot potato. These guys meant business.

I feel it's important to divert here just a bit so as not to leave you the impression these guys were uncaring. Quite the opposite. Alcohol, drugs and even life in general is cunning. What I came to learn was almost no one EVER recovers from an addiction of any sort until they're ready. Not food. Not booze. Not drugs. Not cigarettes or gambling or anything else you can imagine being addicted to. If you aren't ready, it isn't going to happen. I saw it over and over and over again during my seven years in AA and Al Anon. These guys knew that far better than I. So as long as I was willing to "get better," they were willing to help. But the minute I was no longer willing, it was better to move on to someone who was than risk their sobriety.

As melodramatic as it sounds, recovery meant the difference between life and death for guys like these. I understood.

Like the kid who first discovers real food, I was starving for what Larry had and did as I was told. I called every day if only for a moment, told him how things were going and asked for guidance on Step Four. Here's what he told me.

"It's all in the book," Larry said. "It's laid out in easy English and they've even printed an example. Just follow that. You have a week." Parental coddling clearly wasn't part of the program!

The men who wrote the *Big Book* knew how people running from the truth think. Taking a moral inventory as outlined in Step Four is a daunting task, but all you really have to do first is list those situations where YOU feel you have been wronged. In other words, list the things that made you angry or hurt and why. Then you list who did those things to you. Hell that was easy! An easy example would be something like, "I was pissed off and hurt because Rita got drunk and probably screwed the guy she was in California with." Ok, that's not so hard. But I had dozens of examples of places where I'd felt wronged. It was a great exercise in justifying my anger. But then it gets a little trickier.

Once you've listed ALL the places where you've been wronged, the sneaky bastards that wrote the book ask you one simple question: "What was your part in it?" That little part went in column four. It's important to remember that the first three columns are just a set-up so you can easily recall situations in your life where you felt wronged. But this program isn't about pointing out other's faults. It's about exposing your own. Now THAT is a little tougher.

The first three columns only took me a day, but it took the rest of the week to muster the strength to admit my own shortcomings in those situations. Before I was done I had a short thesis that included areas where I had clearly made bad choices and wronged people myself. I called Larry to let him know I was finished. But that was still the easy part. Now I had to share it all with someone.

Larry agreed to meet with me the following day to go over the inventory. He felt it was important we not put it off. I went to his place in Dallas, he said a short "prayer" and I began to tell him every dark little secret I could recall about my life up to that time. It was painful to admit all those shortcomings to someone I hardly knew. He sat quietly as I spilled secret after secret over more than an hour. In the end, he did one of the kindest things ever done for me. (At least until I met Linda, but we're WAY ahead of ourselves now!) He told me some secrets of his own and mine were nothing. This man had been to hell and back. I vomited all the things I disliked about myself. I spewed all the wrongs that had been done to me and then admitted my part in them. I told it all. And then he just smiled and made me feel good about myself, because he had done "worse." Much worse.

And therein lays a very, very important life-lesson that isn't mentioned at the beginning of this chapter. No matter what you've done; no matter what secrets you harbor that keep you from freedom; someone has done worse. You are never, ever alone. Keeping secrets keeps you weak. Letting someone know the real you—and I mean the REAL you with nothing left undone, and then having them validate you and love you anyway—is the most liberating thing there is. But we're getting to that.

Once we finished, I received a bonus from Larry. We completed Steps Six and Seven. I truly became ready to have the God of my understanding remove my defects of character and then asked him prayerfully to do so. I wasn't struck by a bolt of lightning and I didn't feel as though my entire life had changed. What I did feel was a tremendous release from the burden of secrets. I was physically, emotionally and mentally exhausted. It had been a big day. Larry told me how proud he was of me, hugged me at the door and sent me on my way. But he knew something I didn't know yet. There was still more work to be done. And it wasn't going to be easy either.

Lesson Thirty-Two:

IT ISN'T ENOUGH TO SAY YOU'RE SORRY

"Made a list of all persons we had harmed, and became willing to make amends to them all. Made direct amends to such people wherever possible, except when to do so would injure them or others."

~Steps 8 & 9, *The Big Book*

The thick, yellow, acidic bile rose in my throat as the phone rang on the other end. "Don't pick up. Don't pick up. Don't pick up." I pleaded.

"Hello?"

"Hello, Janet. It's Matt," I nearly whimpered into the mouthpiece of the phone. "How are you?"

"I'm fine. What's up?" she inquired with curiosity overtaking the tone of her voice.

Janet and I had not had a successful marriage, but once the dust had settled from our divorce, we did establish a more-than-civil and cooperative relationship when it came to raising our daughter. This was a little different.

"Listen, um, er, uh. You know that Rita and I have become heavily involved in AA and Al Anon, right?"

"Sure," She said, her voice growing with anticipation of what was to come.

"I, um. Well, hell. I wanted to say that I know I wasn't the easiest to live with and I didn't always put your needs first. I had as much to do with our divorce as you and I want to say I'm sorry. If there's anything I can do to make that up to you, please tell me. I'll do anything to set that straight." I spilled as I began finding it hard to breathe. This was even harder than I thought.

My attempt at making amends with Janet was not my first at tackling the long list of people I had harmed and it wasn't my last. It was a grueling yet liberating process of cleaning up my past as best I could without causing further harm. Without exception, everyone I spoke with either in person or by phone, accepted my sincere apology and asked nothing more of me in setting things straight though I had to be willing to do so. There were a couple of instances where my only means of contact was by letter. Cleaning house is hard and satisfying work.

Rita and I had finally settled into what most would consider a "normal" way of life. With the exception of our trips to Nebraska and making AA or Al Anon meetings almost every night, we did what any other married couple did. We worked and played as time and money allowed. Rita became immersed in her life of sobriety and was often asked to tell her story at other clubs. She began to sponsor other women entering the program. She lived her sobriety a lot like she drank. She took it seriously. Living by a guideline was comfortable for me. I liked having rules to play by that didn't insist I adhere to one kind of god or another. I was living the promise that "if you do certain steps you'll feel a certain way. NOT the other way around." It was a good fit.

We "changed our playmates and our playground." We no longer hung out at the clubs or surrounded ourselves with people who liked to party. It was too dangerous. Instead, we made new friends with those living a similar lifestyle. By living in the moment, I began to miraculously take notice of little things that normally wouldn't have caught my attention. The signs were everywhere.

I saw bumper sticker after bumper stick adorned with slogans like, "Live and Let Live," "Let Go and Let God," "One Day at a Time" (sometimes life required living one MINUTE at a time), "Easy Does It," "Higher Powered," and of course, the familiar AA symbol of a triangle surrounded by a circle. I was clearly not alone. Many more just like me had found a guide for living inside the walls of AA and Al Anon. I started to feel as though I belonged to the human race once more.

I feel another side note is in order regarding AA's symbol, which they no longer use by the way due to some type of copyright issues from the late 1980s and 1990s. I have met those that trounce on the foundation of groups like AA because "Their symbol is rooted in Paganism" or "They don't teach Christian values." Whatever. I'd like to put that to rest. The FOUNDATION of groups like AA is that you aren't strapped to any particular belief system. You are free (what a concept) to worship a god of your own understanding. The symbol has no hidden meaning or agenda. The triangle represents the three-part concept of AA—Unity, Recovery and Service and the three levels of the alcoholic illness—Physical, Mental and Spiritual. It isn't some secret lodge plotting to destroy America. And although I am not active in the program today, I know for a fact it has saved the lives of thousands. I witnessed hundreds myself. That speaks loudly enough for me.

In the process of living by a code, I reestablished stable employment with a large utility contractor. It wasn't exactly my cup of tea, but it was a good combination of my management skills from LT&T and my technical skills as a cable splicer. I had my friend Jim again, to thank for the lead and I actually initially worked for him as a foreman. When he left for Indianapolis, I was promoted to Manager of their technologies division. I was good at that job. I was organized, efficient and was respected by my crews. I made my company an enormous amount of money and even produced the top-selling division in the entire nation for one quarter. On top of that, people in recovery just seemed to pop up everywhere. Two of my foremen were recovering alcoholics. The god of my understanding continually put the things in front of me that I needed. Wants were something different.

Even though I was good at my job, I didn't love it and the hours were brutal. God was letting me learn to be grateful with what I had before He'd give me something better. I think it's a good lesson. I began to contact my sponsor less and He was encouraging me to find a more permanent sponsor from Al Anon. I was still active in meetings and I was doing "daily inventory" and righting wrongs as soon as possible. I sponsored two guys from our group and spent every morning in meditation. I got on my knees to pray at night before I went to bed and in the morning before I ever stood up. I was actually living a spiritual life and on most days felt the world was more controllable. To an active mind, beginning to think you're in control is a dangerous thing. More change. More change. More change.

Lesson Thirty-Three:

YOU CAN CATCH MORE THAN GERMS IN A HOT TUB

"By all means let's be open-minded, but not so open-minded that our brains drop out."

~Richard Dawkins

I've always been a guy that likes to follow a routine. I've learned to be more flexible, in fact ENJOY being flexible, as I've gotten older, but having things orderly has always given me a sense of well… order!

As a manager at Fishel Technologies I had a great deal of flexibility in my schedule. I was usually able to finish all my administrative duties at the office before 10:00, which gave me the rest of the day to bid jobs, check on my crews and stamp out fires. It also meant I could work my way home by mid-afternoon with a stop at a fancy gym along the way. Although my workouts varied from day-to-day, my after-workout routine was the same. I always made my way to the dry sauna followed by a dip in the hot tub. It calmed my sore muscles and helped melt away the stress from work. Unless something terribly unusual came up in my schedule, I never missed my dip in the tub.

The smell of sweat-laden chlorine filled my sinuses after a particularly hard work out in the circuit training area. Because

I was going to an AA dance that evening, I skipped the dry sauna and went straight for the effervescent bubbles of the steaming tub. Joining me on this fine afternoon was a VERY large black man and another man I came to know as Ed.

"Ahhhhhhhhhhhhh," I could feel the warm water begin to wash away the lactic acid from my legs and back.

My head rested on the granite edge of the pool as I closed my eyes with only a vague awareness of the others.

"Have you accepted Jesus Christ as your savior?" I heard Ed ask the rather large man next to him.

"I have. I been washed in the blood for many year now," was the immediate response.

"Oh lord," I thought. "All I need is to sit here and listen to a couple Bible-thumpers carry on about Jesus." I began to slowly get up from the pool. I could soak another day.

What happened next I really can't explain. I rose from the pool with some authority in my movement, my mind made up to exit the area. As I lifted one leg to the landing area, the pressure on my shoulders was unmistakable and the voice in my head clear.

"Sit down," the voice said. "You need to listen."

The source of the voice can certainly be argued from a spiritual, supernatural, or scientific perspective, but none of that matters. I don't know the source and today how you explain it means little to me. In that moment, I knew I had to sit back down in the midst of this conversation.

"Just listen," the voice said. "You might learn something."

Instead of avoiding the conversation between the two men, I quietly listened, intent on fueling my spiritual growth in some way. I didn't know how. I became absorbed in "the moment." But very shortly after my reentry to the pool, the large black man got up and left. I was alone with Ed.

Whether or not I ever begin a conversation with a complete stranger is largely a product of my mood. On this day I felt I'd met my obligation of listening and my time in the pool with Ed would involve nothing more than a polite smile. Apparently Ed didn't see it that way.

"Hi there. The name's Ed!" he said almost immediately after his other friend departed.

"Uh. Hello. I'm Matt," I stammered, caught completely off guard.

"That guy is really something," Ed continued. "Used to be a lineman for the Philadelphia Eagles. Helluva guy. Loves the Lord."

"That would explain his size," I smiled back. "Well, I hate to go, but I have a dance to go to tonight. It was nice to meet you."

"What kind of dance?" (We were bordering on "nosey" now.)

"My wife and I are involved in AA and Al Anon. Our group is hosting a dance tonight," I replied almost sheepishly. It was my first real public admission to my part in the program.

"No SHIT?!" Ed fired back. "I've been sober in AA for ten years now and have seven in Al Anon!"

Could this really be happening again? My Higher Power, as yet to be clearly defined, continued to slap me right in the face with people walking my path; or should I say STANDING in my path. Ed gave me a short run-down on his involvement in the program as I stood over him at the edge of the hot tub, water dripping into the frothy bubbles.

"Hey, I know this REALLY great Men's Meeting on Wednesday nights. It's sort of a mix of drunks and Al-Anon's. It meets at 6:00 p.m. every Wednesday just off the toll road. It's a great meeting. Wanna join me this week?" he invited.

"Sounds good to me," I said. "I'll see you Wednesday."

Ed gave me the most contagious smile as I left. All I could do was just shake my head. "The Lord certainly works in mysterious ways," I thought. I went home to share my story with Rita and we left for the dance.

I entered the small, packed conference room filled with men the following Wednesday. Ed spotted me right away and immediately shook my hand and pulled me in to a warm manly embrace. "I'm so glad you could make it!"

The meeting was everything Ed said it would be. There were men from every conceivable walk of life in that room and I can't think of a single one from that first meeting not firmly grounded in "the solution." Not all of these guys had been to skid row and back, but they all shared the same kind of story I'd been hearing in groups across North Texas. I loved it. And after listening to Ed share during the meeting, I felt sure he was the one I needed for a sponsor. I asked him immediately following the meeting.

"Oh my god, I'd be honored!" he beamed. "Where are you in the 12 Steps exactly?"

I gave Ed a brief rundown of my short history in the program and he gave me the same advice Larry had given me only a few months before.

"Hit your knees every morning and call me every day. We'll get together soon," he said as he walked me to my car.

And that's what I did. I called Ed to touch base every day and followed his advice to "hit my knees" in prayer every morning and then again at night before I went to bed. I continued to work and make meetings almost every night with Rita, but also started to find my own way in the program by attending other meetings on my own. I developed a fast friendship with Ed, met with him on occasion and learned about his business. It was during those daily phone calls and visits to Ed's house where I began to get little quips for living from another I perceived as having mastered the program. I later learned there IS no such thing.

During one little low stretch where I was feeling sorry for myself about work and life in general, Ed told me I was to make a "gratitude list," put the list in a box and put the box under the bed. Like a good little pupil I did as I was told, but with one question.

"Why put it under the bed?" I asked.

"Because you'll have to get on your knees to get to it," was the simple reply.

From Ed I also began to learn not to sweat the small stuff. I remember one call to him in particular where I was confused about "what to do next." If my memory bears any accuracy at all, it was related to work or some other silly thing, but I was stuck about how I should proceed with a decision.

"I just don't know what to do, Ed!" I complained into the phone. "I've prayed about it, brought it up at meetings and done everything I know to do. I just can't decide."

"Have you brushed your teeth yet?"

In what was very near an interruption I said, "What? What the hell are you talking about?"

"You asked me what you should do next," you could almost hear Ed grinning on the other end. "I'm simply asking if you've brushed your teeth yet. If you haven't, then do that next. You might follow that with some breakfast and meditation."

"Are you serious, Ed? You want me to brush my teeth?"

"Look, Matt," he clarified. "This really isn't all that difficult. You want an answer to a question whose time may not have come. You asked me what you should do next and I told you. And that's what people like you and I do in a situation like this. If we don't know what we should do, we simply do what's next. The other answers will come in God's time, not yours."

I can't adequately describe with words the look I'm sure I must have had on my face as I just stood there holding the telephone receiver (we were still a bit before cell phones). Dumbfounded comes to mind. And although I was initially frustrated at not getting an answer from Ed, I can't begin to tell you the number of times in my life I have done exactly what Ed told me. When I'm not sure what to do, I do the next thing.

And sometimes that's just brushing my teeth. What Ed taught me was that no one can know what's best for me. I have my own path and seeking a solution from someone else isn't where I'll find my truth. My truth comes from doing the next thing, sitting quietly and accepting an answer will come. I'm amazed at how common a thread that is throughout any religious or spiritual lesson I've read.

On still another occasion I called Ed to vent about someone that had me pissed off. I don't even remember who it was today and that may be the most important lesson of all. It was another one of those "I'm mad as hell and I don't know what to do" moments. Ed found a way to make my mouth hang open again.

"I want you to pray for him for two weeks morning and night," he said.

"You're outta your goddamn mind if you think I'm gonna pray for that bastard," I shot back. "You don't seem to understand."

"I understand perfectly," Ed said. "I understand that you feel wronged and you're angry. And I also understand the only person suffering for that is you. The other guy, whoever he is, couldn't care less. In your head, anger is a dangerous thing. Remember we never allow ourselves to be too 'hungry, angry, lonely or tired' (H.A.L.T.—damn slogans.) This is part of your program, Matt. What he did isn't important. What is YOUR part? You have to look at that. And if you do and find you've harmed him, you have to make amends or risk everything you've worked for in terms of your inner peace."

"Sigh. You're freakin' killin' me, Ed!"

"Just do it. Every day you get on your knees like clockwork and you ask God's highest blessings for this guy. In two weeks or less you'll feel completely different. I promise."

Ed was right except for the fact it took far less than two weeks. I felt better the first time I reluctantly hit my knees, and with a scowl on my face as big as Texas, did what Ed asked.

"I'm really only doing this, God, because Ed says I have to, but I want you to know I want what's best for that guy. I'll do better tomorrow, but it's all I got for now."

The anger was immediately lifted. By the end of the day I'd forgotten I was angry and within two days I'd forgotten what it was I was even sore about. We're going to talk a lot more about prayer later, but this was clearly a lesson provided by the universe to show me that often what's best for me is to offer the best to others. I'm not saying I don't still get angry and frustrated on occasion, but at my core I want only for everyone to live in peace and love. I want them to be happy. It took a little longer to learn I couldn't MAKE them happy, but that's "Progress. Not Perfection."

There were other lessons Ed was able to depart to me on a fairly regular basis and the world around me continued to grow lighter and happier. I had a guide for living and a coach to walk me through the guide. But I hadn't forgotten about the first time I met Ed in the hot tub and knew he was a Christian. Yet Ed never broached that subject with me. He let me bring it to him. I hate it when people are smarter than me.

"So, Ed, we've never talked about the fact that you're a Christian," I began.

"Do you want to?" he smiled.

"Well, I just mean I'm NOT a Christian and I wondered if that was an issue and also if you find it hard to work around in a program like AA."

"Find WHAT hard to work around?"

"Don't toy with me, Ed. There just don't seem to be a lot of people that profess to be Christians in the program."

"There are tons of Christians in AA," Ed continued. "We just don't wear it on our sleeves. This is a program where people are free to choose a god of their understanding. Many have tried a more traditional religious approach and failed. But once finding a higher power, many return to identify that higher power as Jesus Christ."

"So…"

"So to be honest with you, as a Christian myself, I've been concerned about your eternal life," he said.

"What do you mean by that?" I inquired curiously.

"What I mean is that, as a Christian, I believe the only way to Heaven is through accepting Christ as your savior. If you haven't, then I'm afraid you'll be spending eternity in Hell," Ed affirmed bluntly.

"Well that's a helluva thing to say," I said. "You think I'm going to Hell?"

"It doesn't matter what I think," Ed went on. "It's what the Bible says and I believe the Bible to be God's word. Therefore, that's what I believe. Listen, I think you're a great guy. But there are going to be a lot of great guys in Hell and some really 'horrible' people that came to accept Christ spending eternity in Heaven."

"I'm just not sure I buy in to all that stuff, Ed," I shot back. "I spent a lot of time in the Methodist Church and tried reading the Bible. It just seems like a lot of gobbledygook to me. It's wrought with inconsistency and open to interpretation. I just can't get my mind wrapped around it. Besides, didn't MEN write the Bible?"

Ed had a way of looking and smiling at me patiently, waiting for different light bulbs in my brain to be switched on or off. It was one of the things I admired about him and also one of the things that pissed me off. Ed then said the one thing that opened the gates to my influential brain and my starving spirit.

"You might be right," he sighed.

"Huh?"

"You could be right about the whole thing," he said. "The entire story about Christ and his miracles and salvation could all be absolute bullshit. No one knows for sure. But here's the thing. If you're right, you have nothing to lose. But what if I'm right?"

"Um… I'm not following you, Ed."

"If you're right, then when you die you die. But if I'M right, you have plenty to lose because your death will mean eternal separation from God. It's something to think about."

I guess when you looked at it like that, Ed made a valid point. Almost completely unarmed in the ways of religion, I had nothing to say back. On Ed's advice, I bought a Bible that day. And I didn't buy just ANY Bible, no sir. I bought an expensive, quality-bound STUDY Bible that not only had quotes from Jesus himself in red, but had notes at the bottom of the page from panels of "experts" explaining the verses for me. I called Ed to tell him about my purchase.

"That's awesome!" he started. "Now read the Book of John."

"Shouldn't I start at the beginning?" I asked.

"You could. But everything you need to know you'll find in the Book of John," he smiled. "Read it and get back to me in two days."

I armed myself with a highlighter and, with the help of the Contents page, opened to the Book of John. Ed was a smart fellow, for he knew the only way I would ever come to his way of belief and eternal life was to read it for myself. I read the entire Book of John in one day. If you have the most basic knowledge of the Bible, you already know what I found in John.

"For God so loved the world that he gave his one and only Son, that whoever believes in him shall not perish but have eternal life." JOHN 3:16.

I called Ed on the phone immediately. Despite my clouded memory of many facets of my life, I can recall precisely where I was standing when Ed picked up the phone. I was between the kitchen table and "bar" at my rent house in Rowlett, Texas. The sun was streaming through an easterly window. Lying on the faux-wooden table with chrome legs was my new Bible. It was opened to the Book of John.

"I read John," I started.

"Excellent! Excellent!" What did you think?" Ed asked.

"Ed. I've been listening to people talk about being a Christian for a long time. Everyone seems to have their own interpretation of what it is to BE Christian. Like I said, I just finished the Book of John for myself. It can't be this easy."

Silence at first. Then a snicker. "Oh, but it IS that easy," his smile on the other end unmistakable.

"So, according to John and now YOU, all I have to do is say I believe in Jesus Christ and that's IT? Why is everyone always making it so complicated?"

"The gift of salvation, Matt, is just that; a gift. All you have to do is accept it. It's as simple as that. To be placed in the 'Book of Life' and have Jesus in your heart, you need really say only yes. Can you do that?"

"Yes. I can."

"Congratulations," Ed beamed. "You've been saved."

PART FOUR:
BECOMING A "CHRISTIAN"

"I cannot imagine how the clockwork of the universe can exist without a clockmaker."

~Voltaire

Lesson Thirty-Four:

THIRSTY PEOPLE WILL FOLLOW ANYONE THAT OFFERS THEM A DRINK

"To gather with God's people in united adoration of the Father is as necessary to the Christian life as prayer."

~Martin Luther

I wasn't struck by a bolt of lightning or overcome with the Holy Spirit when I said "yes" to the Jesus as described in the Gospel of John from the Holy Bible. My life wasn't instantaneously changed. In fact, I felt much the same as before. The only difference was I had accepted a gift of salvation. I didn't even know what that meant yet.

When I described my misgivings about not feeling a change to Ed and other Christians I was met with much the same response you might expect. From Christians outside the program it was, "It doesn't happen that way for everyone, but don't worry. It'll come as you grow in your relationship with Christ."

From Christians within the program I was answered with more of what I'd already been taught. "You know, Matt. Feelings always follow actions. NOT the other way around." In other words, I was instructed to do as I was told which would lead to feeling different. That was only true in part. I should have been more skeptical from the beginning.

Upon my acceptance of Jesus as my savior, Ed immediately made arrangements for me to "make an outward display of my inward commitment." Through his church, I was to be baptized... again. I guess the first time didn't take. In a display of support, Rita, my Catholic Lite and now sober spouse agreed to also be baptized at the same ceremony along with her daughter, Paige. The three of us were going to be "washed in the blood." By now I was already immersing myself in the Bible, especially the Gospels and I pointed out to Ed that nowhere did I find reference to baptism as a condition of salvation.

"It isn't a requirement, Matt," Ed pointed out. "You're already saved. You belong to Christ. But as a Christian, it's important you show your commitment as a sign to others AND to God."

Like a puppy eager to be house-trained I merely said, "Ok, if you say so."

Already I was finding things about my new-found religion that didn't mesh exactly with my most recent lessons in Al Anon. But I was being vacuumed, albeit willingly, into the world of Christianity. I allowed myself to blindly follow the teachings of Jesus, the Bible, and of course, Ed. Believing in something was better than no belief at all and besides, I was saved. I belonged to Jesus and He would never let go. I had already learned a valuable lesson which was to read things for myself if I wanted an answer. It amazed me then, and puzzles me now how differently MY answers and someone else's can be.

In what turned out to be a momentous event at Ed's church, Rita, Paige and I were donned in white robes and totally submerged in a pool of water under the guiding hands of the church pastor. I wouldn't know the guy if I saw him on the street today.

"I baptize thee in the name of the Father, the Son, and the Holy Spirit. Amen."

Sploosh! Back I went into the pool of water in front of hundreds of cheering spectators. The old Matt was being washed away where a new Matt could emerge.

"Praise the Lord! Praise Jesus!" I could hear them chant.

People were standing, arms outstretched in a showing of openness to Christ. They chanted and prayed and I'm pretty sure some of them even "spoke in tongues." I'm not sure we'll even get into that ridiculous notion, but we won't do it now for sure.

"GASP!" Up from the water I sprang!

"Bless you, Matt. Blessed Jesus. Praise the Lord! You are new in Christ Jesus!" The pastor spoke directly to me and not the crowd.

I only smiled at the pastor, but the question was already developing in my brain and it was hard to keep the thought from forming vibration on my vocal chords. "I am?"

I felt different alright. I felt wet! And I felt I was under the microscopic view of hundreds of people, all who just KNEW I was feeling the rush of the Holy Spirit. I wasn't.

After Rita and Paige took their turns and the church service ended, we all went to Ed's house to celebrate with him, his partner (yes, it turns out Ed was gay) and several friends from our AA and Al Anon groups. Ed was beaming with pride at his success in bringing three lost souls to Jesus. Today, I couldn't even tell you who was at the party, what we ate, or what we talked about. I couldn't even get you close to Ed's house if my life depended on it. Such a momentous occasion should be forever stamped on my soul. This was the day I professed my belief in Jesus Christ and made my intentions known to the world. It's nothing but a blip on the radar of memories. Everyone else was thrilled at my conversion. I wasn't so sure.

Like the Emperor with a new suit in Hans Christian Andersen's famous fable, I dove into Christianity with vigor, never admitting I had doubts of its validity or my worthiness. I became a voracious student of the Bible. I quenched my thirst for knowledge of its contents with daily reading. Armed with pen in one hand, highlighter in the other, I picked through chapter after chapter in search of truth from God's Word. I began every morning with readings and meditation from both the Big Book and the Bible. I hit my knees in prayer before I went to bed and again when I got up.

I would never be pretentious enough to think I became an expert in things biblical, especially compared to those who have spent a lifetime studying its contents. But what I did learn is that I knew more about the Bible itself than almost any Christian I knew. Don't get me wrong here. LOTS of people have forgotten more than I ever learned (in fact I've forgotten a lot myself), but in MY little circle of friends, I was amazed at how many people lived a Christian life with so little idea about the contents of the Handbook written by none other than God Himself.

Two things became apparent to me in a short period of time. First, I was beginning to believe all that I read and took root in the idea that the Bible was God's word inerrant. After all, that's the basis for Christianity and we WILL talk a lot more about that soon. But the second and most baffling thing was what I already alluded to. Many people professed this biblical principal or that, based simply on what they had been TOLD! Very few people (and yes, I know I'm generalizing) had the foggiest notion what the Bible actually SAID about certain topics. And despite what I'd been told about how open the Bible was to various interpretations, I didn't find it that way at all. In fact if you take it verse at a time and in context, it's all pretty clear. At least it was to me.

So chapter and verse at a time is exactly how I read it. Although I wanted to start with Genesis, I read the New Testament in its entirety first at Ed's urging. Then I went back to the beginning and read the Old Testament from Genesis. Once I had the Old Testament behind me, I left it there and studied the New Testament over and over, line by line. I pored over the Gospels and soaked in the teachings of Jesus Christ himself. The Old Testament is full of wonderful stories and prophecy, but it is just as it's titled; old. That fact is exactly why we have the New Testament to begin with. But I'm getting ahead of myself again.

I loved it. I adored learning about this ancient religion (which, by the way, wasn't actually Christianity until about 346 A.D.) and I began to share what I was learning with anyone who might listen. I was beginning to sound like the Bible-thumpers I used to detest. But also within the verses of the Bible were hidden question after question that people couldn't answer to my satisfaction. I continued to call Ed every day in an adrenaline-laced froth asking question upon question about things I had read. And for a long time, Ed tried to swing at every pitch I threw. But even the mighty Ed had his limits. He knew it was time for me to take the next step. I still didn't feel Jesus living in my heart as expected, but I was learning His teachings and developing a relationship with Him nonetheless.

It was time to find a church.

Lesson Thirty-Five:

THERE MAY NOT ALWAYS BE STRENGTH IN NUMBERS, BUT CERTAINLY SOME COMFORT

"For where two or three come together in my name, there am I with them."

~Matthew 18:20

I've visited lots of churches. I grew up in the Methodist church and was a guest at my friend's Christian church. I'd been to Catholic Mass and even visited a "spirit-filled" church in Arkansas. And that's just a small sampling. None of them ever felt like home. Finding a church that fed my spirit was going to be a daunting task.

Rita and I were able to immediately eliminate any association with the Catholic faith. I didn't understand it and she no longer wanted any part of it. Baptist's seemed a bit too intense for me and I already knew I had no interest in returning to life as a Methodist. Lutherans were simply a version of Catholic (I later learned that Methodists were actually an early extension of the Catholic Church) and Presbyterians, well...

I had no idea what they were all about. The large independent churches in the south seemed far too commercial for my taste and I thought the gaudiness of their buildings represented the utmost in hypocrisy. Even though we visited several different churches in an attempt to find a home, none of them seemed to be what we were looking for. We were running out of options.

By mere coincidence (as if there WERE such a thing), someone suggested we try a Bible church located near our AA and Al Anon club. I consulted the local Yellow Pages for information about the church and called the pastor. He actually answered the phone which was the first of many things that impressed me about him. He sounded warm and genuine on the phone and agreed to visit our house to tell us about his church and discuss how we might become members.

In what can only be described as a surreal moment, we sat in the kitchen of our little rent house awaiting the arrival of the man who was to become our spiritual leader; our pastor. It had been a long road from the days of my youth, watching deer and trapping muskrat, to where I was that day, expecting the arrival of a pastor who was actually going to try selling me on his congregation. I found it hard to reconcile my days of youth with the adult still seeking spiritual direction. The life of a "seeker" is funny.

I liked the man immediately. He was on time, youthful, full of energy and excited about bringing a new couple to his flock. He especially liked the fact we were "new to the faith" and was eager to be a spiritual library for all my questions. Like the famous line from Jerry Maguire, he had me at hello. But I still had one pressing question and his response would be the deciding factor.

"Can you tell me how you feel about tithing at your church?" I asked, trying to sound confident and important.

"Absolutely. It's not difficult to find reference in the Bible to God's request for ten percent. But what you give is between you and God. There is only one family from our church of whose contributions I'm aware, and that's mine," he said with a twinkle from his eyes, one of which was "lazy." "Give joyfully and as God moves you to give. My job is simply to lead our congregation and bring souls to Christ. I don't concern myself with money."

Sold. We started attending the Rockwall Bible Church the following Sunday. From the very beginning it was home.

In addition to the warmth of our new pastor and his congregation, what impressed me most about our new church was its philosophy regarding sermons and teaching. Every Bible school, Sunday school and sermon was laid out verse by verse, exactly like I'd been studying. No longer was I exposed to preaching where the pastor drew a weekly subject out of a hat and then jumped all over God's Word citing chapter and verse to support his opinion. Our new pastor took entire chapters, set a course, and preached his sermon based on Bible verses, IN ORDER and IN CONTEXT. Sunday school lessons were tied to the sermon. Wednesday night Bible studies were tied to the sermon. Brad (not his real name) took one line at a time and explained it thoroughly before he moved on to the next. Entire sermons often covered only five or six verses of whatever chapter we were studying. He used historical reference and explained the verses through the eyes of someone who lived in that era. He made the Bible come to life. And because he did it in order, I didn't believe he could possibly be wrong.

For the first time in my young life I felt like a believer. Rita and I were as faithful to our church as we had been to AA and Al Anon although we still went to meetings on the nights we weren't at church.

We went to Bible study EVERY Wednesday. I LOVED Bible study. It was small and intimate. I could ask questions freely and Brad never dodged a question. He always answered every inquiry with honesty. He told me once he'd never known someone with so many questions, yet he felt the questions were good for him as well. They made him think. And they made him study. Although I was timid at first about calling God's Word into question, Brad immediately put my doubts to rest by telling me God appreciated the questions, in fact encouraged them. For in my doubt lied my search for the truth.

We went to Sunday school every Sunday and then to the regular service. We had lunch after church with new friends and truly began to build a life around our new church-home and family. I felt more whole and alive than I had my entire life. I had roots, friends, a God and a purpose. In fact, I was TOLD my purpose in life was to serve God.

The young boy from the early chapters of this book had always had a "hole" that he couldn't fill. Living a spiritual life of serving God, surrounded by those doing the same, was finally starting to fill the hole. I felt peace and I felt protected. But I also still had a lot of questions. And right there at good ole Rockwall Bible Church, I learned that Christians have an answer for everything. It was one of those answers that innocently put a small crack in the foundation of my faith that eventually ended it all.

"The Lord works in mysterious ways. We aren't meant to understand His plan. All of that will be revealed in Heaven. We don't know why bad things happen to good people. God gives us free will. God knew you before you were born. In fact He knew everything you would ever say and do in this life. Jesus died for all sin: past, present and future. He died for YOU," the one-liners went on and on. There was nothing you couldn't explain by blind faith in God the Father.

And then one night while watching our pastor do what his wife called "Stupid Husband Tricks" immediately after Wednesday Bible Study, I dropped the bomb.

"Brad? How do you reconcile the existence of dinosaurs with the Bible?" I blurted. "I mean, there is tons of scientific evidence supporting the existence of creatures never mentioned in God's Word. The time frame doesn't mesh with Genesis and I haven't even mentioned evolution versus creation. Can you explain that?"

"Well, there are two possible explanations," Brad began. "For starters, the time frame in Genesis can most likely be attributed to the fact that 'days' to God are maybe 'centuries' to us. The beginning of Genesis most likely covers thousands of years."

"And the dinosaurs?" I pressed.

"It's likely that the true age of earth is only 10,000 years or so."

Had it been humanly possible my chin would have literally hit the tile floor.

"WHAT?"

"That's right," he went on. "There are huge discrepancies in the validity of carbon dating. Many theologians now agree the earth is likely only around 10,000 years old."

"But how is that possible?" I moaned. "You're telling me that our scientific community's estimate of our universe being billions of years old is wrong?"

"It's easy, Matt," he explained further. "The Lord, our God, built this earth for our enjoyment. Don't you think if God could create ALL of this, He's powerful enough to create it with age built in?"

Just as my dad did with his knowledge of the "small race of yellow people," I began to spread the news of my latest realization the next day. God was SO powerful that He created our planet with age built in. He built it with mountains and volcanoes and remnants of dinosaurs for our amusement! Isn't God grand?

Yeah, despite my best efforts, I wasn't buying it either. And like a micro-crack in the great walls of Hoover Dam, although hard to detect at first, the initial damage was done.

Lesson Thirty-Six:

HAVING A RELIGIOUS IDENTITY DOESN'T MAKE YOU IMMUNE TO CHANGE.

"Dysfunctional systems will fall under their own weight. Let them."

~Bashar

Although undetected by those around me, my faith was clearly shaken by the answers given me by those in religious authority. I loved my pastor, but was growing suspicious of the responses he gave directly from his Baptist upbringing. I didn't fault him directly, but my questions only got tougher and the answers more vague. Be that as it may, Rita and I continued to settle in and live the life of a Christian family with a church home. On the outside, life was "normal." But on the inside, my soul was reaching another time of unrest. A storm was brewing.

Two significant things were weighing heavily on my spirit. The first was something each of us surely goes through at least once in our adult life. I was horribly unsatisfied with my job. The hours were long, the pressure to produce large profits was suppressing, and nothing about the work fed my spirit. Sure, I had a great crew, the money was decent and I had some flexibility, but I remained unfulfilled.

I can still remember doing all the things I was called to do by Al Anon and my church. Every morning began with me hitting my knees in prayer followed by daily readings and meditation. Those meditations always included gratitude for my job. "Fake it, 'til you make it," they used to say. While checking on crews throughout the day (and often at night as well), I'd tell God over and over that I wished only for His will to be done and then asked for the strength to carry it out. The teachings of my friends of faith rang in my ears constantly as I tried living a life of gratitude. Only now do I realize why that wasn't working for me. But it took years.

In addition to the unrest with my job, the pastor at our church hit us with, what I considered, an enormous bombshell. He told us he was leaving to accept a position at a church in Iowa. I was devastated. Selfishly, I felt betrayed. Even though I was beginning to question his wisdom, he was a person I loved and admired. His openness and willingness to field my endless questions made him a figure I respected. He made it clear when he recruited us for his church that he had no plans to go anywhere. I guess plans change.

In retrospect I know that it wouldn't have mattered who the elders chose for a new pastor. No one could have measured up to the man that helped educate me in the faith. But I held out hope that the church would come through with a servant of God that paralleled Brad's charisma. They tried. They failed. After a search that took nearly a year, a man took the reins of our troubled church and I was lost for good. He was a nice guy. But he was inexperienced and less tolerant of my doubts. Everything began to change. Rita and I attended church less. Sunday school and Bible study became less challenging. I blamed it on the pastor. It wasn't his fault, of course, but everything happens for a reason and leaving Rockwall Bible Church was a change I could smell coming from a mile away. It didn't happen quite like I thought. My mother used to say, "That's what you get for thinking!"

In the midst of what my underdeveloped spiritual mind considered turmoil, a plan was unfolding I couldn't possibly have masterminded myself. A friend from church, the tall, masculine half of a wonderful couple with whom Rita and I often ate lunch, was a chief at one of Dallas' suburban fire departments. He was often on the receiving end of my complaints about work and always patiently steered me in a direction of living in gratitude and knowing that "God has us right where we are for a purpose." Then one Sunday morning he asked me how things were going at work.

"Oh, they're going alright." I complained. "Still putting in lots of hours and I don't like it much. Same story, different day."

"Have you thought about trying the fire department?" he asked.

"To tell you the truth, I've never considered it. I wasn't one of those kids that grew up dreaming of being a firefighter. I always dreamed of owning my own business and becoming rich!"

"Well, Matt, the pay is pretty good, the benefits are excellent, and we work 24 hours on and 48 hours off." He pressed.

"What's that again? That last part. You work WHAT?" I asked as my eyes opened a little wider.

"That's right. We work one full day and then get two days off. It's a great schedule and it leaves you time to do other things like start your own business."

In typical impulsive fashion, I broke the news to Rita immediately after church. "I want to be a fireman."

"Well, then that's what you should be," she said.

The next day I began to contact cities around our metroplex asking about requirements for being a firefighter. If anything, I was educationally overqualified, but one thing was sure. Becoming a firefighter, assuming I was lucky enough to land one of the few jobs from thousands of applicants, meant I was going to take a cut in pay. I was going to take a SUBSTANTIAL cut in pay.

While on my employer's clock, I began to take entrance exams between bidding jobs and checking on my crews. I even completed two physical agility tests as part of the process while still meeting the requirements of my employer. In fact, the division I managed was the most profitable in the country two separate quarters. I was doing my job, but I was looking for another. It isn't good business and I should have been more honest. In fact, when I filled out the employment application for Dallas, I marked on the form and then made it clear to the powers-that-be, they were NOT to contact my present employer.

Randy, my boss, entered my office one morning at 7:00 a.m. while I was finishing a bid for Southwestern Bell Telephone. It wasn't all that unusual for him to stop in and drill me about job progress, profitability, etc. But on this particular morning he wore an uncharacteristic and sheepish grin on his face as he leaned back in the chair across my desk and laced his fingers behind his head.

"So, you want to be a fireman, huh?" he started.

I almost fainted. Although enormously fair, Randy was also strict and I had seen him fire more than one employee the minute they gave notice. I feared that's what was now in store for me.

"Yes sir," I stammered. "I'd very much like to be one, although the process is long and the odds of being hired are longer."

"Well, Matt, I've always admired people that want to pursue a life of service," he went on. "How much longer will you be with us?"

"It's really hard to say, Randy, but I promise to give as much notice as possible. I won't leave you hanging."

Within a month I was sitting before a panel of chiefs for my final interview.

"Define courage. Tell us why you'd be willing to take a pay cut to be a fireman. You realize you'll also be a paramedic. Why did you come so close to failing the physical agility test?" These were only a few of the questions and comments they had during my hour-long interview. And then finally, "Wait in the lobby. We'll let you know in a minute."

And then at almost thirty-two years old, the words that changed everything:

"Congratulations, son. Welcome to the Dallas Fire Department. We have a class starting on Monday. Be at the drill tower at 0800 hours."

"MONDAY?" I thought to myself as I left the room, thrilled to have been selected, but feeling bad about the short notice I was going to have to give Randy.

After months of searching, applying, and testing, the "dysfunctional system" that was my life crumbled once more under its own weight. I was going to be a fireman.

Lesson Thirty-Seven:

AFTER A BIG CHANGE, YOU CAN ALWAYS COUNT ON SOMETHING TO FOLLOW: MORE CHANGE!

"At this point trust will help you more than understanding."

~Alan Cohen

The small room was lined with four rows of classroom chairs barely big enough to hold a 4th grader. Air was thick and excitement was high as the newest members of the Dallas Fire Department took our seats for a day of orientation. This was what I had worked for. This was the beginning of a whole new and exciting chapter in my life. This was…

"Welcome to the Dallas Fire Department," the man in the white shirt with oak leaves on his collar bellowed. "You are the members of Rookie Class 236. Today begins a journey like none other. Training starts today. However… "

"Wha…," the thought barely crossed my frontal cortex.

"Not all of you will be starting with this class," he went on.

"Oh shit," I shuddered as the feeling of what was to come filled my core.

"Five of you will be starting with Class 237 sometime in the near future. For now, you will be what we call sub-rookies," he finished as I tried for a breath of what stale air was left in the room. "Blah blah blah blah, Blah blah blah, blah blah blah blah blah, blah blah, and Matt Leatherwood will all be assigned to duty downtown as sub-rookies. Any questions?"

In my eighteen-plus year career as a firefighter, I've actually won awards for my ability to ask questions. I even have a plaque to prove it.

"I'm sorry, sir. What exactly IS a sub-rookie?" I muttered.

"Well, son, it's like this. Rookies are lower than whale shit. Sub-rookies are lower than that. You'll be working downtown, delivering mail, making copies, and running errands until your class starts later this year. Clear enough?"

"Clear enough, sir," I whispered almost under my breath.

The rest of the day was filled with mundane tasks like getting sized for uniforms, and learning about basic rules and regulations. To tell you the truth, the fog was so dense inside my head I can't tell you what else we did that day. One minute I was off to rookie training. The next I was a janitor in a spiffy fire department uniform. Things truly don't always go quite the way you plan. Sometimes they go better.

The next day I reported for duty downtown and became better-acquainted with the other four souls who had received the same news I had only 24 hours earlier. Three of those men became close friends, eventually roommates, and finally lifelong friends. Getting to know these other fine men made being a sub-rookie much easier. In fact, it was almost pleasant. After all, we were guaranteed a spot in the next class, we were on the payroll, and the work was ridiculously easy. For three short months, we delivered departmental mail, cleaned bathrooms, emptied trash, made copies, helped with the department's physical agility test and still found time for paper football and lunch. Life was good. Well, at least life was easy.

Humility is a funny thing and at thirty-two years old I was just getting a taste of it. Although much had been given to me in the way of employment, this job I landed on my own. I did the research, took the exams, and passed the physical. This was something I could claim for myself. And I was proud of that fact. But now I was getting a dose of what it was like for someone else to be in charge. I was told when to eat, when to work, and even needed permission to use the bathroom. At a mere thirty-two years old, I had recruited managers for a Fortune 500 telco, managed a multi-million dollar budget, directly supervised sixty employees, nursed a company through bankruptcy, owned my own business, and earned record profits for a nationwide contractor. Now I was a glorified janitor, making less money than I'd made since leaving college, and had a fat lady with big blonde hair barking orders at me on a daily basis. It was good for me. It actually felt good to have the pressure off. I was officially a number in a bureaucracy. Peace at last.

This book isn't about my life as a firefighter. In fact, that's a book all its own and I hope to write it someday. No. This book is about my spiritual journey and my life as a firefighter is but a miniscule part of that lifelong trek. Sure, there are many things about a career as a public servant that have shaped who I am today. I've seen things most can't imagine and have dealt with people at their very worst on a daily basis. But the stories themselves aren't who I am so I'll save them for the other book. The lessons came despite my career, not because of it. Perhaps more on that later.

My first lesson in diversity and "fairness" came when I learned that the start of Class 237 was delayed because we needed two more Hispanic classmates. But since this book is also NOT about my political views, we'll skip the soap-box delivery of my position on what's fair and what isn't. The point is, Class 237 DID eventually begin training and every day for the next six months was a dream.

A big city was actually paying me to exercise and study. Each morning started with physical training which usually included a mile run and various other resistance exercises. The mile was supposed to be a warm-up, but it eventually became a race between me and another classmate. It was the same every morning. I was being paid to compete. It was like being paid to join a health club, go to college, and compete on the track team all at the same time. It simply doesn't get any better than the days I had at recruit training. I learned about ladders, ventilation, and hydraulics. I got to drive a fire engine, chop holes in roofs and push myself to the limit. Young kids dream of the things I was living. But then again, I had the advantage of knowing what it was like to have a real job. Every day I loved my job more. And with that, I learned to love my wife less.

You may have thought I'd forgotten about Rita, but you'd be wrong. Rita had openly supported my attempt to operate my own business and then provided for our household as it failed. She encouraged me to follow my career as a firefighter and didn't bat an eye at the pay cut I was taking. And now, at thirteen years my senior, Rita was being left behind. Although there probably isn't a good explanation for how things went for us, allow me to try.

As you may recall some chapters back, my first wife left me for another man and took my daughter 650 miles away. I was ready for Janet to go. I was NOT ready for my daughter to go and the pain of that separation was brutal. So I made a little pact with myself that went something like this: "Never again will I ever allow myself to be put in a position where someone can take my children."

In that regard, Rita was perfect. It's clear that the reason for marrying her was ridiculous, but I believe today that everything happens for a reason. She was thirteen years older, her kids were grown, and she could no longer bear children of her own. She was safe. But then a funny thing started to happen.

Being a part of a young group of men and women made me feel invigorated and alive. And even though I'd been diligent in my pursuit of a sound spiritual life, I had also been living a lie. I was being safe. I was hiding. And as I began an exhilarating career in the fire service, Rita was beginning to talk about retirement planning. I was just starting and she was talking about how to finish. And just like sick people don't like talking about funeral arrangements, I couldn't fathom talking about retirement. I was simply too young.

I wouldn't classify it as an affair, but I did develop a fast friendship with a female from our rookie class (I've always been better at relating to women than men) who brought me to realize I had "settled." I had chosen a life of security and safety over one of risk and reward. And although I had made that pact some years back, I now realized I was still young enough to reach again for the wife with two kids, two dogs, and yellow house with white picket fence. What I DIDN'T realize for many more years to come is that I only THOUGHT that's what I wanted. In fact, living within the confines of that scenario isn't even something I'm good at!

Regardless, my restless spirit began to manifest itself at home. Rita picked up on it immediately and I eventually told her of my desire to start over with a family and children. And, bless her heart, she offered to make that a reality for me by being willing to adopt children. But Rita didn't really understand the big picture of my troubled soul and I didn't know how to describe it. We began the agonizing ritual of counseling which probably would have helped if I'd been willing to let it. But I was already completely detached, convinced a new life with a new start was what I needed. I stopped reading my Bible because the passages exposed my "wrongs." I stopped going to Al Anon and AA meetings with Rita and instead hung out with my new, young fireman friends. It was a fraternity of which I never made Rita a part. And although I'm not proud of the way I handled it, I told Rita I was moving out. I asked three of my sub-rookie buddies and now 237 classmates if I could share an apartment with them. They openly agreed to provide whatever was needed for a "brother."

The next morning, with Rita standing in the door sobbing uncontrollably and begging me to stay, I told her good-bye, got in my truck and left for the academy. I saw her only one other time to sign the divorce decree. I selfishly erased her existence and got on with a new life. Sadly, it's not the last time I treated someone that way. Some lessons you just keep learning until you get them right.

Lesson Thirty-Eight:

THE UNIVERSE HAS NO CHOICE BUT TO COME IN TO ALIGNMENT WITH YOUR VISION

"7 Ask, and it shall be given you; seek, and ye shall find; knock, and it shall be opened unto you: 8 For every one that asketh receiveth; and he that seeketh findeth; and to him that knocketh it shall be opened."

~Jesus of Nazareth, Matthew 7:7-8

The above quote by Jesus, the Christ (Christ is a title bestowed, NOT a name) is some of the most glaring evidence that Jesus, himself, knew the secret of our universal existence although it took many more years for me to sort through the religious dogma and arrive at what Jesus meant. You can find the same message by doing a simple Google search for nearly any prophet attached to almost any area of faith. It's a universal truth. What came next in my spiritual journey is evidence enough of that fact for me.

After severing ties with Rita, I applied myself more stringently to my career. I worked diligently at Rookie Training, studied hard at paramedic school and played hard at night with my new roommates. I even began searching for a new church. I was in the best shape of my life and was living a life of hard work and freedom. I had friends. I had a wonderful, exciting new career. A multitude of doors seemed to lie open before me. Cliché, yes, but I had the world at my feet.

And then as faithfully as thunder follows lightning, the weekends came. There were no holes to be chopped, courses to be run or arrhythmias to be ciphered. My friends, much younger than I, went back to their homes and left me to learn the excruciating art of "being alone." I had very little money, no real hobbies, and learned quickly that this thing called loneliness is real and something to be dealt with. I spent many long weekend hours rereading material I already knew for school and watching movies from the small library left by my friends. I was actually relieved to discover Lonesome Dove was an eight-hour movie!

On Sunday mornings I faithfully began to attend a nearby Bible church which I found to be both comforting and saddening. I loved the music and the message, but always sat alone and made no new friends there. Staying immersed in "God's Word" made me feel like a sinner for divorcing Rita. I began to harbor doubts about leaving her, not because I was happy there, but because I wasn't "lonely" there and the Bible said, "divorce was wrong." We all know by now, that's a bad reason to stay. Trust me, we'll get in to all that later.

What I failed to remember with any regularity was that I left Rita so that I could have a family to call my own. Just saying it that way opens a whole new set of thoughts regarding what family IS, but for the time being, a wife with kids of my own was my definition. I wanted a partner to share in my skewed vision of the "yellow house with a white picket fence" fallacy. In the deepest recesses of my subconscious, I continued to send that message to the universe. Although back then, I would have called it praying. There is a very, very important message here that took me years to understand and you can learn it here or learn it on your own. It's your choice. If you ask, the universe delivers… period.

Within a short period of time, with no real effort on my part, the universe delivered a potential mate that came from a "Good Mommy" checklist. Same age, check. Never married, check. Good looking, check. Nice family, check. Christian, check. Nice person, check. Liked my daughter, check. Liked my friends, check. I could keep going, but you get the idea. It's worth noting that there isn't a lot on this list about sharing the same vision, or having similar educations, or having things in common. I wasn't thinking about compatibility. I was clearly thinking about attracting someone that would be good at raising a family. Those are all good qualities. They just aren't ALL the qualities to consider.

Lydia was a multi-generational, west-Texas, Hispanic, Catholic girl. I plunged head-first into the troubling world of Catholicism. No longer was I dealing with Catholic Light as I did with Rita. No sir. This was years of ground-in belief that is apparently impossible to shake. But undaunted, I relished the fact that at least we were both Christians and shared a faith in God and Jesus Christ himself. That's really all that matters, right? That would probably depend on who you ask, but I'll share this much. Lydia was and is a very loving and kind person. But not only was our initial belief structure different, our desire to examine that belief system and turn it inside out was COMPLETELY different. I once asked Lydia why she was Catholic. She responded, "Because I always have been." It's still hard for me to bring my dropping jaw back into alignment when I hear that reasoning.

I learned about things like the Seven Sacraments, Mass, church hierarchy and rules for taking communion. Before my eyes unfolded a world conglomerate of faith, money, and power that to this day make me uncomfortable. Yet we pressed on, Lydia and I, ignoring our differences and capitalizing on our shared desire to have a family. After a courtship that spanned a little over a year, we were married in a rose garden.

"A rose garden?" you ask. "But I thought Lydia was Catholic!"

Stay tuned dear friend. Stay tuned.

Lesson Thirty-Nine:

SOMETIMES YOU JUST DO WHAT YOU GOTTA DO

*"Marriage is a fine institution,
but I'm not ready for an institution."*

~Mae West

As a young girl, Lydia always dreamed of a beach or garden wedding. Even though Catholicism clearly required she be married by a priest in a church, Lydia rebelled just enough to fulfill her wish outside the church. And so we were married in a rose garden surrounded by friends and family. Our fire department Chaplain conducted the ceremony. Calling it a rose garden is probably a bit of a stretch since an epic hailstorm the week before the ceremony stripped every plant of every petal. The heat and humidity neared record levels, but the band played on. Maybe the Universe was trying to tell us something. According to the State of Texas, Lydia and I were now man and wife. The Catholic Church, however, took a different stance.

To make things right meant the marriage would have to be "blessed by the church" which meant (you guessed it) I'd have to go through the annulment process. If you've been keeping up, you know this was my third marriage. I had to make two of those marriages go away in the eyes of the church. Drum roll please as I introduce one of the biggest scams in the history of deception.

The first step in the process is actually writing a check to the Catholic Church for $300. As I signed the check, the local priest attempted to put me at ease about the entire process by telling me, "We only have to annul the first marriage. Since your FIRST marriage was never annulled, the church doesn't even recognize the second."

The amount of man-made dogmatic bullshit was so thick in the room you could taste it as I responded, "Well, I guess that's good news. What exactly IS the process?"

"We'll have you interviewed by a member of our staff who deals with annulments," he went on. "She'll compile the data from the interview and send it to the tribunal in San Antonio who will review your case and issue the annulment. Then you and your, um, wife, will be able to have your marriage blessed by the church."

"Father, I want to make it clear that I am NOT a Catholic and I have no intention of ever becoming a Catholic. I'm here for one reason and one reason only. I want my wife to be able to practice her faith," I retorted.

"I completely understand," he said. "I'll get you scheduled for an interview."

Beginning now, you're finally going to see a gradual shift from actual life experience to editorial. I do actually have an opinion about some of the spiritual information I was being fed and it's yours to absorb or not. I'm not trying to sway anyone to one way of thinking or another. That said, if you're so inclined to read the actual manual that supports your faith (in this case, the Bible), you'll find that nowhere... NOWHERE does the very deity to which Christian's profess their faith require anything like an annulment. You won't find it in the Bible. You won't. I dare you. Look. Read it again. You won't find it. What you WILL find is some references regarding the guidelines for divorce, but you won't find a single chapter or verse regarding annulment. This process is strictly a man-made process that gives the Catholic Church control AND money. The sect that claims to harbor true Christianity veers from biblical truth at every corner. It's a sham of epic proportions.

I met with a lady with no theological or biblical training that recorded an interview meant to poke holes in the entire concept of my previous marriages. She asked for details about my first wife (Rita was never an issue) and our marriage together. She then asked for a list of witnesses which would corroborate my story regarding the details of that relationship. I willingly gave them in the spirit of being a good husband to my Catholic wife. Our interview concluded with me reminding the interviewer of my reason for going through the process in the first place. She assured me there would be no issues and thanked me for my time.

A few months passed with no word from the interviewer or the church. Apparently my annulment "application" was somewhere in Catholic limbo. If you think our government is a bureaucratic nightmare, you should try dealing with Catholics. But eventually the call from my old-lady-interviewer did come.

"Matt, I was wondering if you could come back down to the church and meet with me and a priest from the diocese," she almost whispered through the phone.

"Sure," I said. "What seems to be the issue?"

"There seems to be some inconsistencies in your testimony and that of some of your witnesses," she continued. "We just need to clear a couple things up with the Priest."

"Just tell me when," I countered.

I couldn't wait to sink my teeth in to this little charade.

"Thank you for coming in, Matt," the strange man with the white collar said. The lady who conducted my initial interview sat close by. "We have some questions regarding your annulment interview."

"Fire away, Father."

"When you married Janet, did you feel like it was a permanent arrangement?"

"Of course. It never occurred to me that we might be divorced one day," I responded.

"Do you think Janet felt like it was a permanent arrangement?" he pressed.

"I do. Absolutely."

"Is there a history of divorce in Janet's family?" he went on.

"None. That was a first for her family."

For the first time, I saw the priest glance at the lady next to him with a look that said, "He isn't really giving us the answers we need here."

"How about your family? Has there been a lot of divorce in YOUR family?"

"There hasn't been a lot of divorce in my immediate family," I lied.

And then it became clear to me. This priest was looking for a way to substantiate the fact that there was a basis for making my first marriage invalid. He was looking to save face for the church. It was then I rose straight up in my chair and gazed directly into the eyes of the lady who conducted my initial interview.

"Do you remember why I agreed to this interview in the first place?" I asked.

"Well, I, um, er, well, I...," she stammered.

"I agreed to this entire annulment process because my wife is forbidden from taking part in the sacraments of her faith because of something I did in my past." I asserted angrily. "I want to make this right for HER."

The priest glanced sheepishly at the older woman and said, "I guess we can just say that Janet didn't feel like the marriage was a permanent arrangement."

I cut in immediately, "You do what you have to do, but you make this happen."

The priest, now clearly frazzled and afraid leaned forward in his chair and said, "Don't you worry, son. We're going to make this happen. Don't you worry."

And with that, the deed was done. I called Lydia on the phone to break the news to her.

"I have good news and bad news," I said. "The good news is, the annulment is going to be confirmed. The bad news is, your church is going to lie to make that happen."

In a spirit that puzzles me about religious faith to this day, Lydia was only happy about the result and paid little mind to the manner in which it was done. The small crack in the dam that developed when my old pastor told me he believed the world to only be 10,000 years old was now opening wider; much wider. There were serious issues with religious dogma. I couldn't possibly be the only person to see them. Or could I?

Lesson Forty:

FAITH HAS DEEP ROOTS. YOU CAN'T PULL IT AND YOU CAN'T ARGUE WITH IT

"It is a lie—any talk of God that does not comfort you."

~Meister Eckhart

"Why ARE you a Catholic?" I asked innocently as I looked anxiously at Lydia while standing in our kitchen.

"I don't know," she said. "I just always HAVE been."

In a condescending tone I've learned to regret I retorted, "Being a Catholic simply because you always HAVE been is the sorriest reason to be anything I've ever heard."

The hurt on her face was apparent following the challenge I had just thrown to her faith. The blow was dealt; the damage done, but a seed that eventually began to bear fruit was planted. And I also began to learn the timeless lesson: There simply IS no arguing faith.

Over time, Lydia and I began to live peacefully within a "mixed marriage." She came from a long line of hard core Hispanic Catholics. I was a Christian trying to find reason and truth in something I discovered to be increasingly arbitrary. At every turn I found "holes" in Christian dogma that shook my already cracked foundation.

With the approval of the local priest, we joined a Catholic Church despite my paper trail which identified me as a Methodist. His words were clear. "We have many members here who are from a Methodist background. All are welcome."

It took some time to fully realize that the translation of his welcoming comment was, "We'll be happy to take your money."

And so it was, almost without exception, we attended Mass on Sundays and took our daughter along. She began her journey as a young Catholic by attending classes in preparation for her first communion, while I sat in disbelief reading rules in the hymnal about why I wasn't allowed to partake. I wasn't Catholic. I hadn't been to confession. I wasn't welcome to partake in the sacrament I found most important simply because the largest organization in the history of Christianity found me to be outside the faith. They seemed to think it purified their denomination. I felt as though it merely separated the faiths and on occasion partook of the bread and wine against church policy. To this day, I know in my soul of souls that Jesus himself would never have required anyone to be a member of a church to sit and break bread with him. Remember, Jesus wasn't a "Christian" either. Jesus was a Jew. Jesus was KING of the Jews. But I'm ahead of myself again.

The crack in my Christian faith grew larger along with my apathy. I continued to attend Mass on Sunday in a show of unity for my wife and a daughter who needed a religious foundation I felt ill equipped to provide. I was miserable in trying to be a fatherly pillar. And then the scandal to end all religious scandals hit the news. Priests were molesting young boys. Priests had BEEN molesting young boys for years and then covering it up. But a crack in THEIR dam was opening wider as the public learned more of the atrocities.

To be fair, I must be clear that obviously, not ALL priests were molesting boys, but there were many and the cover-ups were worldwide and went all the way to the Vatican. But whether it was one priest or a thousand, apparently ONE priest in our parish had been one of those molesters. It was before our time at the church, but our current priest, rather than call police, referred the accused to the Bishop where his sins were carefully swept under the rug by nothing more than a transfer to a different parish. Our parish was guilty of taking part in their own little piece of what was eventually exposed as a global phenomenon throughout the Catholic Church. And then, as faithful members of the church, we received a letter requiring our permission on a small matter.

In a continuous effort to put a band-aid on a large, open wound, the local parish was offering a class for the children in Sunday School about how to avoid and recognize sexual abuse by an adult. That's when my foot finally came down.

This time my voice was raised as I approached Lydia. "I've been lied to and kept at arm's length by the church you've embraced. I've sat through Mass, sent our child to Sunday School and sat alone in exclusion while you took communion. I have seen the news, and read the reports and I tell you this. I'll be damned and it'll be over my dead body before I ever let my child take a class about avoiding molestation by the church that's doing the molesting. It. Will. Not. Happen."

And it didn't. In fact, when our daughter was prepared for her first confession, I carefully scrutinized the process to be sure she was never in a confessional alone with a priest. It was done on the pulpit before the entire congregation. The crack in my dam of faith was now clearly opened and I told Lydia, as "spiritual leader" of the household, it was time we found another church. But before we could really begin to search, another symptom of my broken faith invaded our home. The beginning of my true spiritual awaking came in a way you would never expect. God works in mysterious ways.

Lesson Forty-One:

THE GRASS MAY ACTUALLY BE GREENER ON THE OTHER SIDE, BUT IT'S STILL GRASS

"I complained to God when my foundation was shaking, only to discover it was God who was shaking it."

~Charles Weston

At now 50 years old, I've learned many lessons. Several of those lessons I'll share with you later in the book. In this case, I feel compelled to share some lessons before the story. Most importantly, if you view my life through an objective looking glass, even the most amateur in the field of social behavior can chart patterns. And I think that may be the most important lesson itself. The universe behaves in cycles. Our planet behaves in cycles. LIFE behaves in cycles. For some those cycles are minimal. For others the ebb and flow of life happens in extremes. For most those patterns lie somewhere in between. But make no mistake. Life moves in cycles and what follows, although not the first episode in MY life is what made me recognize it for the first time.

I forget things. Not ALL things, but many things. I don't remember what I had for lunch yesterday or where I spent the last holiday. I don't remember exactly where I stood the day

Elvis died and without the use of a planner, I forget important dates easily. And I don't remember the date or even the year I first saw her, but I DO remember exactly where I was. And I remember where SHE was. I used to think I remember it so clearly because she was "the one." But now I believe it's clear because it was the first time God got my attention by shaking my world completely off its foundation based on my free will.

I was standing at my locker early in the morning after a busy shift on the ambulance at my fire station. And by busy, I mean I had just completed at least twenty-five EMS-related calls over a twenty-four hour period. I was beside myself with exhaustion and just stared at the dark void inside my locker, my hand resting on the edge of the door as I held it open. I think the loosely-hinged door was all that held me upright. I let out a small sigh as I swung the door carefully closed. Then I looked to my right.

She was standing near the long, Formica-topped kitchen table, one foot on the aged wooden bench adorning the table, a newspaper opened before her as the sun seeped through the window, silhouetting her shape. I heard it as if God, himself whispered it in my ear. It wasn't just a thought. It was an audible sound. "Uh oh," the voice said.

When I started this book many months ago (yes, I forget the exact date), I thought I would have to go into great detail about this impending relationship. I felt in order to clearly portray my feelings, both good and bad, I would need to turn over every leaf, rock, and pebble. I thought you would need details to understand. I knew I would have to be perfect in my descriptions in order to work through the entire thing and make it clear for you, the reader. I was wrong. A rough sketch is more than sufficient for you to get the idea. And "working through it" is no longer necessary. I've done that, and frankly the book isn't about the relationship. The book is about where that relationship, along with a long list of other events, led me.

The "uh oh" was apparently not about her. It was about what she was going to teach me.

I was now a veteran firefighter and she was the new rookie on "B" shift at our fire station, thrown into the epitome of men's clubs in a sea of testosterone. The place where I worked was known for the ruggedness and sheer tough attitude of those that worked there. Like Vegas, much of what went on at our station STAYED at that station. Rarely did the command staff ever look our way because we took care of business when the bell hit. And that's enough said about that. We were the toughest of the tough and she was sent to work on the toughest shift of all, led by a small Italian-like guy that treated his boys as if he were the Godfather. The most resilient of women would be enormously hard pressed to swim in that sea of testosterone, but she tried.

And whether I truly wanted to be helpful, or saw it as an opportunity to get an upper hand as predator does with prey, I may never be sure. But either way, I made friends with her in a show of support for what she was going through on her shift. I'd ask her about her shift, talk to her about how to deal with the other firefighters on her shift, and on occasion, even came in to ride the ambulance with her to give her a break from the regular crew. We weren't fooling anyone; at least not at the station.

Over a period of several months we developed a close friendship and to her credit, it didn't go beyond that because, as she pointed out often, "you're married." But over several more months I got bolder and she got weaker. Almost overnight it went from platonic friendship to affair. From there I continued to make riskier choices and after lying to Lydia about "needing some time to myself" even drove to Maryland to join her on her vacation with family. Something that overtly stupid and cowardly obviously led to Lydia being suspicious and then discovering the affair.

Upon returning from that long, even magical trip to the east coast, Lydia gave me the opportunity to end the relationship, get help and return home to work things out. I don't know if the correct response is that I couldn't or wouldn't, but I didn't. I put my entire career, home and family second to pursue this dream-life I had with "someone that finally understood me." She was much younger, and much smarter. I moved in with her "temporarily" and began my first real battle with depression. The relationship SEEMED perfect, but the guilt was overwhelming. So I did what many other depressed souls do. I starting taking anti-depressants and sought a good therapist. Those are harder to find than I thought.

I'd like to side-bar here and share some other important lessons about relationships that ring true for me. Use them if they help. Dump them if they don't. I call them "The Checklist." I don't mean for one second that you CAN'T have a successful relationship without these, but I think meeting these four criteria give you a fighting chance from the start.

Are you close to the same age? Granted, age is just a number, but age is also representative of your life experience and life stages. If you get these too far apart, you're going to have some issues.

Are you of similar educational backgrounds? Again, I've known a lot of smart people that never set foot in a college classroom and some terribly ignorant ones that have. Even so, if you aren't equally yoked in the area of education or open-minded intelligence, one of you is going to get bored.

Do you share the same or similar religious beliefs? This one is tricky when you consider the different denominations within a single doctrine like Christianity, but if one of you is Catholic and the other Atheist or Agnostic, you have some major issues to deal with; especially if you have children.

Are your family values the same? If one of you is the type that devotes their entire life to parenting and hanging with family on weekends and the other is a little more "relaxed" in that area, again... more issues.

I'm obviously no professional and I realize those four guidelines are generalizations, but if I'd asked myself those four questions, answered honestly, and then been brave enough to act at the beginning of my relationships throughout life, I think my path would have been smoother. But then we don't always get to choose our path, do we? Sometimes it chooses us. Let's move on.

As I've pointed out, details are no longer important. We lived together for eight months while I trudged through the process of dealing with my depression and guilt. Lydia and I were divorced and my five year old daughter was "crushed" in five year old terms. Daddy went on a vacation, and basically never came back. I saw her ALL the time, but wasn't living under the same roof and tucking her in at night. It was both a wonderful and horrible time for me. On the wonderful side, I was staying with someone that met all "The Checklist" but one. On the horrible side, I completely put my own impulsive urges before my family and it took years to understand that. You'll see.

As is almost always statistically the case in these types of affairs, the age difference and the stress of me dealing with my guilt led to a breakup of sorts. I moved out on my own to "learn the art of being alone," got an apartment and she and I began to communicate less and less. It was one of the lowest and most painful periods of my life, but as it turns out, necessary in a big way.

I spent roughly six months basically living at the fire station while I saved money for an apartment. I worked more and took a part time job teaching CPR. I visited at least three therapists in search of the "right" one and gave up the anti-depressants because they made me feel lethargic. The first therapist violated her oath of secrecy. The second fell asleep during our session after telling me, "It sounds like you already have it all figured out." And finally, the one that saw right through me; the one that cut right through the bullshit; was a little lady named Shirl. She worked part-time at the Christian Counseling Center of all places. I credit Shirl for saving my life on SO many levels. You'll get to hear more about her soon.

I was divorced (AGAIN!) in my late thirties. I was basically separated from the affair, living at a fire station, going to therapy and sleeping wherever I could. It was a shake-up from the universe of epic proportions. (I fully realize in the big scheme of things this is just "life," but for ME, it seemed epic at the time.) I felt broke, sad, alone, and stupid. I purposely kept my shotgun and the shells in separate places. I felt like a failure. And then things got worse; or better. It's all about perspective.

Lesson Forty-Two:

LIFE TURNS ON A DIME

"I intend to live forever. So far, so good."

~Stephen Wright

"Matt! Are you ok?" the class member asked. "You don't look so good."

"I'm fine. I just need to lay my head down for minute," I stammered.

"Is this a drill?" he chuckled.

Fade to black

The mellow taste of the avocado from the one and only bite I took from my California Club sandwich lingered on my tongue as the room suddenly became equally divided into two of everything. There weren't blurry lines of things moving together and apart. Instead there was a distinct line in my field of vision that created an environment of twins. There were two of every chair, table and person in the entire conference room.

As an adolescent and young adult I had been a frequent sufferer of Classic Migraine, complete with auras. To myself, I thought this was merely the prelude to the mother of all migraines. I responded to the initial question raised by one of my class, but never got to answer the second about the drill. Everything just went black.

The comical part of the episode I'm about to describe in more detail, is that just before lunch the CPR class I was teaching HAD been doing drills where I acted out the part of a person with this malady or that, hoping the First Responder Team they represented could figure the appropriate Basic Life Support treatment. This logically seemed like an extension of the fun we'd already been having. This, however, was not a drill.

I began to regain consciousness as I heard paramedics from a nearby suburb enter the room. I was flat on my back, feet elevated, oxygen mask firmly affixed to my face. My class had performed perfectly. The Basic Life Support they provided was textbook for someone who had experienced an episode of syncope (fainting spell). I was confused and proud at the same time. The paramedics took over.

"Can someone tell us what happened? Hi, Matt. Are you hurting anywhere? Do you know where you are right now?" The questions kept coming.

As if having an out-of-body experience, I could hear my class describing the events prior to the arrival of the medics. I then found the strength to speak.

"I think my sugar just got low," I whispered. "Just check my D-stick and give me some D50. I'll be fine in a minute. I have to leave for my daughter's graduation in the morning."

Early in the process, the medics on scene could see something I couldn't, yet I continued to attempt self-treating as the medics performed tests. I was a medic too, after all, and I knew what I'D be doing to treat a patient like me. Apparently medics and doctors make lousy patients. I was no exception.

"We think you need to go to the hospital, Matt." They went on. "Which would you like to go to?"

"I don't NEED to go to the hospital. Just check my D-stick, dammit!"

"We did check your D-stick, Matt. It was normal. We need to get you checked out," they persisted.

"Fine, then take me to Baylor," I managed to utter. "Just hurry up so we can get this over with."

And as if I had scripted the words myself, they asked the VERY question I would have asked. "Are you sure you wouldn't like to go somewhere closer, like RHD?"

"Fine. Take me to RHD. I'm leaving in the morning anyway."

I have no real recollection of being loaded on to the cot or being wheeled through the pharmaceutical factory where I was teaching. I don't remember being loaded into the ambulance or even the sensation of moving. What I do remember is hearing one of the medic's voices on the radio talking to Biotel, our medical control center.

"Biotel, this is Farmers Branch Med 1 requesting a list of today's stroke centers."

"That's odd," I thought. "It would seem to me they're too busy with a patient (ME!) to be worrying about stroke centers. I mean, I'm feeling pretty g... "

"Matt. Listen buddy, we're going to divert to a different hospital. We're taking you to Presbyterian instead," the upside down face told me as I gazed half-conscious toward the ceiling of the ambulance.

I didn't answer because I couldn't. I faded again into a state of semi-consciousness. I recall nothing else about the trip until I heard the burst of air as we passed through the doors of the ER.

"Matt, I'm Doctor Kwan," I heard a man say. "I need you to lift your left arm for me." I shot my right arm straight into the air.

"Matt. I need you to raise your LEFT arm for me." Up went my right arm.

"Your left arm, Matt. I need you to lift your left arm." Again my right arm pierced the cold emergency-room air.

"Wiggle the toes on your left foot for me," he pushed. My right toes wiggled.

"Can you feel this?" he asked as he raked some sharp instrument up the sole of my left foot.

"Feel what?" I answered in a voice reserved for people in heavy sedation.

Time and space began to get fuzzy at this point. Again, I have no real memory of my trip for a CT scan or any of the other events surrounding my little hospital visit right up until the doctor came back in the room to give me some news. (I have no idea how I got BACK in my room!)

As our fire department Chaplain stood by my side holding my hand (When did HE get here and what the hell is he DOING here?), Dr. Kwan told me the following: "Matt, you're a candidate for a clot-busting medication called TPA. Your scan shows negative for a bleed so we want to go ahead with the TPA to break up the clot in your brain. However, you should know that it does come with about a five percent mortality rate after treatment."

"Wha... what?" I stammered. "Look, doctor, I'm not dead yet. Why on earth would I let you give me something that might kill me?"

I was confused beyond reason. People were everywhere and all of them were telling me things that made no sense. What was this clot business and why did I need some drug meant to kill me? In, out. In, out. I just couldn't stay awake.

"Fine, Matt," the doctor said patiently. "We don't have much time so you think about it and I'll be back in a minute." I could see the Chaplain holding my left hand, but couldn't feel it.

"OK, Matt," the doctor was now standing back over my head. "We need to give you the TPA. It's what you need."

"No way, Doc," I whispered in a rare moment of clarity. "You guys are overreacting. I have low blood sugar and I'm leaving in the morning for Nebraska."

The doctor sighed as he walked away, "I'll be right back."

"You really need to do this, Matt," the chaplain finally spoke. "This medicine will make you better."

"Fine," I said defeated. "You guys all do what you have to do, but get me outta here by morning."

Things turned terribly fuzzy again after that. I don't recall receiving the medication or the short visits by my guys from Station 6. I faintly recall talking to my mother and my oldest daughter, explaining to them in barely audible words I'd still be there tomorrow. And then I DO remember something fascinating. Lydia walked in.

After dragging her through an affair, a divorce, and all that goes with it, I had forgotten to remove her as emergency contact at work. So when things looked bad, the chaplain called Lydia. And Lydia came. I think that says glowing things about her character.

And then miracles began happening. Within twenty minutes of receiving the intravenous TPA, I began to get feeling back in my left side. I was able to wiggle my toes slightly, move my left arm, and the left side of my face began to take its rightful place. Then I was moved to ICU where, by ten o'clock that night, I was sitting up in bed, working a crossword puzzle and begging the nurse for some food. Miracles were happening and information began flowing at an exponential rate.

A neurologist I didn't recognize walked cheerfully into my room the following morning.

"I feel great. Can I go home now?" I asked without saying good morning.

He just smiled and said, "I'm afraid we're going to need to keep you in ICU for a few days to monitor your condition, but let me run a couple of simple tests first."

I stood, bent over, touched my toes, touched my nose and a variety of other sobriety-test-type things and watched the doctors puzzled look.

"You don't seem to have any deficit whatsoever," he said while scratching his chin.

"Yeah, I know," I shot back. "Deficit from WHAT?"

"Young man," the doctor's kind eyes met mine. "You've suffered a major stroke. I'm afraid you'll need to be considering another line of work from now on."

"No. No. Nonononononononono," I stammered. "You must be in the wrong room. I just had a fainting spell and some low blood sugar. I'm ready to go!"

"I'm afraid that's not possible, young man," he said. "But your recovery after the TPA is miraculous. You had absolutely NO left sided sensation last night. It's beyond paralysis really. We call it Left-sided Neglect. As far as your brain was concerned, you had absolutely no left side. And this morning, you appear completely normal. I've never seen a recovery like this. Just rest and I'll be in later to check on you."

Stunned, I sat in utter silence and let the doctor's words roll over me. "Major stroke, different job, few days…." This couldn't be happening.

But it was happening and it was happening to me. The odd thing is that I DID feel great! But according to the neurologist, TPA requires a 2 or 3 day stay in ICU to monitor internal bleeding and then a couple more days in a regular room. I was stuck and I was missing my daughter's high school graduation. On top of that, someone I hardly knew informed me I was going to need a different kind of work, because as he put it, "I would never release you to do your kind of work on the heavy blood thinners you're going to be on. For a young man with a big clot with no known cause, blood thinners for life are usually the treatment."

Later that morning, the chief of our department and his assistant chief came to my room and put my mind at ease about work. With kind, cheerful faces they told me we'd worry about that after I was better. But I WAS better!!

Lydia stayed at the hospital during almost all of my stay there. She told me that even though we were divorced, I was still the father of our child and she saw no need in me going through this alone. Like I said, Lydia is a kind soul with sound character. But we'll get to that.

After two long days in ICU which included every neurologist for miles around poking and prodding and telling me what a miracle I was, I moved to a regular room. It was there I finally got a call from "her."

Through sobs she said, "Oh my God! I just heard you had a stroke and they thought you were going to die! I'm so scared!"

"Where are you now?" I asked.

"I'm at the airport. I was about to board the plane for Maryland when I got the news!"

"So, what does the stroke do to change anything?" I pressed further.

"It just makes me realize how much I really do love you and thought I was going to lose you!" she cried.

"Go on your trip. Everything here is fine. I'm not going to die after all. Go."

And that's precisely what she did. She got on the plane. It may be entirely unfair to judge her for that and in reality I don't. But I do believe she made a choice that day. If what she told me on the phone were true, she'd have been on the way to the hospital the second she got word. Instead, she got on the plane. I still loved her then, but that decision told me all I really needed to know. A woman who professed her love for me went on vacation instead. Another woman who was victim to my impulsive urges stood by so I wasn't alone. I think that speaks volumes.

The rest of the saga is really just about tests and procedures and recovery. In the end, they DID discover a genetic heart defect that caused my stroke and with a simple procedure, fixed it. I had one minor setback in the form of an arrhythmia that resolved itself and within three months I was back to work and off the blood thinners. My cardiologist put it like this. "You are no more likely to have a recurring stroke now than anyone else in the general population. You're cured."

I think if we'd been on the football field he'd have smacked me on the butt as I left his office. I was a walking miracle and he was pleased that disaster had been averted. I believe this may be what others would call a "second chance."

I've told you this very long story about my brush with mortality because more than any other I've told you hence, THIS is where the rubber met the road. This is what got the ball rolling toward my spiritual discovery. It happened in two ways.

The first was my recollection of the paramedics entering the room when I first collapsed. For weeks and weeks I pondered how I felt at that moment and I'm still not sure I can adequately describe it more than eight years later. It was like this. I was here one minute. Then I was back. Notice I don't mention the feeling of being gone. There wasn't one. I was teaching a class, my vision went nuts, and then I woke up. And even though I had been unconscious for at least five minutes, there was NOTHING in between one second and the next. What does that mean exactly?

For me it means this. There was no bright light or actual out-of-body experience. I didn't see my life pass before my eyes and I felt absolutely NO fear whatsoever. In fact I didn't feel any fear through the entire process. Now I fully realize I wasn't dead. I did, however, according to my neurologist, have the oxygen completely cut off to my brain for that period of time. By sheer luck my collapse dislodged the clot so it could travel deeper into my brain causing the paralysis. Since that time, I have never looked at death the same way.

All I know is that with no oxygen to my brain, there was nothing. Cold, black, nothingness.

That missing piece of time truly made me begin to question absolutely everything I believed about an afterlife. Is there a heaven? Do you follow a light? Do we have a soul? Where does it go when we die? I actually DO believe we have a soul. It's how I explain self-awareness. But following that day, I have had absolutely NO fear of dying. Because for me, whether you have a soul that leaves the body in search of another life, (which sounds pretty cool!) or when this body dies there is only unawareness and darkness in which case you wouldn't even KNOW you were dead, neither is something to fear. Both are spiritually painless.

The second wasn't so much an awakening as a set up for a future awakening. We now know Lydia stood by me through my hospital stay and recovery. We also know that "she," the woman who finally understood me, did not. And although we all know relationships born of tragedy are risky, I began to see Lydia in a different light and we began to date again. I refer you to "The Checklist" one more time and remind you that I ignored it... again. After some time, Lydia and I decided we should make a go of marriage again and agreed to renew our vows. Only this time, it came with a condition. It went something like this:

"I'll agree to remarry you, as long as you promise to work on growing in your spirituality," she said.

"I think you are absolutely right," I replied. "My spirituality needs some work. I promise."

And with that, Lydia and I were remarried with a small ceremony in our living room. My, isn't it amazing how one little sentence can change everything. Buckle in.

PART FIVE: INTRODUCING SCIENCE

"Science is simply common sense at its best."

~Thomas Huxley

Lesson Forty-Three:

NO MATTER HOW MUCH YOU THINK YOU KNOW, THERE IS MUCH TO LEARN

"I laugh when I hear the fish in the water is thirsty."

~Kabir

Lydia meant, "You need to go to church and spend more time reading your Bible."

I meant, "I'll work hard at examining my spiritual life."

It goes without saying that we probably should have worked out those details from the beginning. On the other hand, if the faith we professed, Christianity, were true and inerrant, no amount of research I did could prove it wrong. To be clear, I didn't set out to disprove it to begin with. My intent was to validate it.

I began by asking various friends from the Christian belief about recommendations they might have concerning my journey. I got more than one hit on a book called *The Case for Christ*, by Lee Strobel. That's where I started. Mr. Strobel is a former journalist and former pastor of a mega-church who sets out, from a journalist's point of view, to prove that Jesus of Nazareth was the risen Son of God. I didn't research his background before I read the book or I'd have been suspect from the beginning. But again, I was looking to validate my belief, not change it.

Mr. Strobel actually does a remarkable job of validating the events surrounding the death and resurrection of Jesus. That is, assuming the story is true to begin with. To thwart the argument that Jesus never actually died on the cross, which would explain his empty tomb three days later, Mr. Strobel lays down some hard medical evidence about how the wounds Jesus suffered on the cross would be nothing less than mortal.

He does a remarkable job of explaining events of the death and resurrection story by pointing out journalistic cues that would validate it was possible for them to happen as told.

After reading the book I came to a solid conclusion. Although a sound work in validating how the events could have happened as told, there was absolutely no address to the truth of whether the events occurred in the first place. To my recollection, there was no historical data that even began to touch on the truth of Jesus's existence as fact. Nothing came close to explaining the virgin birth or the missing pieces of Jesus's life or Christianity's claim to Jesus as Messiah or in the Greek, Cristo or Christ. The book simply took the stand that Jesus was, in fact, the Holy Son of God and set out to defend how those things could be journalistically explained. In the end, it was hollow reading.

The second text on my reading list was *The Purpose Driven Life*, by Rick Warren. Mr. Warren is a Christian author who lays out a 40-day spiritual journey based on God's five principles for humans on Earth. This choice of material came about by other well-meaning friends who felt as though my faith merely lacked direction. And I'll be honest. The material in Mr. Warren's book made perfect sense to me at the time and I even attempted following the principles outlined in his book. But in the end, *The Purpose Driven* Life, although a decent book, was still based on the assumption that the God of Christianity was real. Deep down, that's the answer I was truly seeking. I couldn't live a life based on the rules of the Christian God (or any other "God" for that matter), without some basic evidence of His existence. Some are led by "blind faith." I wasn't born one of those souls.

After two failed attempts at material meant to light my spiritual spark, in addition to daily reading in my once heavily-used Bible and review of other literature already on hand like The Big Book of Alcoholics Anonymous, I found myself standing before a large wooden shelf at the local library. I could have spent exhaustive hours at the computer doing Google searches, but the spirit within me, although not yet clearly defined, longed to hold a book containing a wise author's insights. I love the smell of the polished oak and deteriorating leather of the library. Something about that place just leaves me feeling closer to wisdom. I guess like church does for some folks.

As I stood before the shelf, two full rows of books on religion and Christianity beckoned back at me. I caught sight of another volume on the adjacent shelf. *Quantum Physics for Dummies*, by Steven Holzner, practically called my name out loud. Although clearly not a work of literary genius or a volume debating the existence of God, it called to me like the fall winds of Nebraska. As I picked it up and began to leaf through the pages, I recalled my own experience with physics in high school. Like strong narcotics, walking into that class made my eyelids heavy and I usually succumbed, sleeping through nearly all of it. Lest you think I joke, my classmates presented me with the Satin Pillow Award, complete with an actual small pink pillow I still have today, some thirty-two years later.

I nearly failed Physics and Calculus along with it. Although necessary for my college-prep curriculum, I just didn't get it and frankly didn't care. But at nearly fifty years old, I found myself fascinated with the concepts of Physics and wished I'd paid more attention. So in my warbled little mind, I changed my focus from "spiritual growth" to "I want to learn about things I should have learned when I was younger." Little did I know that the pursuit of knowledge I missed in my youth would ultimately point me in a direction of the spirit. It was a novel, *From the Corner of His Eye*, by Dean Koontz, that first rekindled my interest in the quantum. Now I had the interest and time to see what this mysterious science was all about.

Quantum Physics, Mechanics, or Theory, call it what you want, is enormously complex. I don't pretend to understand the mathematics of even the basic elements. Even Einstein, who helped develop the theory, had some issues with it. In fact, much of what we know about physics today is rewriting history in terms of Einstein's Theory of Relativity. Yeah, I don't know what that really means either. But what I do seem to understand is some of the underlying implications that come with something as grand as Quantum Physics and the subatomic world we live in.

In the novel, *From the Corner of His Eye*, there is a boy who walks into his house from a blinding rainstorm, bone dry. His mother asked him how that was possible. The boy simply replied, "It's easy, Mom. I just walked where it wasn't raining."

Of course, the implication from the above conversation and the story in general is that we all live on a single plane in a 2 dimensional world. But there are many planes and dimensions. This boy simply knew how to pass between them. I can tell by the deep sigh and telepathic eye-roll I just received by you, the reader, that this sounds a little insane. Well, I agree with you. It does. That is until you begin to read about the long term possibilities of Quantum Theory. Someday, should mankind survive long enough to harness its power, Quantum Mechanics could be the key to things like long-range travel to other galaxies and even time travel. It may even solve the debate between The Big Bang and Creationism once and for all.

More than one source I've investigated has implied that what we perceive as real is nothing more than a dream state brought about by imprinting we received as a child. In other words, we create our own reality. Everything you see and do is brought about by "popping" or interpreting all things that merely exist in "waves." If I understand my reading correctly, Quantum Theory suggests that everything exists in the form of waves on different frequencies and don't become real until you "pop the wave" and make it so.

I know your eyes are still rolling and frankly, even as I write it down it sounds crazy. But just because we don't understand it doesn't mean it isn't true. It's simply beyond our current understanding.

Another fascinating fact I learned from my mostly inadequate research is that two particles, once introduced are affected in the same way by stimuli to one, regardless of how far apart they become. Put differently, if you introduce two particles and then separate them by the equivalent of millions of miles and then stimulate one of the particles, BOTH particles respond the same… even the one that didn't receive the stimulus. You can use that information any way you see fit, but this is what it said to me.

All people and all things are made of the same material; energy. We are all universally interconnected. So if you and I meet at the Starbucks and shake hands, nothing that happens to me from that moment forward happens without also effecting YOU and vice versa. Sure, it mostly happens on a level we can't see or feel, but it's true nonetheless. It's proven science, at least at the sub-atomic level. You are me and I am you. Every person you meet or touch; every THING you touch becomes part of you on a sub-atomic level forever. Creepy, right?

But, not so fast. Even the great religious leaders of the modern and not-so-modern era had a firm grasp of the implications found in Quantum Theory.

Jesus of Nazareth (whether you believe him to be a real person or manifestation from ancient lore) said, "Yes. I am with you always, until the very end of time." And, "Remain in me, and I will remain in you. No branch can bear fruit by itself; it must remain in the vine. Neither can you bear fruit unless you remain in me."

Buddha himself said, "In the sky, there is no distinction of east and west; people create distinctions out of their own minds and then believe them to be true." And, "The foot feels the foot when it feels the ground."

And from the Dalai Lama, "From the viewpoint of absolute truth, what we feel and experience in our ordinary daily life is all delusion. Of all the various delusions, the sense of discrimination between oneself and others is the worst form, as it creates nothing but unpleasantness for both sides. If we can realize and meditate on ultimate truth, it will cleanse our impurities of mind and thus eradicate the sense of discrimination. This will help to create true love for one another. The search for ultimate truth is, therefore, vitally important."

It's true you can interpret these quotes most any way you see fit based on the context in which they were said, etc. I wanted to merely point out a few examples from thousands where religious icons we recognize seemed to have grasped an absolute truth of our universe. What many recognize as religious doctrine, I feel is simply a firm grasp of the quantum.

And now let's discuss Antimatter. On second thought, let's not.

Lesson Forty-Four:

YOU HAVE TO READ BETWEEN THE LINES

"And there were in the same country shepherds abiding in the field, keeping watch over their flock by night. And, lo, the angel of the Lord came upon them, and the glory of the Lord shone round about them: and they were sore afraid. And the angel said unto them, Fear not: for, behold, I bring you good tidings of great joy, which shall be to all people. For unto you is born this day in the city of David a Saviour, which is Christ the Lord. And this shall be a sign unto you; Ye shall find the babe wrapped in swaddling clothes, lying in a manger."

~Luke 2:8-12

He was born of a virgin on the Winter Solstice, December 25th. He was considered the way, the truth and the spiritual light doing battle with darkness. His twelve companions followed him on his travels as he taught of evil being made good through his favor. He performed miracles and was "God's" eternal source of grace. He was known as redeemer, savior and Messiah. People identified him with both the lion and the lamb.

The Messiah was the source of life, redeemer of dead souls into a better world, did ceremonial baptisms and partook in a sacred meal of bread, water and wine. His followers held Sunday as sacred and celebrated his mysteries at the Spring Equinox, our modern-day Easter.

The Savior spoke of a great flood near the beginning of history, and preached the immortality of the soul, last judgment and resurrection of the dead. He foretold of a great, final conflagration of the universe. His followers became an organized church which taught meditation, atonement, and salvation. He was both human and divine.

Upon the teacher's death, his body was placed in a tomb from which he rose after three days. His resurrection was also celebrated each year at the Spring Equinox.

You're probably thinking the above story is a bit of set-up on my part and you'd be right about that. What you read above is the story of Mithras a god and religion that pre-dates Jesus by six centuries. Some sources state the modern-day Vatican is actually built upon the grounds once devoted to Mithra's worship. The hierarchy of the Mithraic religion is almost identical to that of Orthodox Christianity and they share many of the same rituals.

Is the story of Jesus and his followers real or the retelling of an ancient story? Was Jesus himself real or is he yet another savior-god brought to life by the skilled hands of writers from that era? The simple answer is that no one knows, although millions of people still pledge their undying faith to Jesus of Nazareth. There are probably sound historical reasons for the development of Christianity, but that doesn't necessarily make it true.

In addition to the story of Mithras, history tells us of dozens of savior/gods dating as far back as 10,000 BCE. In ancient Egypt they worshiped Osiris/Horas, born of the virgin, Nepthus.

The Hindu God, Krishna who dates back to 1200 BCE was on earth to atone for the sins of man. Although there is some dispute about his "virgin" birth, there is lore-laced evidence to describe his mother's conception as "without a sexual union."

The Greek God Prometheus became flesh to save mankind and had a friend named Peter, who happened to be a fisherman. Prometheus was referred to as Logos (the Word) and was crucified. He rose from the dead causing the earth to shake and graves to open up.

Zoroaster was a mythical god, born of a virgin, baptized in water, and tempted by the devil. His ministry is said to have begun around age thirty.

There are literally dozens of accounts from history, both real and mythical, that parallel the Jesus Story in some way or another. All of them predate Jesus by hundreds, if not thousands of years. Is Jesus a myth?

Scholars have devoted their entire lives to the pursuit of validating Christianity's claims to eternal life through belief in Jesus Christ. Still others have devoted THEIR lives to proving otherwise. And there is little doubt, the library and internet are full of books, research, and documents to support either claim. It depends on which side of the issue you care to look. You want so find support for your faith? It's a Google Search away. Would you care to disprove the essence of Christianity? Tweak your search a bit and the same Google sight will take you to thousands of references in support of your quest.

But there is ONE thing that sticks out for me when I'm reading about this fascinating topic. Most all those in support of Christianity cite the Bible as their primary source and then interlace some historical reference from the Mideast of those times to validate it. In order for the Bible to be a reliable reference, you'd have to believe it to be an accurate document in the first place. And that, my friend, is suspect.

Ask most any Fundamentalist Christian and they'll tell you the Bible is God's Holy Word inerrant, passed down through prophets like Moses and Noah. What that means is the Bible is flawless and is meant to be taken literally as God's timeless message to all who read it. Both the Old and New Testaments are timeless works of God's Holy message. You must take all of it literally including creation, the flood, Moses's trip to Mount Sinai, the parting of the Red Sea, the murder, prostitution, slavery, and incest at the hands of kings and of course, the teachings of Jesus, himself.

Let's start at the beginning. Are we to believe God created Heaven and Earth in seven days? Is that time-frame literal? It's true and literal if you're Fundamentalist, yet popular science and physics have shown indisputable evidence that the universe was created at some point by a Big Bang; a sort of cosmic explosion created when matter met antimatter. Couple that with the fact we also have evidence our universe continues to expand at an exponential rate and I start to scratch my head a little.

Recent DNA mapping has proven beyond any doubt human-kind could not have been the populated by the joining of two original people, Adam and Eve. Again, you'll find similar beginnings in a number of religions and even American Indian lore. If you are to take the Bible literally, you're forced to believe we're all related to the original pair. It isn't scientifically possible.

How about a great flood? The Bible tells of Noah and his great Ark, meant to preserve all life in the aftermath of God's wrath. Once again, several religions adhere to a story about a great flood on Earth. For the sake of argument, let's assume there is some truth to the story. Although most likely lore passed from generation to generation, let's open our minds to the possibilities. Isn't it reasonable to think a large flood in that time could easily be assumed to have covered the whole earth?

After all, if what you see is water all around you, in those times believing the entire earth was underwater would seem reasonable. Today we know it isn't scientifically plausible, yet must be taken as truth to the Fundamentalist.

I think you get the message. The Bible, like any other work of its time is historically unreliable and impossible to prove scientifically. Yet if you're a fundamentalist, it can all be easily explained by assuming God created everything with age built in only 10,000 years ago. To not find the word "fairy tale" buried in there somewhere to anyone with a minimal sense of reason is baffling to me.

It may seem as though I'm nit-picking at the Bible and I understand your sentiment. It just happens to be the document with which I'm most familiar. Christianity, although not what I practice now, is the formal religion most familiar to me. But it would be unfair to single out the most widely purchased book on the planet. There are plenty of others and they all have similar holes. And I'll get to those in a more generalized sense.

As I began to drink less of the Christian Kool-Aid and do more reading on my own, I learned some things I believe would cause a reasonable person to pause. To begin with, the Bible was originally written in Greek, Hebrew, and Aramaic. I don't know about you, but I find those languages to be vastly different than the English translation we see today, whether it be King James, New International or otherwise. Converting a text in that manner, using the tools of the time had to be grueling work. And by its nature, would seem to be subjective and difficult to transcribe. The "experts" will tell you the greatest minds of the time worked to interpret and then AGREE on the interpretation of the Bible. But it just didn't morph from Greek to English. No sir. We had Latin and some others to start with. The original Greek word now read in every Bible as "virgin" was originally "young woman." That's a pretty important one to get right, don't you think?

Even if you buy in to the fact the Bible is God's Holy Word, imagining it to be inerrant after all those human transpositions is ludicrous. The "greatest minds" theory is priceless, because frankly, there isn't a legitimate way to deny or defend it. We don't know for certain who they were or even if they WERE great minds. One can only assume.

And speaking of authors; here's another small issue that piqued my interest. The authors of the modern-day gospels not only didn't write them until thirty to eighty years after the death of Christ, which means they didn't even know Him or live in His time, their names weren't even Matthew, Mark, Luke, and John. These names were assigned to anonymous authors at a later date. Yet today, we take those names as "Gospel." What else are we missing?

Many practicing Christians today still refer to Jesus of Nazareth as the original Christian. Even my daughter's geography lesson on World Religions named Jesus as the "founder" of Christianity. History, once again, proves this to be suspect at the very least, completely false at the other extreme.

To be clear, the man's name, if he ever existed, was NOT Jesus Christ. The word Christ is an English version of the Greek Christos, transliterated from the Hebrew word Messiah. Christ isn't a name. Christ is a title. It means Jesus was the Messiah or if you prefer, the Anointed One, whose birth, ministry, death, and resurrection were foretold by prophets in the Old Testament. But remember, there were dozens, if not hundreds, of saviors predicted by "prophets" throughout history. You can make just about anything fit if you try hard enough.

Okay, maybe just one more and we'll give it a rest. Jesus was crucified for His claim to be King of the Jews. Not only is this evidence he was NOT the first Christian, but it also lays claim to his birthright. Jesus was by many accounts, rightful heir to the throne of David, which can be traced through the "Virgin" Mary's bloodline. Joseph isn't part of the picture. He wasn't Jesus's father, remember? If you trace Mary's bloodline back biblically, you'll find that Jesus was in fact, King of the Jews. It gets convoluted from here when you consider Herod and Pontius Pilate and the entire debacle that led to Jesus's crucifixion and frankly, for purposes of this text, it isn't necessary.

If you want to examine the bloodline of Jesus, there is much you must take at face value. You have to assume the Old Testament is historically accurate. You have to assume Jesus existed in the first place. And you have to sign off on the notion that His conception was indeed, immaculate; that Jesus was the only Son of God, born of the Father, God in the flesh. It's just too much for me to swallow.

But wait! There's more! NOW how much would you give?

Lesson Forty-Five:

THE BIBLE WAS NOT WRITTEN BY GOD!!!

"God has no religion."

~Mahatma Gandhi

Santa Claus, the Tooth Fairy, the Easter Bunny, Jesus Christ, Muhammad, Buddha; they all have roots in lore and what we could now arguably consider ancient history. And depending on your geographic location, the religious beliefs of your parents, and local spiritual principles, you've probably been exposed to all of them in some fashion. We all know the story of St. Nicholas and his gift-bearing benevolence toward children. Who of us has not left a tooth under the pillow (or in some cultures, buried it) to find money in its place the next morning? What child from the majority of homes in North America has not risen on Easter morning in anticipation of the gifts left by the Easter Bunny? Who hasn't hunted a colored Easter egg? It's ok!

And lastly, who hasn't heard the Christmas story that tells of the virgin conception and birth of Jesus, the Nazarene? You know the one. He was conceived by God, himself, in the womb of the virgin, Mary. We talked about this two chapters ago! He was born in a manger because there was no room at the inn. He was visited by three wise men who brought gifts of frankincense and myrrh. Shepherds followed the star that shined upon the location where the Messiah was born! The child-God grew to be a famed teacher, and as foretold by great prophets of the Old Testament, was crucified and buried for his alleged claims to be the Son of God, or King of the Jews. He rose from the tomb after three days, during which time he descended to Hell to defeat sin, and ascended to heaven to be seated at the right hand of God. His sacrifice and resurrection paid the price for all our sins. It's a WONDERFUL story full of magic and hope. But it's just that; a story. And it's much less believable than the story of St. Nicholas.

By the time we reach the age of twelve (and many much sooner) we have clearly determined that the present-day roles of Santa, the Tooth Fairy and the Easter Bunny are ALL played by our parents. The evidence is just too overwhelming and eventually the parental figures cave to the prodding of young minds. The truth is revealed. And yet when it comes to the story of virgin births, bright stars and mangers, despite overwhelming evidence that brings the entire story in to question, our children's minds are continually imprinted with the undying devotion that the entire story is true. No one wants to recant the story because, by the very nature of Christianity itself, to not believe comes with too high a cost. Better to believe and be wrong than to NOT believe and be wrong. Let's take a look at that. I know. It's confusing.

What exactly does it MEAN to be a Christian? Actually, few things in scripture are clearer than the definition of what it means to be a Christian, that is, to hold your place in the Book of Salvation and be saved through Christ Jesus. In other words, your ticket to heaven is free and easy. Referred by some as the "Gospel in a Nutshell," John 3:16 sums it up perfectly.

"For God so loved the world that he gave his only begotten Son, that whosoever believeth in Him should not perish, but have everlasting life."

You can read the entire Bible from front to back if you wish, but the only chapter and verse that really mean anything is found right there in John. In simple English is says without ambiguity, if you believe in the birth, death, and resurrection of Jesus, you're going to heaven. Period. It's not open for debate. For Christians of every single denomination it boils down to that; belief.

You don't have to tithe, go to church or sing in the choir. It isn't necessary that you give to the poor or be kind to your fellow man. The Ten Commandments really become just "Ten Suggestions" because acting on them has absolutely nothing to do with your salvation. I'll take it a step further. If you're Christian and believe the Bible as written, then by your very claim you must ALSO believe there will be murderers and rapists in heaven. Some wonderful earthly people will spend eternity in Hell because they never accepted Jesus as their personal savior. And this is where it gets convoluted.

Time and time again I have met "Christians" who hadn't the foggiest notion what that claim means. I've met those that believe you must only believe "in God" and when pressed about the bad people going to heaven, back-pedal and begin the process of picking and choosing those parts of the user's manual (the Bible) that best fits their needs. Some of the Bible is easy to swallow; some of it, not so much. For the parts somewhat less palatable, people defer to those verses that feed their spirit. For the life of me I'll never understand how those that claim the Bible to be God's word inerrant can also be the sort that behave outside its teaching. It's like trying to have it both ways. You can't. And therein lays the root of why I no longer adhere to its message. Who wrote this thing anyway? If not God, who?

What I'm about to share with those of faith in the Bible may sting a little. Sorry about that. It has to be done. You see, even those of the Christian faith can't agree on the Bible's content.

In fact, it's been in dispute since it was first written. Does that puzzle you in the least? It means the book commissioned and inspired by God is different depending on your denomination. I can't speak for you, but I don't think God would leave His Word open to interpretation. Any god I chose to follow would make it crystal clear. The beauty of the entire explanation offered by those of theological background boils down to things like "we're just not meant to understand some things." That's no different than the parental explanation of "because I said so." The entire faith and many religions like it are packed with empty explanations to keep you faithful. It's a money and power thing. We'll get to that soon.

There is no common version of the Bible. Let me repeat that. There is no common version of the Bible. How can that be? I'll agree there is a MOST common, i.e. the Christian Bible we see most often in North America, but not one that is common between denominations within the same faith. Scary.

The Bible is from the Greek biblia or The Books. It is made up primarily of writings or religious texts from Judaism and early Christianity. Even within Judaism anywhere from 5 to 24 original texts are recognized depending on where your Judaist allegiance lies. There are 24 texts of the original Hebrew Bible which are divided in to 39 books of the Old Testament. Complete Christian Bibles (both Old and New Testament) range from sixty-six books of the Protestant canon to eighty-four books for the Eastern Orthodox. The Jewish Bible is recognized in three parts, the Christian Bible, two. Christian Bibles contain the same books as the Jewish, but in different order. Early church fathers compiled gospel accounts of the life of Jesus sometime during the first century. They chose four. There were hundreds to choose from. Need I go further?

The Bible may have been compiled by men who meant well, but it clearly wasn't inspired by a perfect deity. If it had been, don't you think it would be perfect? Isn't it at least minimally plausible, that if God intended us all to worship Him, he would have produced a manuscript that united us without question?

"Some things we just aren't meant to understand," I can hear them say. "God wants us to come to Him of our own free will."

Or my personal favorite, "Satan is planting seeds of doubt."

Good grief.

Unless a supreme deity is just playing us for purposes of his grand entertainment, a loving god would have made it clear. He didn't. And for me that settles it.

But since we're on the subject of Free Will, let's address that little slight-of-hand for just a moment. It has always been one of the things that sticks in my craw regarding religion. Now seems like as good a place as any to address it.

The American Heritage Dictionary defines Free Will as "the ability or discretion to choose; free choice." It simply means that each and every human on Earth has the ability to make choices. Some might call it discernment or "weighing our options," but the premise is the same. At every corner, every second, we are able to make a choice about what comes next. Sure, some things happen seemingly without our choosing. Or do they? We'll see more about that later, as well. But for now, let's adhere to the confines of a discussion comparing God's Will for us and our own free will. It's a wonderful paradox.

I don't recall exactly where I was the first time someone told me God had a plan for me. I was told (and referred to scripture) that God knew me even before I was born. He knew everything I would ever do, both right and wrong. He knew every decision I would make. He knew every choice, every turn, every breath… before I was born. God was omnipresent and omnipotent. He was everywhere and everything. Every part of my life was preordained by a loving god. At the time, that notion seemed pretty fascinating. It was comforting.

But as has been the case most of my adult life, I began to ask questions.

"Let me get this straight," I would start. "God knew I would be divorced more than once? He knew I would question His very existence and even try to argue the fact the story of His Son was myth?"

"Yes," they would say. "God knew all those things. He knew there would be murderers and horrendous criminals. He knows of great floods, droughts, and wars. He knows there will be great sorrows for people. He knows everything. And he loves you anyway."

"I don't understand," I would counter. "If He can foresee every bad thing that's to happen, why would He allow it? If there's a heaven, why not make it right here on Earth? That doesn't sound like a loving god to me."

"Ah, my child," I would hear. "The most precious gift God gave to mankind was free will; the power to choose."

"Wha… ?"

"That's right. God is love. And God is perfection. He allows bad things to happen so we can appreciate the good. And he allows us to turn from Him so that we can return to His love of our own choosing. He doesn't make us love Him. He waits for us to choose His love."

"But I thought you said God knew everything. I thought you said God already knew every choice I would make. I thought my life was preordained by God."

"It is," they would continue to lie. "And God cries for your mistakes and longs for you to love Him as your heavenly father. He wants only the best for you."

"Well, if He wants only the best for me, why not just create me that way? Aren't we created in His image?"

"In His image, my son, but not exactly like Him."

"So which is it?" I would press. "Do I have free will or don't I?"

"You do."

"But if my life is preordained by God, then I'm not choosing ANYTHING!" I would assert with clenched fist.

"Some things we just aren't meant to understand, my child," they'd console. "All our questions will be answered when we're in the presence of God. And the only way to God is through Jesus."

It's a shell game. Christianity, and many religions that follow a particular dogma that can't be adequately supported, play a game of "blind faith." They make it impossible to understand and then promise our understanding one day if we adhere to the principles of their faith. Trust me. If you start playing the religious shell game, you'll never find the marble. If you get too close, the marble gets moved. It reminds me of a bumper sticker I once read. "Just when I thought I had all the answers, they changed all the questions."

It's like that with religion. To expose their sham is to crumble their empire. And thanks to the gullibility of people and absolute NEED to believe, religion will live on. It's like this. You can put lipstick on a pig, but it's still a pig.

Let's take a look at the real reason religions protect their secret so carefully. Let's do what any good investigator does. Let's follow the money.

Lesson Forty-Six:

THE CHURCH IS A CORRUPT MEGACORP

"One must beware of ministers who can do nothing without money, and those who want to do everything with money."

~Indira Gandhi

I can still see the grin on my old pastor's face as I asked him about tithing to his church. You may recall the conversation from an earlier chapter. His answer is what brought me to his flock. He seemed to only be interested in bringing souls to Christ. He didn't care about the money. But he should have. Church is big business. But most of them are in the wrong business.

It wasn't long after I first got the "Earth is 10,000 years old" speech I began to notice the enormous size and ornate look of many "houses of God." And by enormous, I mean gigantic! Just one of the many churches I attended during my years as a follower needed hired police officers to direct traffic on Sunday. And they didn't need it for just one service. They needed traffic control for BOTH! People flocked to hear the flamboyant pastor by the thousands.

He was a gifted speaker. He dressed nice and used expensive props on stage and had his sermons simulcast to satellite buildings and on radio. It was impressive. The building that housed these thousands of faithful followers, fancy props, and symphony orchestra for "music time" covered acres of land and was valued at several million dollars; millions of dollars raised by the members. I forget. Did Jesus, Buddha, Muhammad, or Krishna preach in such a building?

The church I attended MOST recently (before I walked away from organized religion) was already too large in membership to fit in to one gargantuan building. It took two buildings in separate areas of town. To begin making room for the huge following, the church founders began a campaign to raise money for a NEW church which came with a price tag of $10 million! Ten. Million. Dollars. All raised by the members of the church. I believe Jesus called people to give up all they had and follow him. He asked his followers to share the message. Not once did he say, "Come to my church. Sign a membership card and pledge ten percent of everything you make to support my cause."

It doesn't take money to spread the word of salvation through Christ Jesus. It takes time. It takes commitment. But it doesn't take money. What DOES take money is supporting the inflated salaries and overhead that come with a mega-church. Heck, it takes a lot of money to support a SMALL church!

Why do we do it? Why do we build bigger and bigger buildings to bring in more and more followers? Why do we as a human race spend BILLIONS on the salaries and overhead of big churches? Have you seen the size of the house your pastor lives in? Have you seen the car he drives? I tell you why we do it, and it isn't to save souls. We do it for one reason; convenience.

Sure, an argument can be made regarding a bigger building required to harbor more souls, but are these elaborate shrines really necessary? Not one of the great teachers of recorded history taught in such a place. Jesus himself said, "Where two or more are gathered in my name, there am I also." And I get that there is comfort in going to church and being surrounded by other "believers," but again; why the giant mosque?

Since the earliest stories of the Bible, people have been purchasing their salvation. To do wrong, meant there had to be atonement to offset the sin. There had to be a sacrifice to God. Kill someone, slay the fatted calf. Commit adultery, sacrifice your prize lamb. Nearly every culture you examine has some form of sacrifice built into its belief system. If the god's are angry, you can calm their spirits by tossing a virgin into the volcano. It's an ancient and redundant story. And it's what makes the story of Jesus so fascinating. People got tired of slaughtering their prized livestock or first-born daughter or son to make atonement for wrongs. Let's face it. We ALL "sin" at one time or another. It's part of the human existence.

Enter Jesus of Nazareth. He's like the quintessential bankruptcy attorney who wipes your slate clean for all eternity. All debt is paid. He is the sacrificial lamb for all those who believe. But that's just a little too simple, in my opinion. It's everywhere you turn in nearly every religion. How do we pay our way to God? How much is enough? Is it ten percent? Is it all your worldly possessions? The Bible tries spelling it out for us by declaring God wants ten percent of everything, but then we're right back to who wrote it, aren't we?

If you follow the money trail like any good investigator, you'll probably find, like I did, that the trail begins at the Council of Nicaea at or around 325 A.D. This council of Rome was called by the Roman Emperor Constantine and consisted of 250 to just over 300 Christian Bishops. There were four main purposes of the council. They were there to settle the relationship between Jesus and God the Father, write early versions of the Nicene Creed, agree on a date for Easter, and develop canon law.

I want to be clear at this juncture about what jumps out at me regarding this council. It was men, not God, who were establishing Christian guidelines (law). Remember, this council actually arrived at an agreement regarding Jesus's divinity. Jesus had been dead for 325 years! It would seem to me that God himself would have made that clear without a council meeting. He didn't. If Easter was to be a celebration of the Risen Christ, it seems to me that would be indisputable as well. It wasn't. It took a council to agree on the date. Up until the Council of Nicaea, Jesus was "officially" just a man. People proclaimed his divinity, but it wasn't recognized officially by the "church." It took a meeting to make that happen. And it took a panel of bishops to develop a creed by which to live. I thought Christians already had a guidebook.

Why was this council necessary? Opinions vary and like most things, you'll find evidence to support what you believe, although much of it is clearly flawed. But this is what I believe based on what I've studied.

Constantine wasn't even a Christian! By most accounts, Constantine had been a practicing Pagan. Modern Christianity has twisted "paganism" to mean "devil worship," but that's clearly a smear campaign. Paganism is simply a relationship with nature. It doesn't matter. What matters is that a practicing Pagan called a council of Christians. I couldn't quite get my mind wrapped around that one either until I considered the political climate of the time. Christianity was gaining momentum all over the region and people were divided throughout the kingdom as per their beliefs about Jesus. Constantine was no dummy. He saw the need of a united kingdom for political and economic reasons. Christianity was the latest and greatest thing. Constantine's Council of Nicaea united the factions. His kingdom united.

The "church" has been protecting its kingdom since that time. Enormous amounts of political and financial pressures have been asserted to protect the kingdom. The Catholic Church alone, although their assets are heavily secret, is worth billions and billions of dollars. Some sources cite the Catholic Church as the world's largest conglomerate. Bigger than Walmart. Bigger than GM. Bigger than the largest oil company you can think of. Their gold and priceless art collections are estimated to be in the billions of dollars alone. Their Bishops and Cardinals, although living under a Vow of Poverty, live in the lap of luxury under the protection of the Vatican. They wear the finest clothes and jewels and drive the finest cars. Yet worldwide, people who took no vow to be destitute go hungry. This, my friends, is so far outside the teachings of Jesus, himself, I can't even adequately define the hypocrisy. And yet, we continue to support them.

It wouldn't be fair to pick on Catholics just because they're the biggest. The Nation of Islam is also reported to have hidden assets in the billions. But what about television? Jim and Tammy Fay Bakker, Billy Graham, Kenneth Copland, Jerry Falwell, Benny Hinn, Oral Roberts, and Robert Tilton, to name a few, have built EMPIRES on their fear mongering. They live in mansions, fly on private jets and hold millions in assets all from the twisting of biblical principles to scare you in to sending money. Month after month, people from every walk of life send their social security checks to an organization run by a phony, all for the purpose of atonement. That's right. People are still trying to buy their salvation. It's still easier to slay the fatted calf than it is to live a life of goodness. It's just more convenient.

If you're still a Christian, listen to that little voice in your heart and remember what Jesus taught. It's all found in John 3:16. It doesn't cost a penny to get to heaven. You need only believe. Anything you hear otherwise from another soul claiming to be a godly man or woman, is simply a lie. Don't take my word for it. Read it yourself. You'll be amazed at what your religion teaches.

The older I get, the more appalled I become at the millions of dollars churches of all religions spend on themselves, while millions on Earth go hungry. What shocks me further is that people continue to bury their heads in the sand about it in the name of convenience. Going to a multi-million dollar church and pledging a portion of your paycheck isn't what makes you a good person. We're all good, perfect, spiritual beings. The great teachers got that. The opportunistic "spiritual leaders" of today's mega-churches have it wrong; dead wrong.

The Catholic Church alone could wipe out poverty in a dozen third-world countries. Does it not make you raise your eyebrow just a bit to wonder why they don't? It's because today's "church" isn't here to serve you. It's here to serve itself. Don't get me wrong. I do realize that churches do some good with the money they have. They just don't do NEARLY what they're capable of. Maybe, instead of tithing at church, we could sponsor a hungry child. Maybe, instead of building a mega-church, we could build a hospital in Darfur. Maybe someday we'll all realize the truth hidden behind the altar curtain. Someday. Maybe. Here's something I'll borrow directly from Christians themselves. What would Jesus do?

Lesson Forty-Seven:

THE ANSWERS ARE IN THE STARS

"It is clear to everyone that astronomy at all events compels the soul to look upwards, and draws it from the things of this world to the other."

~Plato

We can't go much further without taking a look at Sun Worship. After all, you can trace almost every modern-day religion's roots to that topic: worship of the Sun. Even our friend, Constantine, from the previous Lesson, was a Pagan. More accurately, sources state Constantine actually worshiped Sol Invictus or, "The Unconquered Sun." The Roman Empire actually celebrated the "birth" of the new sun each year at the winter solstice. Many confuse this with worship of Mithras, whom we discussed earlier, due to the similarities with Sol Invictus. Regardless, Constantine's worship status at least begs the question, "Through the Council of Nicaea, did Constantine incorporate his sun worship in to Christianity?" It seems at least possible. We'll get back to that.

Hinduism is based in sun worship. Early Hinduism consisted of Adityas; deities of classical Hindu worship that were of a "Solar" class. One of their earliest sacred hymns is dedicated to one of their principle solar deities. Hinduisms Sun God is highly revered. In more modern times, the Vedic Adityas (solar group of deities) have lost identity and basically "morphed" in to one god, Surya or, the Sun. From Surya, there were offspring that make up the "clan of the sun." We can go on.

Ancient Egyptian religion was entirely about worshiping the sun. Their mythology brings us such deities such as Isis, Horus, and Ra. From Ra, we get Hathor, the horned cow. Ancient Egyptians believed the sun (Ra) moved across the sky in a kind of "solar boat" and drove away a demon of darkness at dawn each morning. I'll make my own comparison here and liken this story to Jesus doing battle with Satan: Light versus Darkness.

Ancient Chinese have recorded mythology that tells of ten original suns. Ten were too many so nine were shot from the sky with bow and arrow.

Buddhist cosmology recognizes the supremeness of the Sun.

The Munshi Tribe in Africa believes the sun bore a son, Awondo.

The Aztecs worshiped the sun god, Tonatiuh who ruled over Tollan, or Heaven. They believed that Tonatiuh required human sacrifice or he would refuse to move across the sky. One source states as many as 20,000 people a year were sacrificed on Tonatiuh's behalf. Makes you wonder if the Aztecs were wiped out by disease, doesn't it? It also supports our discussion from the previous Lesson about people buying favor with god; in this case, the Sun.

Indonesian mythology recognizes the Sun as "father" or "founder" of their tribe.

Even I'm getting bored bringing light to all these cultures who worshiped the brightest star in our solar system. There are more. There are a LOT more! Story after story tells of the Sun (insert appropriate deity name here) descending into the underworld to do battle with darkness (insert appropriate demonic name here). All of these cultures were seeking understanding of their awareness through the only means at their disposal; the sky. And what better place to look? If you're looking for a place to find wonder and power and vastness, you need look only to the sky. Try looking directly at the sun. You can't. And if you're an ancient astronomer or holy person trying to find definitions to things you don't understand, why not the night sky? Where do you think all the consternations came from? SOMEONE had to map them and name them. Human beings, from the beginning of time, have been wondering how we got here. And humans have been finding ways to explain the unexplainable over the same period. Man seeks the answer to his awareness. Something as wondrous as the sky seems only logical. So let's get back to Christianity. In fact, let's get back to the Christmas Story.

The parallel I'm about to draw will bring eye rolls. It will especially draw conspiracy theory backlash and shouts of "this is the work of Satan" from the Christians among you. I get that. But if you look at the evidence I'm about to share, add that to the long history of Sun worship, and the limited knowledge afforded Man at the time, and don't at least CONSIDER the Christmas Story has some roots here, then blind faith surely becomes you. To look at the mounting evidence modern science and research affords about the questionability of religion, especially Christianity, and then ignore it or at least QUESTION it, befuddles me. I can only present to you that which brought a change in me.

The authors of *Astrotheology & Shamanism, Christianity's Pagan Roots* state it better than I.

• • •

> *New Year and Christmas are essentially the same holiday, the celebration of the birth of the sun. But how can you tell when this happens, like our ancestors did? There is a simple technique to recognize when this time of year occurs. As the typical story goes, three kings, or magi, follow a star in the east to the birth of the Christ child.*

The three wise men, or the three kings, are anthropomorphisms of the three stars of Orion's Belt. Like the sun, Orion's Belt also rises on the eastern horizon. In early December, Orion's Belt will rise above the horizon approximately an hour after sunset. In mid-January, it will rise above the horizon approximately an hour before sunset. However, on Christmas Eve it will rise above the eastern horizon just after the sun sets. This occurs on the evening of December 24 to the morning of December 25. Symbolically, the three kings (Orion's Belt) are following the star of "Bethlehem," known as Sirius (also called Sithus by the Egyptians).

The tale tells us that these kings traveled a great distance. This is because on this day, the three stars of Orion's Belt begin their journey across the night sky immediately at twilight. When this alignment with Sirius occurs, it appears to point straight down at the earth as if it were pointing down to the place where the sun in the sky is about to rise. On this night, we know that God's son, the sun in the sky, is about to be born. When this occurs it is Christmas morning. It is the dawning of God's sun/son, the beginning of the (real) New Year, and the first day of the sun's journey to the north.

• • •

What the authors are trying to explain in a way I initially found difficult to follow is this: The entire story of Jesus's birth can be explained by the alignment of Orion's Belt in relation to the sun. Sure, it leaves out the whole "immaculate-conception-born-in-a-manger" thing, but it draws a significant light on how ancient cultures could turn the alignment of the stars into a story that took root. Three stars (wise men) in perfect alignment with the birth of the new sun (son).

Some will find that a bit of a stretch. But by this time I think it would be easy to see how ancient cultures could birth such a story and have it eventually written as fact. There simply are too many parallel stories to ignore it; at least there have been for me.

This little lesson is in no way close to inclusive of all the history (both fact and fiction) surrounding Sun Worship. It isn't meant to be. As difficult as this chapter is to read (it isn't a cute little story like Lesson One), it is a vital link in the chain that has been my journey of spirituality. I don't know if any of its true. It doesn't matter. What matters to me is that there is no more evidence to support the story of Jesus, (or Muhammad, Buddha or Krishna for that matter) than there is to support the theory of how stars tell the history of religion. Satan hasn't planted these seeds of doubt in my mind to separate me from Jesus. A little research and common sense has done that.

We've come a long way, you and I. From the stories of my youth to the research on religion, much time has passed. I can't ignore the facts about Sun Worship, the stories of parallel saviors and every religion's claim to the truth. My journey has brought me to a place where organized religion plays no part in my existence. And if you've hung in there this long, it's brought you to an explanation of where all this has been going.

Lesson Forty-eight:

BE THE VERY BEST "YOU" YOU CAN BE

"Your time is limited. Don't waste it living someone else's life."

~Steve Jobs

"Maybe it's time you finally accepted who you are," she stated bluntly. Shirl's eyes met mine as I looked up from my cupped hands where tears from my swollen eyes were puddling once more.

"What?" I blubbered. "What do you mean?"

"Matt," she said while trying to sound consoling. "You've been coming here a long time. We've talked about a lot of things. And Lord knows I've tried everything I know to help you get where you feel like you need to be. But maybe where you think you need to be isn't where you're SUPPOSED to be. Maybe, it's time. Maybe it's time you finally just accepted who you are."

I don't believe every life has one defining moment. I tend to think every life is nothing BUT defining moments. One moment leads to the next. But if I were expected to choose ONE defining moment out of all the moments I've lived, this would be the one. This is where I finally got permission to be the person I am, instead of the person I longed to be.

I started seeing Shirl, my counselor/therapist, when Lydia and I split for the first time. But she wasn't where I started. There was a series of incompetent and disinterested therapists leading the way, most of whom had no business counseling others in human behavior.

My first was a lady I should have reported to whoever it is that takes reports on folks like that. In a desperate attempt to salvage a marriage I was destroying with an affair, Lydia and I went to see a female therapist who decided to share our secrets with the people who recommended her. We saw her as a couple once and individually twice more before we realized she wasn't keeping her oath.

From there I branched out on my own and found a man in a nearby suburb that came highly recommended. As I shared my story with him on my first visit, he began to doze off, being awakened only by his bobbing head. In the end, after investing nearly an hour telling him all about "that girl" and my impending divorce and my guilty feelings about my daughter, ad exhaustion, he had this to say, "Sounds to me like you have it all figured out."

And that was the end of THAT!

In an audacious attempt to find competent help with my spiraling emotions, I consulted the Catholic Church where Lydia and I had been members. Their referral services, coupled with my dwindling funds, pointed me in the direction of help I would never have imagined. They sent me to the Christian Counseling Center. I didn't care. I was getting desperate. And besides, I hadn't yet completely severed my ties with organized religion.

Shirl, a slight woman of nearly seventy, opened the door to the waiting room and asked gently, "Matt?"

"That's ME," I said as I stood to move toward the door and shake the hand of the woman who was to be my savior.

Although petite, she was dressed to the "nine's" and had intense, short auburn hair and a smile that told me everything was going to be alright. But she also had an experienced aura that said, "I'm about to call you on all your bullshit." And she did; all of it. I knew from the first handshake I had found the person I needed.

Many years and sessions with Shirl have passed and I no longer recall the exact order of business from each hour I spent with her. But over the course of nearly eight years, sometimes weekly and sometimes yearly, Shirl slowly peeled back the layers of onion that kept the "little voice" of Matt Leatherwood prisoner.

It started simply enough. As I took my place on the low-slung sofa, next to the tissue and directly across from Shirl, who sat in an antique-armed chair adorned with a flowery pattern, the tears began to flow… and flow… and flow… and flow. She listened patiently as I told her the history of my life you've read throughout the course of this memoir. It took several sessions just to get that far. At every encounter, she assured me things would be alright. She spoke little and listened intently, always scribbling notes on a basic yellow legal pad. My file began to grow.

"Matt, I have to ask you," Shirl began at our first meeting and at the beginning of most meetings long after. "Do you feel like hurting yourself?"

That question, although I knew it was coming, caused me pause as I looked at Shirl with unrelenting tears streaming down my cheeks. And then I smiled.

"You know, Shirl," I started. "I've been a paramedic for a long time. Therefore, I realize fully that even stating I wish to hurt myself is against the law in the State of Texas. It would give you cause to have me hospitalized. I don't want that. So, for the record, let me assure you that, no, I don't wish to kill myself. And if I ever do, let me also clearly aver that I won't tell you about it first."

Shirl gave me a look that told me immediately she knew I would be challenging as she said, "That's fair enough."

The truth is I did want to kill myself. More accurately, I just wanted the emotional pain associated with my life to go away. To say I never considered ending my life would be an untruth. Today I know that the events of my life at the time weren't all that horrible, but I purposely kept the bullets and the gun in two separate areas of my apartment nonetheless. 'Nuff said.

Shirl did insist on one thing at our first meeting. She insisted I see my doctor about taking an anti-depressant "to get my emotions under control" before we moved forward. I did as I was told, not because I necessarily believed I was depressed, but because I trusted Shirl's judgment. I intuitively knew I was in the best of hands.

Although a woman of Christian faith, Shirl never once pressed that issue with me. We talked about it and even "argued" about many of the things you've read in this manuscript. But she never made it a prerequisite for helping me. She recognized a troubled soul when she saw one and I truly believe the woman may have lost sleep at night puzzling over how to make progress with me. At one point during the process she even told me, "I don't really think I'm capable of helping you any further." She was exasperated.

"Shirl, please," I begged. "I think you're the only person that CAN help me!"

And she did; in ways she may never fully realize. Shirl knew I was smart (I know that sounds arrogant) and had an interesting way of letting me set my own traps. Clearly, Shirl was much smarter. She realized that deep down, what I sought was "permission." My emotions were fueled by my decisions and all I wanted was for someone to let me off the hook. I wanted someone I trusted to tell me I was doing the right thing. And she often did. But she was cunning.

Because of my shaky emotional state, Shirl gave me her cell number so I could call any time of the day or night. She was generous like that. Like yesterday, I remember the Sunday afternoon I called her from my truck. I was bouncing off the walls with excitement.

"Shirl! Shirl!" I shouted into the phone. "I think I have this all figured out. I'm going to stay with "that girl" and my daughter will be just fine! Everything is going to be just fine! I know I'm doing the right thing!"

"I'm so happy for you," she started with that patient little voice that was starting to piss me off. "If you think that's right, then it probably is. Congratulations."

"So you think I'm doing the right thing?" I asked, my enthusiasm already starting to ebb.

"It doesn't matter what I think," she said. "What matters is what YOU think. If you feel okay about this, then go for it!"

Damn it! Once again, I was seeking permission and Shirl was more than happy to give it. But she also knew my "little voice" would tell me more than she ever could. And just like that, the excitement was gone. I had more work to do.

That's how it was with Shirl and me for eight years. Sometimes she wouldn't see me for months at a time and then I'd be in for another sob session, begging her to help me. We talked about my affairs, my relationships, my writing, and my religion. Her file on me is thick with notes and even manuscripts of some of my early writing. With the exception of Linda, there isn't a person in the world that knows me better than Shirl. I hope she isn't still losing sleep over my stubbornness to improve.

Every new round of sessions always started with me restarting rounds of anti-depressants. Over the course of weeks we'd talk about the same old pattern regarding my life-long behaviors. You could chart them on a graph. The jagged lines of ups and downs prompted Shirl to suggest I see an actual psychiatrist. Once more, I did as I was told and after filling out a ten-question test and talking to a quack for fifteen minutes, was diagnosed with bi-polar disorder and given bottles of medications from boxes scattered around the shrink's office. I never took them and I never went back. Not EVERYTHING Shirl suggested was a good idea. Or was it?

Like *Tuesday's With Morrie*, I could write an entire book about my years seeing Shirl in the little office on the low-slung sofa. But the details of all those sessions, where I continued to seek permission for my behaviors from another person, aren't nearly as important as the permission that person finally gave me. After years of trying to get to the core of who I am, it turns out we were trying to get to the core of who I thought I SHOULD be. Those are two completely different things and when we had exhausted all else, Shirl realized what it was we'd been doing. She most likely saved me from killing myself in the early years. And then this slightly framed little lady, who I considered my friend, albeit professional, did the most amazing thing of all. She gave me my life back. She gave me the REAL permission I'd been seeking all along without even realizing it.

"Maybe it's time you finally accepted who you are," she said.

And although I'm a work-in-progress, I believe I am learning to accept who I am and share it with those around me. Finally, it's time for us to take a look at just who Matt Leatherwood is.

EPILOGUE

"We cannot assume the sacredness nor spiritual livingness of the earth or accept it as a new ideology or as a sentimentally pleasing idea. We must experience that life and sacredness, if it is there, in relationship to our own and to that ultimate mystery we call God. We must experience it in our lives, in our practice, in the flesh of our cultural creativity. We must allow it to shape us, as great spiritual ideas have always shaped those who entertain them, and not expect that we can simply use the image of Gaia to meet emotional, religious, political, or even commercial needs without allowing it to transform us in unexpected and radical ways. The spirituality of the earth is more than a slogan. It is an invitation to initiation, to the death of what we have been and the birth of something new."

~David Spangler

Rainy days, birthdays, and the New Year always seem like a good time to reflect on life and take stock of lessons learned. As I sit here listening to the soft rain so tortuously needed in the region, it has occurred to me that those few days a year have never been enough for me. I've always been a seeker. I've always asked the hard questions. When I haven't been satisfied by the answers, I dug deeper until I found a place within my soul where the answers to all things live. I believe we were born with all we need to know. I believe we are all Spirit. The difficult part is realizing it… awakening.

As a child I grew to love smallness and simplicity. Small village life and the experience of distinct seasonal changes taught me that with each winter there is a promise of spring; with each scorching summer, the promise of death and renewal. I slowly learned to embrace my feelings of solitude and the "special" label so eloquently placed by my mother. My obsession with death, illness, and mortality has ultimately brought me to a place of living. Death is merely a stage of life.

Shirl's gift of permission to accept who I am was liberating and, at the same time, challenging. It's taken me places I never imagined on levels I didn't know existed. As a child, all I ever imagined being was a husband and father, living the dream in a yellow house with white shutters, white picket fence, two kids and two dogs. It's what everyone's dream is supposed to be, right? Regardless, it's what my imagination of an adult life looked like. When it didn't go as planned, I spent YEARS trying to mold myself into the guy that fulfilled that vision. As it turns out, that simply isn't who I am. That was incredibly hard to swallow at first. But learning to accept Matt Leatherwood with all his flaws and quirks has been a journey to rival space exploration. I've been liberated.

I pined for months over how to bring this memoir of sorts to a close. And doing just that has taken on many forms. Do I start a Part VI complete with five new chapters or do I simply wrap it up with an epilogue? What should those chapters be? For reasons lost on me, I knew there were five, but WHAT those five topics were has changed, spun on the roulette wheel if you will, until I landed on what makes up who I am today. It's important to note that it's who I am TODAY, for I'll be someone else tomorrow. We all will be. As much as I wanted to bring my story about a spiritual journey to a close, it simply isn't possible. Spiritual journeys never end.

Learning to view our UNIVERSE in terms beyond human understanding has been the foundation of my core beliefs. No religion, dogma, or human perspective can adequately put our existence in to some neat little box. Quantum physics is only just beginning to unmask the mysteries of who we are and why we're here, but even that fascinating science is clouded with human frailties… "interpretation", if you will. The truth is, no one is ever going to know until we move on to what is next. And even then, who's to say? I am now a man that no longer spends wasted energy concerning myself with what's next. I'll find out when I get there. No amount of speculation will provide a clear answer. The only way to know is to go. I'll go when it's my time and not a moment sooner… or later.

Today there IS no heaven or hell for me. Those two places simply don't exist anywhere but the heart and mind. We are all "spirit." Of that I am sure. That little spark that defines each of us individually comes from somewhere. God? Higher Power? Mother Ship full of Aliens? I have no earthly idea. And it no longer matters. I simply know that in a universe expanding exponentially every second of every day, I'm both enormously significant and completely insignificant at the same time. I'm not a human having a spiritual experience. I AM "spirit" having a human experience. And that, my friends, has changed everything.

The most profound change brought about my new understanding of the universe, is my position on WAR…

KILLING, if you will. It's no secret at this juncture I've done my share of ending innocent life over the past fifty years. Sure, it was "wildlife" mostly, but I've also sat in the back of a speeding ambulance and watched the life slip away from dozens of people. I didn't "end" those lives, but I certainly was powerless to save it many times. Other times not, but I don't take the credit.

What could have been an entire chapter on the subject of killing just boils down to this. I believe life is life. There is no distinction between the life of a muskrat or that of a human. Life is a force; a force to be respected and cherished. Even the Ten Commandments were clear about this. "Thou Shalt Not Kill." I think it's important to take notice that it doesn't say, "Thou Shalt Not Kill Humans." I don't believe these commandments were passed down by God to Moses on a mountain. Seriously. But they're a good set of guidelines and not killing things is a great place to start.

So, what does that mean? It means I don't swat flies if I can help it. It means I help a trapped moth to find his way to the door and it means I don't burn ants with a magnifying glass. It means every living thing has as much right to be here as I do. And it means I see war as a tragedy beyond all tragedies. You may think war has won our "freedom" or changed the face of the planet. You can bet your sweet behind that it has, but not in a positive way.

As a firefighter, I was one of the first to jump on board the war train during the tragic events of 9/11. But despite raising the death toll from that event from 3000 to well over 12,000 through the process of war, nothing has changed. We're no "safer" than 9/10. Killing each other is never, EVER the answer. Life is a force. It lives on regardless of the change in form you give it. Killing accomplishes nothing. Until humans learn to give instead of take; until they drop the "Us vs. Them" mentality; until we realize we aren't Americans or Mexicans or Canadians or whatever, bent on protecting our borders; until we learn we're all humans sharing the same planet... the same universe, the killing will continue. But it changes nothing.

This will cause anger for some of you and I completely understand. I simply no longer consider myself American. I am enormously grateful for the many lives sacrificed in the name of freedom, ad infinitum. I am thankful beyond words that I live in a part of our world where food and shelter are abundant. But I'm a human, sharing the planet with other humans; sharing the universe with everyone. Nothing more. Nothing less.

Life is a fragile force meant to be respected and loved. In order for humans to survive, we'll have to learn that. I'm still holding out hope it can happen. Yet there are two very human factions at work that make it unlikely.

In recent months I was introduced to the practice of Zen... or more specifically Zazen which is really just practicing the art of sitting quietly and focusing on breathing or "the breath." Although it sounds easy, it's more difficult than it sounds. Sitting quietly, or meditating, while you concentrate on only your breathing or "the breath" is incredibly challenging. It takes... well, practice! It was during one of these "sits" that I realized almost every set of beliefs comes with some set of rules. Even though there is no dogma attached to the practice of Zen, there is an appropriate way to sit, to hold your hands, to bow, etc. And that ended my Zen practice in an organized way.

Since the beginning of man (and no, it was NOT Adam and Eve) there have been wars and killing fought in the name of RELIGION. Not one... not one (and I've researched many) of the religions I've researched has promoted, encouraged or supported killing. Yet, here we are centuries and centuries later, still battling over which religion is the true religion. Almost every war ever fought has some type of religious undertone. The Crusades are a glowing example at the hands of Christians, but the Middle East has been at war for thousands of years over something as simple as who has the "right" religion. In addition to that, not one person who practices any of these said religions has ever been able to adequately explain any of that. It baffles me. Here is my religion: Love. I don't care what it is you "practice." What I'm concerned with is how you treat me, my family, and my fellow man. I don't attend church. My prayer is my daily walk with whoever is listening. I continually do my best to send positive energy into the universe. I believe it comes back. I believe we all share that energy.

Stop killing in the name of religion. Not only does no one possess ownership of the truth, but killing over it goes against your religion… yes… YOURS.

We can't address killing and religion without summarizing my view on POLITICS. Ten years ago I would have labeled myself a staunch Republican. I think today people like to use the word "Conservative", whatever the hell that means. I no longer care much for labels and don't identify myself with either "party." Those that DO enjoy the use of labels would likely brand me a Democrat or "Liberal." I moved from the far right all the way back to the far left. Or have I?

There hangs a necklace on the mirror of my jeep, embossed with the Sanskrit symbol for "Balance." It's something I look at every day and it serves as a reminder that balance is what is most important to me. I wish it was more important to everyone. You see, just like in every other walk of life, if you participate in the political game there isn't just one way or the other of seeing things. It isn't a matter of "my" side versus "your" side. There are good ideas coming from both sides of the floor in our country. We should use the best of each and quit throwing the baby out with the bath water.

Debating politics isn't really within the scope of this book. If it were, I wouldn't be writing it. I no longer take place in the process. It's negative energy and it's best left alone. Besides, if you do your homework and examine political history, you'll find that regardless of who held the office of President of the

United States, things still got done. We're no better or worse off. We're simply where we're supposed to be. We survived "Bush." We'll survive "Obama."... or whoever.

Without a doubt, the most profound progress I've made in my journey has been in the area of LOVE and RELATIONSHIPS. Without question, there have been many and there are those out there that would call them "failed" relationships. I know. I used to think that way, also. But I choose to not look at them that way now. Each and every relationship I've ever had and will have, teach me something about myself and the universe we live in. I wasn't "failing." I was learning.

Relationships can be challenging and I applaud those who have found that one person with whom to spend their entire life on earth. I really, really, really wanted that for myself, remember? But for whatever reason, that just hasn't happened for me... yet. Here's what's different now. I no longer need for it to happen. Part of being a successful spirit in human form is learning to embrace the spirit that I am; completely perfect and whole all by myself. Until you grasp the concept of being okay in your own skin, no person on earth will ever be able to make it okay for you. For me, love just doesn't work that way.

So how DOES love work? For me, love is just like life. It's a force. It just is. It doesn't come with strings or expectations. Love. Simply. Is. Ironically enough, I think the Bible probably comes closest to a clear definition in 1 Corinthians.

I've been married in the eyes of "God" and various states enough times to know I need not go down that road again. I'm learning to love in an unselfish way and no longer need a deity or a government to define my commitment to another person should I be fortunate enough to find the one that complements who I am. What's even more important is that I complement who THEY are.

So I thank each and every person who has crossed my path to teach me about love. I especially owe thanks to my children. They seem to love me with all my frailties. And I love them in a way that is truly defined without condition. If you have children and want to know what the real deal feels like, look no further than them. They get it. I promise you. They get it.

There you have it. This is where I am today. I don't pretend to have all the answers and I, by no means, feel like my growth is somehow over and there is nothing left to learn. Quite the contrary. With the curtain finally raised, my heart is open to finding all the wonders that surround us all.

I told you at the beginning, this isn't meant to be a self-help book. I fully realize my path is not your path. If anything, maybe you'll find similarities in my journey and yours. And maybe that will give you courage to keep searching. If that happens, all this writing will be worth it.

I also have never intended to sound like I was "picking" on one religion or another. What works for you is what works for you. I have only tried spelling out my truth as I see it. I don't pretend to know yours.

So, thank you for making it all the way to the end of this part of the journey. With any luck you've found it entertaining, enlightening, and perhaps even a little disturbing. May your path always be covered with just enough leaves to cause you reason to stop and clear a way to better understanding. And may the best of your past be the worst of your future. We're all going to end up in the same place. I love you.

Namaste,
Matt

Made in the USA
Monee, IL
03 May 2026

49438431R00194